THE
healthy
sides
COOKBOOK

THE
healthy
sides
COOKBOOK

**EASY VEGETABLES, PASTAS, AND
GRAINS FOR EVERY MEAL**

From the Editors of

Cooking Light

Oxmoor House

Kale, Brown Rice,
and Quinoa Pilaf,
p. 86

Contents

Sweet and
Sour Cipollini,
p. 291

Introduction

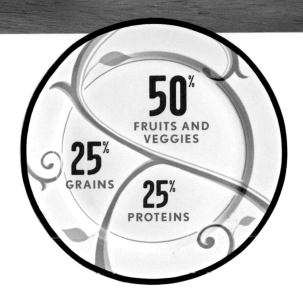

The book you hold in your hands is packed with more than 300 recipes for a wide variety of delectable sides. Still, we almost wish we could give side dish a different name. Why? Because side dish tends to imply something marginal, an afterthought to the main course, something that takes up less space on the plate—and maybe even less of the cook's attention—than the protein. But the fact is that what we call side dishes (the fruits and vegetables, the salads, the grains and legumes) are often where the most vibrant flavors, textures, and colors can be found. Packed with vitamins, minerals, and fiber, they're also where a great deal of the meal's most important nutrients come from, too.

Thankfully, the days when side dishes were relegated to second-class status are over. More and more restaurants are allowing diners to create a whole meal out of a variety of

Building a healthy plate means filling it with sides: Ideally, protein should take up only a quarter of the plate; grains, another quarter (at least half of them whole); and fruits and vegetables, fully half the plate, according to the USDA.

sides on the menu, and why not? The truth is, changing the proportion of foods in your diet to include more plant-forward dishes is a fundamental way to decrease your risk of heart disease, cancer, diabetes, and obesity. And restaurant chefs and home cooks are recognizing that a more vegetable- and grain-based way of cooking in which meat plays a smaller role is satisfying, tasty, and rewarding.

What used to be referred to as the starch—rice, pasta, or potatoes—was typically always pale in color, and could often be lacking in flavor. If you start to think of that category as the "grain," it opens a wider variety of foods to choose from. The main decision used to be whether the rice would be brown or white. Now, home cooks have more grain choices at the grocery store than ever before—everything from quinoa to farro, barley to bulgur—that can be turned into fabulous hot and cold grain-based dishes. These nutty, chewy, flavorful grains can go in everything from pilafs to risottos to stuffings to salads, with flavors that will carry you and your family around the globe.

And don't forget the legumes. Beans, lentils, and peas are as versatile as they are nutritious. Inexpensive and easy to use, they can be turned into any number of hearty, delicious dishes. Conveniently, they come dried, fresh, canned, and frozen, and each type has a place in a healthy kitchen.

Add a burst of color and interest with fresh in-season fruits and vegetables. Grill peaches. Steam eggplant. Roast squash. Regardless of what you choose, you'll find unparalleled flavor and unique texture from peak-season produce.

Use this book to explore new ingredients and cooking methods you may not have experimented with before. You'll find everything from superfast and fresh salads to our favorite classics for holiday feasting. Regardless of what you choose to make, you'll discover an infinite number of ways to bring excitement to any meal.

Full of bright, bold flavors, vivid colors, and satisfying textures—not to mention all that nutrition—these side dishes are poised to move from character actor into the starring role on your plate.

How to use this book

Each chapter in this cookbook includes recipes that offer a range of healthful side dishes that are reliable, flavorful, fuss-free, and versatile. Some recipes share a main ingredient but showcase different preparations; others will hopefully inspire you to try a new vegetable or grain for the first time.

And as with every *Cooking Light* recipe, nutritional information per serving, including calories, fat, carbohydrates, and protein, is clearly stated. For more on our nutritional information, turn to page 354.

Last, to help you quickly look for the right recipes, we've included a list of our holiday favorites (page 22–page 27) and added a Pairs With Guide (page 346) so you can find dishes that work with the lean protein of your choice.

Try **kohlrabi** in our recipe on page 194.

Awendaw, a spoon bread, goes well with shrimp.

Did You Know?

There are tons of interesting facts about food. You'll find tidbits about food history, ingredient information, and more in each chapter.

Simple Swap

Side dishes invite creativity and many ingredients can be easily substituted. Look for simple swap information throughout the book.

Look for these icons throughout the book to help you prepare these recipes and customize them to suit your tastes.

Prep Pointer

These simple tips give you smart advice for preparing some of the sides in this book, including make-ahead tips to help ensure your dishes taste delicious.

Superfast

These recipes are the speediest in this book. They cook up in 15 minutes or less so you can get a fresh meal on the table in minutes.

When pairing mains with sides, it helps to visualize the plate. In addition to a balance of protein, whole grains, and vegetables, consider a variety of colors and textures, as well as hot and cool elements (a spicy curry marries well with a cool cucumber-yogurt salad; smoky barbecue chicken and a fresh, crisp slaw are a great pair). Sides also allow you to play with the season's best produce in new ways, especially if you tend to lean on the same main dishes year-round.

1 Double or triple vegetables. Combining two or three vegetables adds appeal. Mix peppers, onions, and spinach in a simple sauté or roast a few vegetables with chopped herbs, shallots, and garlic. Vary the shape, color, taste, and texture of ingredients to boost interest.

2 Keep it colorful. A good rule of thumb is to have a mix of colors on the plate, both for visual interest and to obtain the widest variety of nutrients. The compounds that give plants their color work as immune boosters, antioxidants, and anti-inflammatories in our bodies. Plus, the deeper the color, the more of these beneficial compounds the plant contains.

3 Play with texture. As flavorful and colorful as your plate may be, it's missing something if your food all has similar textures. Try varying crispy, crunchy, chewy, and creamy. Wake up a dish of tender sautéed chard or escarole with a sprinkling of toasted slivered almonds. Add a dollop of creamy cheese to crisp salad greens or make a steaming bowl of fluffy couscous more exciting with chewy raisins.

4 Try new ingredients. If kohlrabi, sorghum, or red lentils are unfamiliar to you, try them. Try to experiment with one new ingredient a week.

5 Use familiar ingredients in different ways. Even your favorite side dishes can become boring if you prepare them the same way time after time. Keep them interesting by using new flavors or cooking techniques. Jazz up rice with spices, fresh herbs, or toasted nuts. Try roasting green vegetables rather than steaming or boiling.

13

Scale it up

What distinguishes a side dish from a main course? Sometimes the answer is clear, as when the side consists of a single starch, like Roasted Rosemary Fingerling Potatoes (page 271), or a fruit, such as Pickled Watermelon Rind (page 258). While it might seem like a lot of fun to make a meal out of Diner-Style Onion Rings (page 290), it wouldn't be a sensible choice.

But sometimes the distinction between side and main is blurry. With a recipe such as Pea, Pancetta, and Lemon Farfalle (page 37), for example, the dish has it all: a grain, a vegetable, and a protein. The only thing keeping this pasta out of the center of the plate, then, is the ¾-cup serving size. Happily, the recipe, like so many dishes in this book, is easily doubled. (You might also consider swapping out the mini farfalle called for in the original recipe for a regular-sized bow tie shape.)

Hoppin' John's Cousin (page 132) incorporates a mixture of vegetables, beans, and sausage. With an entrée-sized portion and a fresh green salad on the side, there's no reason this couldn't be dinner. Similarly, Arroz Con Gandules (Rice with Pigeon Peas) (page 51) is a balanced meal in itself—complete with rice, beans, and a cubed pork chop. To scale this up, you might want to add a little more meat and increase the serving size.

Side dishes that don't involve protein can often be turned into mains simply by adding some. Many of the salads in this book can be transformed into satisfying stand alone dishes with the addition of a handful of cooked shrimp, shredded leftover chicken, or grilled tofu. Have some leftover steak or roast pork? Cut it into strips and add it to the Bitter Greens Salad with Spiced Mirin Dressing (page 175). Frisée Salad with Persimmons, Dates, and Almonds (page 186) becomes a light, elegant entrée with a few large seared sea scallops on top of each portion.

Many of the bean dishes in this book, such as Fiery Chipotle Baked Beans (page 115), are easily turned into mains by adding slices of chicken sausage or turkey franks. Similarly, Fava Beans with Tomato and Onion (page 134) would make an enticing entrée tossed with some crumbled sweet or hot Italian sausage.

Remember that even with main-dish recipes, the protein needn't be the predominant feature. A little goes a long way, and most Americans consume more than we need.

Pea, Pancetta, and Lemon Farfalle, p. 37

Fiery Chipotle Baked Beans, p. 115

Hoppin' John's Cousin, p. 132

Bitter Greens Salad with Spiced Mirin Dressing, p. 175

15

Making substitutions

Cookbooks can be as much about inspiration as they are instruction, and the recipes in this one are often fairly flexible. Salads, in particular, invite creativity, and it's easy to swap out one green for another.

The kale called for in Barbecued Beans and Greens (page 112)? Go ahead and substitute another hearty dark leafy green such as chard or spinach. Chard can take the place of kale in a variety of kale-based recipes, from Spicy Soy-Kale Salad (page 164) to Wilted Kale with Toasted Shallots (page 311). Likewise, kale will happily stand in for chard in Chopped Chard Salad with Apricot Vinaigrette (page 171).

With myriad pasta shapes out there, it would be a shame to feel constrained by a recipe. Remember, though, to stay within the general guideline of long or short, depending on which category the recipe calls for. Long pastas such as spaghetti are better with smoother sauces—so feel free to swap in linguine, angel hair, or fettuccine—whereas short pastas like penne go well with chunkier ones. Rotini, cavatappi, or farfalle make fine substitutes.

Also, you can be creative with grains. Millet is a wonderful substitute for bulgur. It takes a bit longer to cook, so adjust your timing accordingly. The same goes if you're trading wheat berries for quinoa—they're similarly nutty and flavorful, but be sure to check the cooking times, as wheat berries take longer on the stove. Farro is a super substitute for barley, and vice versa, and both can be swapped in for short-grain rice in risottos. Again, adjust as necessary.

Of course Tuscan White Beans (page 124) wouldn't be the same made with red or black beans, and Louisiana Red Beans (page 119) pretty much require kidneys. But generally, you can let your imagination and good sense be your guide.

DON'T LOVE **KALE?**
Substitute **spinach** or
Swiss chard in the
recipe instead.

MIX IT UP!
There are myriad
pasta shapes to try.

Keep it stocked

With a well-stocked pantry, you'll always have the makings of many a meal—and by pantry, we don't just mean the cupboard or closet where you keep the rice, pasta, and canned goods. Broadly speaking, the pantry is your stock of staples; the items you can use to whip up a variety of dishes on a moment's notice whether they're store in your pantry or your fridge or freezer. With these items, you'll be on your way to infinite side-dish possibilities:

▲
Onions and garlic

Anchovy paste and chile paste

◄ *Mustards*
Dijon and grainy

Sauces
fish sauce, Sriracha, Worchestershire, and lower-sodium soy

Vinegars
white wine, red wine, balsamic, and apple cider

Oils
an everyday olive oil and a very good one for drizzling, canola, nut (such as hazelnut or walnut), and seed (such as toasted sesame)

Cheeses
Parmesan, feta, goat, and blue
▼

Spices and dried and fresh herbs

Nuts

Beans
black, red, white, garbanzo; dried, fresh, canned, and frozen; lentils: brown, orange, and small green such as lentils de Puys; and split peas

Couscous

Rice
not just white and brown, since so many interesting types are available, from black to red to Italian short-grain to basmali

Pasta
variety of shapes and sizes, both regular and whole wheat

Grains
quinoa, freekeh, farro, barley, spelt, bulgur, and wheat berries

Boxed or canned broths and stocks
lower-sodium beef, chicken, and vegetable broth and unsalted chicken stock

Canned or boxed tomatoes
crushed, diced, and whole and tomato paste (canned or in a tube)

Dried fruit
raisins, apricots, figs, cranberries, and cherries

19

Buy it

More and more Americans are shopping seasonally and locally. Often (but not always), the farther fruits and vegetables travel, the less fresh and flavorful they will be.

Think about the difference between a supermarket peach that you might pick up in October and one you buy in July at the local farmer's market. Each looks like a peach, but the former lacks fragrance and flavor while the latter is bursting with both. Same goes for strawberries, available year-round at the grocery store. Most are flown in from California, and if you cut into one, you'll see that the inside is more white than red. Pop it in your mouth, and you'll miss the intense berry flavor and juicy texture of local strawberries picked at the peak of their season in the spring. Check out our seasonal produce guide on page 352 for more information.

If you followed this local-and-seasonal guideline strictly, however, you'd have to give up certain things. Most of us would never get to eat a fresh mango or a pineapple, for example, and we're not advocating that. If you can become aware of what grows in your area and when, and you can wait for it to appear, that's a big step. The produce simply tastes extraordinary, and your taste buds will thank you.

Lucky for us, many fruits and vegetables are also available frozen. It's widely acknowledged that flash-frozen peas can be sweeter and more tender than fresh ones, since the sugars in fresh peas turn to starch so quickly after they're picked. And the same goes for other fruits and vegetables. Frozen fruit—berries, mango—can be defrosted and pureed into sauces, and frozen vegetables such as corn, green beans, and peas can be added to risottos, stews, and salads.

WINTER

SPRING

FALL

SUMMER

Buy local produce by season to get the freshest, most intense flavors.

New Year's Day

Hoppin' John's Cousin, p. 132

Steamed Spinach with Curry Butter, p. 317

Fresh Peas with Spicy Pepper Relish, p. 127

Warm Spiced Lentils, p. 141

Balsamic Collard Greens, p. 313

Mushroom-Ginger Noodles, p. 44

Easter

Spinach with Garlic Vinaigrette, p. 168

Fresh Pea Salad with Radishes, Tomatoes, and Mint, p. 205

Spring Vegetable Skillet, p. 267

Asparagus with Balsamic Tomatoes, p. 319

Radishes in Browned Butter, p. 289

Sautéed Chard Agrodolce, p. 314

4th of July

Corn with Feta-Mint Butter, p. 331

Peach Salad with Tomatoes and Beets, p. 238

Tomato, Fresh Mozzarella, and Basil Salad, p. 182

Jalapeño-Lime Slaw, p. 179

Quick Classic Baked Beans, p. 113

Pickled "Fried" Green Tomatoes with Buttermilk-Herb Sauce, p. 339

24

Thanksgiving

Farro Stuffing with Butternut Squash, Red Onion, and Almonds, p. 81

Mixed Lettuce, Pear, and Goat Cheese Salad, p. 161

Three-Ingredient Cranberry Sauce, p. 236

Acorn Squash Wedges with Maple-Harissa Glaze, p. 295

Simply Herby Stuffing, p. 99

Sherried Green Beans, p. 328

Hanukkah

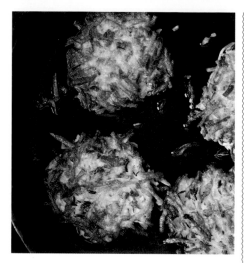

Classic Potato Latkes, p. 274

Chunky Spiced Applesauce, p. 245

Winter Citrus, Escarole, and Endive Salad, p. 176

Moroccan-Spiced Baby Carrots, p. 284

Christmas

Wild Rice Dressing with Roasted Chestnuts and Cranberries, p. 67

Butter-Pecan Mashed Sweet Potatoes, p. 278

Brussels Sprouts Gratin, p. 307

Shaved Fennel with Orange and Olives, p. 193

Lemony Broccolini, p. 308

Glazed Winter Vegetables, p. 264

Tah Dig (Persian Rice), p. 60

Two-Cheese Mac and Cheese, p. 43

Wild Rice and Carrots, p. 64

pastas, rices, and grains

The average American should eat six servings of grains each day, typically half of which should be whole grains. Try expanding your repertoire and explore the variety of grains, pastas, and rices out there. Chewy, toothsome starches add texture, substance, and even an element of comfort to the plate.

Know Your Grains and Pastas

Affordable, quick-to-cook pastas and rices are among the most common side dishes served. While these versatile dishes are always pleasers, expand your horizons to other grains. Whole grains are particularly important. Many of them take longer to cook, but they are chewy, hearty, and higher in fiber and nutrients than refined grains. Grains, especially whole ones, have oils that eventually turn rancid, so buy only what you plan to use within a few months.

Pastas

Pasta comes in a wide variety of shapes and sizes and can be made from refined or whole-grain flour. The new generation of whole-grain pastas boasts hearty, full flavor and can be another way to fill your daily whole-grain quota.

Long pastas
Noodles are good with dressings or sauces to coat them. Shapes include spaghetti, bucatini, fettuccine, linguine, pappardelle, and tagliatelle.

▼

Short pastas
Good companions with diced vegetables, beans, or meats. Shapes include casareccia, cavatappi, farfalle, gigli, orecchiette, penne, penne rigate, rigatoni, fusilli, and rotini.

Grains

With their mild flavor and chewy texture, grains make a delicious base. Whole grains include the germ, endosperm, and bran of the grain, making them high in fiber and other nutrients and good for heart health and digestion.

▲

Barley
Pearl barley is the more common, quick-cooking form of barley, but it has been refined. Hulled barley is more nutritious and a whole grain.

Buckwheat
The flavor of buckwheat ranges from nutty to earthy and pairs well with smoky flavors.

Bulgur (cracked wheat)

Bulgur consists of wheat kernels that have been precooked, dried, and cut (cracked). It has a nutty flavor and can be used in pilafs, soups, and stuffings.

Farro (emmer)

An ancient Italian wheat grain that has a chewy bite. It's often confused with spelt, but they're two distinct varieties of wheat.

Teff

A tiny grain that cooks in 20 minutes. It's porridgy, like polenta, with a deep, toasty flavor.

Millet

Resembles couscous in texture and has a sweet, nutty flavor. It is fast, nearly foolproof, and fluffy—great as a pilaf and perfect for spicy, highly seasoned recipes.

Quinoa

This small, round, high-protein grain is an excellent source of iron—it supplies your entire daily recommendation in 1 cup. It is a good alternative to rice because of its lightness. The tiny seeds cook in about 20 minutes, but be sure to give quinoa a good rinse before cooking (see p. 33).

Spelt

Higher in protein than more common wheat varieties, spelt provides 12 grams in ½ cup. It's also a good source of fiber.

Sorghum

Mild and slightly sweet, like a chewier version of Israeli couscous when cooked. It needs at least an hour to simmer. Great to make in batches and freeze.

Wheat berries

Simply whole-grain wheat. They are big and chewy and take about an hour to cook.

Rices

Though long-grain white rice is most familiar, there's a host of other options—more than 40,000 of them.

▲

Arborio

This popular Italian rice is used to make risotto. Each medium-length grain has a white "eye" that remains firm to the bite, while the rest of the grain softens and lends creaminess.

Basmati

Sometimes called "popcorn rice," this long-grain variety is highly regarded for its fragrance, taste, and slender shape. Whole-grain brown basmati rice is also available. ▼

Black

Both medium- and short-grain, this whole grain gets its color from the black bran that surrounds the endosperm, or kernel. When cooked, the rice might turn purple or lavender.

▼

Brown

Rice hulled with bran intact. The bran lends chewy texture and nutty flavor, and contains vitamins, minerals, and fiber. This whole grain requires a longer cooking time because the bran is a barrier to water.

Wild rice

The only grain native to North America, this is actually an aquatic grass and is considered a whole grain. It's often sold mixed with long-grain white rice. ▶

Jasmine

Thailand's favorite, this aromatic rice has more amylopectin, or sticky starch, than other long-grain rices, so it's moist and tender. Brown jasmine rice is also available.

▲

Sushi

This short-grain sticky rice is glassy and smooth.

Instant/precooked rice

This rice has been partially or completely cooked and dried; it takes only a few minutes to prepare.

How to Prepare

BASIC PASTA

Use a Dutch oven or a stockpot to allow room for the pasta to move freely in the boiling water. For 8 ounces of dried pasta, use 4 quarts of water.

❶ Fill the pot with water, cover, and bring the water to a full rolling boil over high heat before adding the pasta. It isn't necessary to add salt (for flavor) or oil (to prevent the pasta from sticking) to the water.

❷ Add the pasta, and start timing the cooking when the water returns to a rolling boil. If you use fresh pasta, remember that it cooks more quickly than dried. After adding the pasta to the boiling water, put the lid on the pot, but prop it open slightly so the water doesn't boil over.

❸ Start testing the pasta for doneness a few minutes before the end of the indicated cooking time. Pasta that offers resistance to the bite but has no trace of brittleness is al dente, and that's how you want it. If an undercooked piece of pasta is cut in half, a white dot or line is clearly visible in the center. Al dente pasta has only a speck of white remaining. Drain the cooked pasta in a colander, and shake it well to remove the excess water.

BASIC RICE

To make perfect rice every time, select a broad saucepan, deep skillet, or sauté pan with a snug-fitting lid.

❶ For 1 cup of uncooked rice, bring 2 cups of water to a boil in a medium saucepan. Add the rice. Cover, reduce heat, and simmer 18 minutes or until the liquid is absorbed and the rice is done. Do not lift the lid or stir while the rice is cooking. Lifting the lid allows steam to escape, and stirring the rice will release more starch, causing the grains to stick together in lumps.

❷ Remove the pan from the heat, and let the rice stand for 5 to 10 minutes. Uncover the pan carefully— try not to let the condensation on the lid drip onto the rice. Fluff the rice with a fork.

QUINOA

For a tasty change, try cooking your quinoa in unsalted chicken stock instead of water. The stock imparts a lot of flavor to the quinoa without big nutritional changes.

❶ Thoroughly rinse your quinoa under cold water, and drain it in a fine-mesh sieve. Better yet, let the quinoa soak for about 15 minutes in cold water, and then drain through a fine-mesh sieve. Quinoa has a natural protective coating called saponin. If you don't rinse it well, the quinoa will be bitter because of this coating. Much of the quinoa sold in the United States is pre-rinsed. If the box or bin does not say the quinoa is prerinsed, assume it's not and rinse it anyway. An extra rinse or soak won't hurt the quinoa or affect the cooking process.

❷ Combine 1¼ cups water and 1 cup of the rinsed quinoa in a medium saucepan; bring to a boil. Cover, reduce heat to low, and simmer for 10 to 20 minutes or until the liquid is absorbed. You'll know the quinoa is finished cooking when it appears as if each grain has "popped" open. Remove from heat; fluff with a fork.

Prep Pointer

Reserve ¼ cup pasta cooking liquid when draining the pasta and add as necessary to help bind the other ingredients to the pasta. Gradually add to ingredients in pan with the pasta, and simmer until slightly thickened.

Asparagus Farfalle ▶

HANDS-ON TIME: 8 MIN. | **TOTAL TIME:** 8 MIN.

4 ounces uncooked mini farfalle
8 ounces medium asparagus, trimmed and cut into 1-inch pieces
4 teaspoons olive oil, divided
⅔ cup thinly sliced leek
2 garlic cloves, minced
3 tablespoons dry white wine
2 tablespoons chopped fresh mint
¼ teaspoon freshly ground black pepper
⅛ teaspoon kosher salt
1 ounce pecorino Romano cheese, grated (about ¼ cup)

❶ Cook pasta according to package directions; drain.

❷ Sauté asparagus in 2 teaspoons oil over medium-high heat for 4 minutes. Remove asparagus from pan. Add 2 teaspoons oil to pan; swirl to coat. Add leek; sauté 2 minutes. Add garlic; sauté 30 seconds. Add wine; cook 30 seconds. Add pasta, asparagus, mint, and remaining ingredients; toss.

SERVES 4 (serving size: ¾ cup)

CALORIES 203; FAT 7.3g (sat 2.5g, mono 3.3g, poly 0.5g); PROTEIN 7g; CARB 26g; FIBER 2g; CHOL 8mg; IRON 3mg; SODIUM 206mg; CALC 97mg

Tomato, Feta, and Thyme Farfalle

HANDS-ON TIME: 7 MIN. | **TOTAL TIME:** 7 MIN.

4 ounces uncooked mini farfalle
1 cup sliced leek
4 teaspoons olive oil
2 garlic cloves, minced
1 tablespoon fresh lemon juice
1 cup quartered cherry tomatoes
2 teaspoons minced fresh thyme
⅓ cup crumbled feta cheese

❶ Cook pasta according to package directions; drain.

❷ Sauté leek in olive oil over medium heat 2 minutes. Add minced garlic; sauté 30 seconds. Stir in lemon juice, pasta, cherry tomatoes, thyme, and feta cheese; toss.

SERVES 4 (serving size: ¾ cup)

CALORIES 195; FAT 7.3g (sat 2.4g, mono 3.8g, poly 0.6g); PROTEIN 6g; CARB 27g; FIBER 2g; CHOL 9mg; IRON 2mg; SODIUM 127mg; CALC 79mg

◀ *Lemon-Orange Orzo*

HANDS-ON TIME: 7 MIN. | **TOTAL TIME:** 24 MIN.

1 tablespoon butter
¾ cup uncooked whole-wheat orzo
1½ cups unsalted chicken stock
   (such as Swanson)
2 tablespoons chopped fresh flat-leaf
   parsley
½ teaspoon grated lemon rind
½ teaspoon grated orange rind
¼ teaspoon kosher salt

❶ Melt butter in a medium saucepan over medium heat. Add orzo; toss to coat. Add stock to pan; bring to a simmer. Cover, reduce heat, and simmer 17 minutes or until liquid is absorbed. Stir in parsley, lemon rind, orange rind, and salt.

SERVES 4 (serving size: about ½ cup)

CALORIES 147; FAT 3.5g (sat 1.8g, mono 0.8g, poly 0.1g); PROTEIN 6g; CARB 23g; FIBER 5g; CHOL 8mg; IRON 0mg; SODIUM 195mg; CALC 12mg

Pea, Pancetta, and Lemon Farfalle

HANDS-ON TIME: 7 MIN. | **TOTAL TIME:** 7 MIN.

4 ounces uncooked mini farfalle
1 cup frozen peas
1 ounce pancetta, diced
2 garlic cloves, minced
3 tablespoons dry white wine
1 tablespoon butter
½ teaspoon grated lemon rind
¼ teaspoon salt
¼ teaspoon pepper

❶ Cook pasta according to package directions, adding frozen peas during last 2 minutes of cooking; drain.
❷ Sauté pancetta 3 minutes. Add minced garlic; cook 30 seconds. Add wine; cook 30 seconds. Add pasta mixture, butter, lemon rind, salt, and pepper; toss.

SERVES 4 (serving size: ¾ cup)

CALORIES 180; FAT 4.6g (sat 2.5g, mono 0.8g, poly 0.2g); PROTEIN 6g; CARB 27g; FIBER 3g; CHOL 10mg; IRON 1mg; SODIUM 267mg; CALC 18mg

Prep Pointer

Fresh lemon and orange perfume the orzo. You can use one citrus or both.

Prep Pointer

Try this with healthy, whole-wheat orzo.

Orzo with Garlicky Spinach

HANDS-ON TIME: 9 MIN. | **TOTAL TIME:** 9 MIN.

¾ cup uncooked orzo
1 tablespoon butter
4 cups spinach
2 teaspoons minced garlic
1 ounce grated Parmesan cheese
¼ cup fat-free, lower-sodium chicken broth
1 tablespoon white balsamic vinegar
¼ teaspoon salt
¼ teaspoon crushed red pepper

❶ Cook pasta according to package directions, omitting salt and fat.
❷ Melt butter in a skillet over medium heat; cook 1 minute or until browned. Add spinach and minced garlic; cook 1 minute. Stir in orzo, Parmesan cheese, chicken broth, vinegar, salt, and crushed red pepper.

SERVES 6 (serving size: about ⅓ cup)

CALORIES 148; **FAT** 3.8g (sat 2g, mono 0.9g, poly 0.1g); **PROTEIN** 6g; **CARB** 23g; **FIBER** 2g; **CHOL** 9mg; **IRON** 2mg; **SODIUM** 250mg; **CALC** 68mg

Orzo with Pecorino and Mushrooms

HANDS-ON TIME: 9 MIN. | **TOTAL TIME:** 9 MIN.

¾ cup uncooked orzo
1½ tablespoons butter
3 cups sliced cremini mushrooms
½ teaspoon freshly ground black pepper
⅜ teaspoon salt
¼ cup fat-free, lower-sodium chicken broth
1 tablespoon white balsamic vinegar
¼ cup minced fresh chives
1 ounce pecorino Romano cheese, shaved (about ¼ cup)

❶ Cook pasta according to package directions, omitting salt and fat.
❷ Melt butter in a large skillet over medium heat; cook 1 minute or until lightly browned. Add mushrooms, pepper, and salt; cook 4 minutes or until mushrooms release their liquid, stirring frequently. Add broth and vinegar; stir in orzo and chives. Top with cheese.

SERVES 6 (serving size: ½ cup)

CALORIES 156; **FAT** 5.1g (sat 3g, mono 0.8g, poly 0.2g); **PROTEIN** 6g; **CARB** 22g; **FIBER** 1g; **CHOL** 13mg; **IRON** 1mg; **SODIUM** 304mg; **CALC** 48mg

Pasta with Sugar Snap Peas and Ricotta Cheese

HANDS-ON TIME: 13 MIN. | **TOTAL TIME:** 14 MIN.

4 ounces uncooked trottole pasta
4 ounces sugar snap peas (1¼ cups)
½ cup part-skim ricotta cheese
1 tablespoon chopped fresh chives
¼ teaspoon kosher salt
⅛ teaspoon freshly ground black pepper

❶ Cook pasta according to package directions, omitting salt and fat; add sugar snap peas during last 3 minutes of cooking time. Drain. Combine pasta mixture, ricotta cheese, chives, salt, and pepper.

SERVES 4 (serving size: about ¾ cup)

CALORIES 158; FAT 2.9g (sat 1.7g, mono 0.7g, poly 0.1g); PROTEIN 8g; CARB 25g; FIBER 2g; CHOL 10mg; IRON 2mg; SODIUM 161mg; CALC 103mg

Broccoli and Penne with Asiago

HANDS-ON TIME: 12 MIN. | **TOTAL TIME:** 12 MIN.

4 ounces uncooked penne pasta
2 cups broccoli florets
1½ ounces shredded Asiago cheese
1 tablespoon extra-virgin olive oil
⅛ teaspoon kosher salt
⅛ teaspoon freshly ground black pepper

❶ Cook pasta according to package directions, omitting salt and fat. Add broccoli florets during last 3 minutes of cooking; drain. Add cheese, olive oil, salt, and pepper.

SERVES 4 (serving size: about ¾ cup)

CALORIES 185; FAT 7.3g (sat 2.5g, mono 2.5g, poly 0.4g); PROTEIN 7g; CARB 23g; FIBER 2g; CHOL 9mg; IRON 1mg; SODIUM 174mg; CALC 98mg

Superfast

Ready in 15
minutes or less!

Simple Swap

Sub 2 cups penne,
macaroni, or other
hot cooked pasta for
the cavatappi.

Cavatappi with Arugula and Cannellini Beans ▶

HANDS-ON TIME: 15 MIN. | **TOTAL TIME:** 15 MIN.

2 cups hot cooked cavatappi pasta
2 cups packed arugula
1 cup unsalted canned cannellini beans,
　rinsed and drained
1½ tablespoons extra-virgin olive oil
1 tablespoon fresh lemon juice
⅛ teaspoon kosher salt
⅛ teaspoon freshly ground black pepper
1 ounce shaved Asiago cheese

❶ Combine first 7 ingredients in a large bowl. Top with shaved cheese.

SERVES 4 (serving size: about 1 cup)

CALORIES 226; **FAT** 8.4g (sat 2g, mono 3.7g, poly 0.6g);
PROTEIN 8g; **CARB** 29g; **FIBER** 4g; **CHOL** 6mg; **IRON** 1mg;
SODIUM 151mg; **CALC** 87mg

Lemon-Parsley Pasta

HANDS-ON TIME: 12 MIN. | **TOTAL TIME:** 12 MIN.

6 ounces uncooked whole-wheat
　spaghetti
¼ cup chopped fresh parsley
1½ tablespoons extra-virgin olive oil
1 teaspoon grated lemon rind
1 tablespoon fresh lemon juice
¼ teaspoon kosher salt
¼ teaspoon freshly ground black pepper

❶ Cook spaghetti according to package directions, omitting salt and fat. Drain. Combine pasta, parsley, olive oil, lemon rind, lemon juice, salt, and pepper; toss.

SERVES 4 (serving size: ⅔ cup)

CALORIES 196; **FAT** 5.7g (sat 0.8g, mono 3.8g, poly 0.8g);
PROTEIN 6g; **CARB** 33g; **FIBER** 5g; **CHOL** 0mg; **IRON** 2mg;
SODIUM 126mg; **CALC** 24mg

Two-Cheese Mac and Cheese

HANDS-ON TIME: 26 MIN. | **TOTAL TIME:** 36 MIN.

10 ounces uncooked large elbow
   macaroni
2 tablespoons canola oil
3 garlic cloves, crushed
2¼ cups unsalted chicken stock (such
   as Swanson), divided
½ cup 2% reduced-fat milk
8 teaspoons all-purpose flour
4 ounces ⅓-less-fat cream cheese
½ teaspoon salt
¼ teaspoon freshly ground black pepper
Cooking spray
3 ounces extra-sharp cheddar cheese,
   shredded (about ¾ cup)

❶ Cook pasta according to package directions, omitting salt and fat; drain. Set aside.
❷ Preheat broiler to high.
❸ Heat a Dutch oven over medium heat. Add oil to pan; swirl to coat. Add garlic to pan; cook 3 minutes or until garlic is fragrant, stirring frequently (do not brown). Stir in 1 cup stock; bring to a boil. Cook 1 minute. Combine 1¼ cups stock, milk, and flour; stir with a whisk until well blended. Add milk mixture to garlic mixture, stirring with a whisk. Bring to a boil; cook 5 minutes or until mixture begins to thicken. Remove milk mixture from heat; add cream cheese, stirring until smooth. Stir in salt and pepper. Add cooked pasta to milk mixture, tossing to coat. Let stand 5 minutes.
❹ Pour pasta mixture into a 2-quart glass or ceramic baking dish coated with cooking spray. Sprinkle cheddar evenly over pasta mixture. Broil 3 minutes or until cheese melts and begins to brown. Let stand 5 minutes.

SERVES 12 (serving size: about ½ cup)

CALORIES 179; FAT 7.5g (sat 3.1g, mono 2.8g, poly 1g); PROTEIN 7g; CARB 20g; FIBER 1g; CHOL 16mg; IRON 1mg; SODIUM 205mg; CALC 85mg

Prep Pointer

Don't overcook the macaroni. Boil it just until al dente. It will cook more after it is mixed with the sauce and put in the oven.

Prep Pointer

Rice noodles are very versatile and come in a variety of thicknesses. Make sure not to overcook them, as some noodles can get mushy quickly.

Mushroom-Ginger Noodles ▶

HANDS-ON TIME: 16 MIN. | **TOTAL TIME:** 16 MIN.

5 ounces uncooked rice noodles
2 teaspoons dark sesame oil
1 teaspoon minced garlic
1 teaspoon minced peeled fresh ginger
1½ cups sliced shiitake mushrooms
½ cup sliced onion
1 tablespoon lower-sodium soy sauce
¼ teaspoon kosher salt
½ cup sliced green onions

❶ Prepare rice noodles according to package directions; drain. Heat sesame oil in a skillet over medium-high heat 30 seconds; add garlic and ginger, and sauté 30 seconds. Add mushrooms and onion; sauté 4 minutes. Stir in rice noodles, soy sauce, and salt. Sprinkle with green onions.

SERVES 4 (serving size: about 1 cup)

CALORIES 164; FAT 2.4g (sat 0.4g, mono 0.9g, poly 1g); PROTEIN 2g; CARB 34g; FIBER 1g; CHOL 0mg; IRON 1mg; SODIUM 261mg; CALC 24mg

Noodles with Carrot and Onion

HANDS-ON TIME: 10 MIN. | **TOTAL TIME:** 10 MIN.

4 ounces fresh udon noodles
1½ tablespoons canola oil
1 small onion, thinly sliced
1 garlic clove, minced
½ cup shredded carrot
1 tablespoon rice wine vinegar
1 tablespoon lower-sodium soy sauce

❶ Cook udon noodles according to package directions, omitting salt and fat. Heat a skillet over medium-high heat. Add oil to pan; swirl to coat. Add onion; sauté 3 minutes. Add garlic; sauté 30 seconds. Remove from heat; stir in carrot, vinegar, and soy sauce. Add noodles; toss to coat.

SERVES 4 (serving size: ²⁄₃ cup)

CALORIES 170; FAT 6.1g (sat 0.4g, mono 3.3g, poly 1.5g); PROTEIN 5g; CARB 24g; FIBER 2g; CHOL 0mg; IRON 1mg; SODIUM 150mg; CALC 20mg

Couscous Pilaf

HANDS-ON TIME: 10 MIN. | **TOTAL TIME:** 10 MIN.

2 teaspoons olive oil
½ cup chopped onion
½ cup finely chopped red bell pepper
1 cup fat-free, lower-sodium chicken broth
1 cup uncooked couscous
⅛ teaspoon salt
⅛ teaspoon freshly ground black pepper
2 tablespoons pine nuts, toasted

❶ Heat a nonstick skillet over medium-high heat. Add oil to pan; swirl to coat. Add onion and bell pepper; sauté 7 minutes.
❷ While vegetables cook, bring broth to a boil in a medium saucepan; gradually stir in couscous. Remove from heat; cover and let stand 5 minutes. Fluff with a fork. Stir in onion mixture, salt, and black pepper. Sprinkle with nuts.

SERVES 4 (serving size: about ¾ cup)

CALORIES 225; FAT 5.5g (sat 0.6g, mono 2.5g, poly 1.8g); PROTEIN 7g; CARB 37g; FIBER 3g; CHOL 0mg; IRON 1mg; SODIUM 192mg; CALC 17mg

Tomato and Cucumber Couscous

HANDS-ON TIME: 9 MIN. | **TOTAL TIME:** 9 MIN.

1¼ cups water
¾ cup Israeli couscous
½ cup halved grape tomatoes
½ cup diced seeded cucumber
¼ cup chopped red onion
1 tablespoon fresh lemon juice
⅛ teaspoon salt
1½ ounces crumbled feta cheese

❶ Bring water to a boil. Add couscous. Reduce heat to medium-low; cover and simmer 8 minutes or until liquid is absorbed. Stir in tomatoes, cucumber, onion, lemon juice, salt, and feta cheese.

SERVES 4 (serving size: about ½ cup)

CALORIES 156; FAT 2.6g (sat 1.6g, mono 0.5g, poly 0.1g); PROTEIN 6g; CARB 27g; FIBER 1g; CHOL 9mg; IRON 0mg; SODIUM 194mg; CALC 60mg

Pecorino and Parsley Couscous

HANDS-ON TIME: 9 MIN. | **TOTAL TIME:** 9 MIN.

1¼ cups water
¾ cup Israeli couscous
¼ cup chopped fresh flat-leaf parsley
2 tablespoons shaved pecorino Romano cheese
1 tablespoon toasted pine nuts
1 teaspoon grated lemon rind
¼ teaspoon salt
¼ teaspoon freshly ground black pepper

❶ Bring water to a boil. Add couscous. Reduce heat to medium-low; cover and simmer 8 minutes. Stir in parsley and remaining ingredients.

SERVES 4 (serving size: about ½ cup)

CALORIES 148; FAT 2.9g (sat 1g, mono 0.4g, poly 0.7g); PROTEIN 5g; CARB 25g; FIBER 0g; CHOL 4mg; IRON 0mg; SODIUM 219mg; CALC 38mg

Did You Know?

Pecorino Romano is a hard Italian cheese made entirely from sheep's milk. In fact, "pecora" means "sheep" in Italian.

Curried Currant-Couscous Pilaf

HANDS-ON TIME: 11 MIN. | **TOTAL TIME:** 16 MIN.

1 tablespoon olive oil
¼ cup finely chopped shallots
¼ teaspoon curry powder
1 cup uncooked couscous
1¼ cups fat-free, lower-sodium chicken broth
¼ cup dried currants
1 tablespoon chopped fresh flat-leaf parsley

❶ Heat a small saucepan over medium-high heat. Add oil to pan; swirl to coat. Add shallots and curry powder; sauté 2 minutes or until tender. Stir in couscous; sauté 1 minute. Add broth and currants; bring to a boil. Cover, remove from heat, and let stand 5 minutes. Fluff with a fork. Stir in parsley.

SERVES 4

CALORIES 230; FAT 3.9g (sat 0.6g, mono 2.6g, poly 0.5g); PROTEIN 7g; CARB 42g; FIBER 3g; CHOL 0mg; IRON 1mg; SODIUM 275mg; CALC 28mg

Simple Swap

In summer, substitute green beans, corn, and zucchini for the butternut squash and chickpeas.

Couscous with Winter Vegetables

HANDS-ON TIME: 25 MIN. | **TOTAL TIME:** 33 MIN.

2 tablespoons butter
1 tablespoon olive oil
½ cup chopped shallots
1 jalapeño pepper, minced
3 cups chopped peeled butternut squash
1 (15-ounce) can unsalted chickpeas (garbanzo beans), drained
1 cup uncooked couscous
1¾ cups boiling water
¾ teaspoon salt
¼ cup coarsely chopped fresh flat-leaf parsley
2 tablespoons fresh lemon juice
1 ounce vegetarian Parmesan cheese, grated (about ¼ cup)

❶ Heat butter and oil in a large straight-sided skillet over medium-high heat, stirring until butter melts. Add shallots; cook 3 minutes or until soft, stirring occasionally. Add jalapeño; cook 1 minute, stirring frequently. Add butternut squash; cook 8 minutes or until tender, stirring occasionally. Add chickpeas; cook 1 minute, stirring occasionally. Add couscous, and cook 1 minute, stirring constantly.

❷ Stir in 1¾ cups boiling water and salt; remove pan from heat. Cover and let stand 8 minutes. Fluff couscous mixture with a fork. Add fresh parsley and lemon juice; toss gently to combine. Top with Parmesan cheese.

SERVES 10 (serving size: about ¾ cup)

CALORIES 162; **FAT** 4.8g (sat 2.2g, mono 1.8g, poly 0.3g); **PROTEIN** 6g; **CARB** 25g; **FIBER** 3g; **CHOL** 8mg; **IRON** 1mg; **SODIUM** 254mg; **CALC** 74mg

Red Pepper Couscous

HANDS-ON TIME: 15 MIN. | **TOTAL TIME:** 15 MIN.

4 teaspoons olive oil
¾ cup chopped red bell pepper
½ cup chopped red onion
¾ cup Israeli couscous
1¼ cups water
¼ teaspoon salt
¼ teaspoon black pepper
3 tablespoons fresh lime juice
2 tablespoons chopped fresh cilantro
1 jalapeño pepper, seeded and finely
  chopped

❶ Heat a large skillet over medium-high heat. Add oil to pan; swirl to coat. Add bell pepper and onion to pan; sauté 3 minutes. Add couscous, 1¼ cups water, salt, and black pepper; bring to a boil. Reduce heat to medium-low; cover and simmer 8 minutes. Stir in juice, cilantro, and jalapeño.

SERVES 4 (serving size: about ½ cup)

CALORIES 179; FAT 4.9g (sat 0.6g, mono 3.3g, poly 0.5g); PROTEIN 5g; CARB 29g; FIBER 1g; CHOL 0mg; IRON 0mg; SODIUM 150mg; CALC 9mg

Prep Pointer

Israeli or pearled couscous is best for pasta-like sides. Save smaller couscous for curries and tagines.

◄ *Arroz con Gandules*
(Rice with Pigeon Peas)

HANDS-ON TIME: 17 MIN. | **TOTAL TIME:** 37 MIN.

1 teaspoon annatto oil
½ cup chopped onion
2 garlic cloves, minced
1 (4-ounce) boneless center-cut loin
 pork chop, cubed
2 cups uncooked medium-grain rice
1 cup water
¼ cup lean smoked ham, cubed
½ teaspoon dried oregano
¼ teaspoon salt
2 (14-ounce) cans lower-sodium beef
 broth
½ cup Spanish stuffed olives, sliced
2 tablespoons chopped fresh cilantro
1 (15.5-ounce) can pigeon peas, rinsed
 and drained
Cilantro leaves (optional)

❶ Heat oil in a large Dutch oven over medium-high heat. Add onion, garlic, and pork; sauté 5 minutes. Stir in rice. Add 1 cup water and next 4 ingredients (through broth); bring to a boil. Cover, reduce heat, and simmer 20 minutes or until liquid is absorbed and rice is tender. Stir in olives, cilantro, and peas. Garnish with cilantro leaves, if desired.

SERVES 10 (serving size: about ¾ cup)

CALORIES 241; FAT 3.4g (sat 0.8g, mono 1.5g, poly 0.7g); PROTEIN 11g; CARB 41g; FIBER 4g; CHOL 10mg; IRON 3mg; SODIUM 224mg; CALC 38mg

Did You Know?

Look for canned pigeon peas in the Latin foods aisle at the supermarket.

Double Sesame Rice

HANDS-ON TIME: 13 MIN. | **TOTAL TIME:** 13 MIN.

2 cups hot cooked long-grain white rice
2 teaspoons dark sesame oil
1 teaspoon toasted sesame seeds
¼ teaspoon kosher salt
¼ teaspoon freshly ground black pepper
2 diagonally sliced green onions

❶ Combine all ingredients in a medium bowl.

SERVES 4 (serving size: ½ cup)

CALORIES 129; FAT 2.9g (sat 0.4g, mono 1.2g, poly 1.2g); PROTEIN 2g; CARB 23g; FIBER 1g; CHOL 0mg; IRON 1mg; SODIUM 150mg; CALC 15mg

Prep Pointer

To cook long-grain white rice (see page 33), use 2 cups of water for every 1 cup of uncooked rice. One cup uncooked rice will generally yield about 3 cups of cooked rice.

Golden Saffron Rice

HANDS-ON TIME: 16 MIN. | **TOTAL TIME:** 21 MIN.

2 cups hot cooked long-grain white rice
1 tablespoon hot water
⅛ teaspoon saffron threads
1 tablespoon extra-virgin olive oil
¼ cup minced fresh onion
¼ teaspoon kosher salt

❶ Combine first 3 ingredients, and let stand 5 minutes; stir. Heat olive oil in a saucepan over medium heat. Add onion; cook 5 minutes, stirring occasionally. Combine rice mixture, onion mixture, and salt.

SERVES 4 (serving size: ½ cup)

CALORIES 137; FAT 3.6g (sat 0.5g, mono 2.5g, poly 0.4g); PROTEIN 2g; CARB 23g; FIBER 1g; CHOL 0mg; IRON 1mg; SODIUM 121mg; CALC 10mg

Thai Cilantro and Serrano Rice

HANDS-ON TIME: 10 MIN. | **TOTAL TIME:** 10 MIN.

1 tablespoon canola oil
1 tablespoon grated peeled fresh ginger
1 tablespoon sliced garlic
2 serrano chiles, seeded and thinly sliced
¾ cup chopped fresh cilantro
¼ teaspoon kosher salt
2 cups hot cooked long-grain white rice

❶ Heat a small skillet over medium-high heat. Add canola oil; swirl. Add ginger, garlic, and chiles; sauté 1 minute. Stir ginger mixture, cilantro, and kosher salt into rice.

SERVES 4 (serving size: ½ cup)

CALORIES 139; FAT 3.8g (sat 0.3g, mono 2.3g, poly 1.1g); PROTEIN 2g; CARB 23g; FIBER 1g; CHOL 0mg; IRON 1mg; SODIUM 122mg; CALC 13mg

Yogurt Rice with Cumin and Chile

HANDS-ON TIME: 5 MIN. | **TOTAL TIME:** 5 MIN.

2 (8.5-ounce) pouches precooked white basmati rice (such as Uncle Ben's)
1 tablespoon canola oil
1 tablespoon minced fresh ginger
1 teaspoon cumin seeds
1 serrano chile, thinly sliced
2 tablespoons chopped fresh cilantro
½ teaspoon kosher salt
1 (6-ounce) container plain low-fat yogurt

❶ Heat rice according to package directions.
❷ Heat a large skillet over medium-high heat. Add oil to pan; swirl to coat. Add ginger, cumin, and chile; sauté 30 seconds. Stir in rice, cilantro, salt, and yogurt; cook 1 minute.

SERVES 6 (serving size: ½ cup)

CALORIES 173; FAT 4.6g (sat 0.8g, mono 2.1g, poly 1.4g); PROTEIN 5g; CARB 29g; FIBER 1g; CHOL 2mg; IRON 1mg; SODIUM 185mg; CALC 56mg

Superfast

Ready in 15 minutes or less!

Prep Pointer

Using whole packages of rice and yogurt saves the time of measuring. Be sure to use standard yogurt here; Greek is a bit too thick.

◄ *Curried Sweet Potato–Apple Pilaf*

HANDS-ON TIME: 7 MIN. | **TOTAL TIME:** 30 MIN.

3 teaspoons olive oil
¼ cup chopped green onions
1 garlic clove, minced
½ cup uncooked long-grain white rice
1 cup water
⅔ cup diced peeled sweet potato
1 cup cubed peeled Granny Smith apple
2 tablespoons currants
¾ teaspoon curry powder
½ teaspoon ground cumin
¼ teaspoon salt

❶ Heat oil in a medium saucepan over medium-high heat. Add onions and garlic; sauté 1 minute. Stir in rice; sauté 1 minute. Add 1 cup water and sweet potato; bring to a boil. Cover, reduce heat, and simmer 15 minutes or until liquid is almost absorbed. Stir in apple and remaining ingredients; cover and simmer 3 minutes or until thoroughly heated.

SERVES 5 (serving size: ½ cup)

CALORIES 123; FAT 1.7g (sat 0.2g, mono 1.1g, poly 0.2g); PROTEIN 2g; CARB 25g; FIBER 2g; CHOL 0mg; IRON 1mg; SODIUM 130mg; CALC 21mg

Prep Pointer

Adding the apples at the last minute keeps them crunchy, giving texture to this fall-flavored side dish.

Pine Nut, Butter, and Parsley Rice

HANDS-ON TIME: 10 MIN. | **TOTAL TIME:** 10 MIN.

2 tablespoons toasted pine nuts
2 tablespoons minced fresh flat-leaf parsley
1 tablespoon butter, melted
¼ teaspoon kosher salt
2 cups hot cooked long-grain white rice

❶ Stir pine nuts, parsley, melted butter, and kosher salt into rice.

SERVES 4 (serving size: ½ cup)

CALORIES 157; FAT 6g (sat 2.1g, mono 1.6g, poly 1.6g); PROTEIN 3g; CARB 23g; FIBER 1g; CHOL 8mg; IRON 1mg; SODIUM 147mg; CALC 12mg

Prep Pointer

Thinly slice the pepper and onion so they cook quickly.

Fried Brown Rice with Red Pepper and Almond ▶

HANDS-ON TIME: 14 MIN. | **TOTAL TIME:** 14 MIN.

1 tablespoon peanut oil
½ cup thinly sliced onion
1 teaspoon minced fresh garlic
1½ cups sliced red bell pepper
¼ cup sliced almonds
1 (8.8-ounce) pouch precooked brown rice (such as Uncle Ben's)
1 tablespoon fresh lime juice
2 teaspoons yellow curry paste
¼ cup cilantro leaves
¼ teaspoon salt

❶ Heat a large wok or skillet over medium-high heat. Add oil; swirl. Add onion and garlic; stir-fry 1 minute. Add bell pepper and nuts; stir-fry 2 minutes. Add rice; stir-fry 1 minute. Stir in lime juice, curry paste, cilantro, and salt.

SERVES 4 (serving size: ¾ cup)

CALORIES 169; FAT 7.7g (sat 0.8g, mono 3.3g, poly 1.8g); PROTEIN 4g; CARB 23g; FIBER 3g; CHOL 0mg; IRON 1mg; SODIUM 221mg; CALC 23mg

Nutty Rice

HANDS-ON TIME: 20 MIN. | **TOTAL TIME:** 20 MIN.

1 cup basmati rice
¼ cup thinly sliced green onions
2 tablespoons toasted slivered almonds
¼ teaspoon salt
¼ teaspoon freshly ground black pepper

❶ Cook basmati rice according to package directions. Stir in green onions, almonds, salt, and black pepper.

SERVES 4

CALORIES 184; FAT 2g (sat 0.1g, mono 1.3g, poly 0.5g); PROTEIN 4g; CARB 37g; FIBER 1g; CHOL 0mg; IRON 0.7mg; SODIUM 148mg; CALC 30mg

Basmati Rice with Almonds

HANDS-ON TIME: 13 MIN. | **TOTAL TIME:** 28 MIN.

1½ teaspoons olive oil
⅓ cup chopped onion
2 garlic cloves, minced
¾ cup uncooked basmati rice
2 tablespoons slivered almonds
¼ teaspoon salt
¼ teaspoon freshly ground black pepper
1 cup fat-free, lower-sodium chicken broth
¾ cup water

❶ Heat olive oil in a medium saucepan over medium-high heat. Add onion to pan; sauté 3 minutes. Add garlic; sauté 1 minute. Add rice and almonds; sauté 2 minutes. Add salt, black pepper, broth, and ¾ cup water to pan; bring to a boil. Cover, reduce heat, and simmer about 15 minutes or until liquid is absorbed and rice is tender.

SERVES 4 (serving size: about ⅔ cup)

CALORIES 170; FAT 3.3g (sat 0.4g, mono 2.2g, poly 0.5g); PROTEIN 3g; CARB 32g; FIBER 1g; CHOL 0mg; IRON 1mg; SODIUM 216mg; CALC 32mg

Simple Swap

Brown rice can be substituted for basmati rice, leeks or celery for the onion, walnuts for almonds, and beef for chicken broth to suit your taste or to use what you happen to have on hand.

◀ Red Coconut Rice

HANDS-ON TIME: 3 MIN. | **TOTAL TIME:** 33 MIN.

1 teaspoon canola oil
2 garlic cloves, minced
1 tablespoon red curry paste
½ teaspoon grated peeled fresh ginger
½ cup water
½ teaspoon salt
1 (13.5-ounce) can light coconut milk
1 cup uncooked jasmine rice
¼ cup organic dried coconut flakes (optional)

❶ Heat a large saucepan over medium-low heat. Add oil to pan; swirl to coat. Add garlic; sauté 30 seconds. Add curry paste and ginger; sauté 30 seconds. Add ½ cup water, salt, and coconut milk, stirring with a whisk. Bring to a boil; add rice. Cover, reduce heat, and simmer 20 minutes or until liquid is absorbed. Remove from heat, and let stand 5 minutes; fluff with a fork. Garnish with coconut, if desired.

SERVES 8 (serving size: ½ cup)

CALORIES 94; FAT 1.2g (sat 0.5g, mono 0.4g, poly 0.2g); PROTEIN 2g; CARB 19g; FIBER 1g; CHOL 0mg; IRON 0mg; SODIUM 183mg; CALC 11mg

Did You Know?

Many rice cultures have crunchy-rice dishes. In Persian cooking, partially cooked rice is drained and cooked in a dry pan with butter and oil, forming a gorgeous, golden crust.

Tah Dig
(Persian Rice)

HANDS-ON TIME: 10 MIN. | **TOTAL TIME:** 62 MIN.

4 cups water
1 cup uncooked long-grain basmati rice
½ cup plain 2% reduced-fat Greek
   yogurt
1 teaspoon kosher salt
⅛ teaspoon crushed saffron threads
1½ tablespoons unsalted butter
2 teaspoons canola oil

❶ Place 4 cups water in a saucepan over medium-high heat; bring to a boil. Add rice; cook 10 minutes. Drain. Rinse with cold water; drain.
❷ Combine yogurt, salt, and saffron in a medium bowl. Add rice to yogurt mixture, stirring well.
❸ Melt butter in a medium nonstick sauté pan over medium heat. Add oil to pan; swirl to coat. Add rice mixture to pan, lightly packing rice down. Wrap a clean, dry dish towel around lid, tying it at the handle; place prepared lid on pan. Cook rice, covered, over medium heat 20 minutes (do not stir or uncover). Reduce heat to medium-low; cook 20 minutes or until rice is tender on top and a golden crust forms on bottom.
❹ Loosen edges of rice crust with a rubber spatula. Place a plate over the top of pan, and invert the rice onto plate, browned side up. Cut into 8 wedges, and serve immediately.

SERVES 8 (serving size: 1 wedge)

CALORIES 129; FAT 3.6g (sat 1.7g, mono 1.3g, poly 0.5g); PROTEIN 3g; CARB 23g; FIBER 1g; CHOL 7mg; IRON 1mg; SODIUM 245mg; CALC 10mg

Cashew Rice

HANDS-ON TIME: 10 MIN. | **TOTAL TIME:** 35 MIN.

1 cup uncooked sushi rice
1¼ cups water
¼ teaspoon kosher salt
⅓ cup chopped unsalted, dry-roasted cashews
¼ cup thinly sliced green onions
¼ cup chopped fresh cilantro
2 tablespoons thinly sliced serrano pepper
1 tablespoon rice vinegar

❶ Place uncooked sushi rice in a fine-mesh sieve. Rinse under cold water, stirring rice until water runs clear (about 30 seconds). Combine rice, 1¼ cups water, and salt in a small saucepan. Bring to a boil; cover, reduce heat, and simmer 15 minutes. Remove from heat; let stand 10 minutes. Uncover and fluff rice. Stir in cashews, green onions, cilantro, serrano pepper, and vinegar.

SERVES 4 (serving size: about ½ cup)

CALORIES 138; FAT 5.4g (sat 1.1g, mono 3.2g, poly 0.9g); PROTEIN 3g; CARB 20g; FIBER 1g; CHOL 0mg; IRON 2mg; SODIUM 204mg; CALC 11mg

Coconut-Ginger Rice

HANDS-ON TIME: 8 MIN. | **TOTAL TIME:** 23 MIN.

1 cup water
½ teaspoon minced peeled fresh ginger
¼ teaspoon salt
1 bay leaf
1 cup uncooked jasmine rice
¼ cup light coconut milk
2 tablespoons chopped fresh cilantro

❶ Bring water, ginger, salt, and bay leaf to a boil in a small saucepan. Add rice and coconut milk to pan; bring to a boil. Reduce heat to low, cover, and cook until liquid is absorbed and rice is done (about 15 minutes). Discard bay leaf; fluff rice. Stir in chopped fresh cilantro.

SERVES 4 (serving size: about ½ cup)

CALORIES 194; FAT 1.2g (sat 0.8g, mono 0.1g, poly 0.1g); PROTEIN 4g; CARB 41g; FIBER 1g; CHOL 0mg; IRON 2mg; SODIUM 153mg; CALC 15mg

Did You Know?

Amylopectin, a sticky starch, is higher in short-grain rice and, when cooked, produces soft grains that cling together. This kind of rice is popular in Asian countries but is less familiar in the United States.

Risotto with Porcini Mushrooms and Mascarpone

HANDS-ON TIME: 43 MIN. | **TOTAL TIME:** 43 MIN.

1½ cups boiling water
½ cup dried porcini mushrooms
   (about ½ ounce)
1 (14-ounce) can lower-sodium beef
   broth
Cooking spray
1 cup uncooked Arborio rice or other
   medium-grain rice
¾ cup chopped shallots
2 garlic cloves, minced
½ cup dry white wine
1 ounce grated Parmigiano-Reggiano
   cheese (about ¼ cup)
1 ounce mascarpone cheese
   (about ¼ cup)
1 tablespoon chopped fresh or
   1 teaspoon dried thyme
½ teaspoon freshly ground black pepper
⅛ teaspoon salt

❶ Combine 1½ cups boiling water and mush-rooms; let stand 10 minutes or until soft. Drain through a colander over a bowl. Reserve 1¼ cups soaking liquid; chop mushrooms.
❷ Bring reserved soaking liquid and broth to a simmer in a small saucepan (do not boil). Keep broth mixture warm over low heat.
❸ Heat a large saucepan over medium-high heat. Coat pan with cooking spray. Add rice, shallots, and garlic to pan; sauté 5 minutes. Add wine; cook until liquid evaporates (about 2 minutes).
❹ Add 1 cup broth mixture to rice mixture; cook over medium heat 5 minutes or until the liquid is nearly absorbed, stirring occasionally. Add remaining broth mixture, ½ cup at a time, stirring occasionally until each portion of broth mixture is absorbed before adding the next (about 25 minutes total). Add mushrooms, Parmigiano-Reggiano and mascarpone cheeses, thyme, pepper, and salt; stir gently just until cheeses melt. Serve warm.

SERVES 6 (serving size: ⅔ cup)

CALORIES 195; **FAT** 4g (sat 2g, mono 0.4g, poly 0.1g); **PROTEIN** 7g; **CARB** 32g; **FIBER** 3g; **CHOL** 10mg; **IRON** 1mg; **SODIUM** 248mg; **CALC** 71mg

Prep Pointer

Medium-grain rice like Arborio or Carnaroli gives off lots of starch during cooking, which combines with hot stock to yield a creamy texture. Stirring frequently and gradually adding hot liquid are key to ensure creaminess.

Simple Swap

If you can't find precooked wild rice, substitute boil-in-bag or precooked brown rice.

Wild Rice with Tomatoes and Pine Nuts

HANDS-ON TIME: 15 MIN. | **TOTAL TIME:** 15 MIN.

1 (8.5-ounce) package precooked wild rice (such as Archer Farms)
1½ tablespoons unsalted butter
¼ cup pine nuts
8 cherry tomatoes, quartered
1 tablespoon chopped fresh basil
½ teaspoon freshly ground black pepper
¼ teaspoon salt

❶ Prepare rice according to package directions.
❷ Melt butter in a large nonstick skillet over medium heat. Add pine nuts and quartered cherry tomatoes to pan; cook 8 minutes or until tomatoes are tender, stirring frequently. Stir in rice, basil, pepper, and salt; cook 1 minute.

SERVES 4 (serving size: ½ cup)

CALORIES 163; FAT 10.4g (sat 3.2g, mono 2.7g, poly 3.2g); PROTEIN 4g; CARB 16g; FIBER 2g; CHOL 11mg; IRON 1mg; SODIUM 152mg; CALC 10mg

Wild Rice and Carrots ▶

HANDS-ON TIME: 15 MIN. | **TOTAL TIME:** 15 MIN.

1 (8.5-ounce) package precooked wild rice (such as Archer Farms)
1½ tablespoons unsalted butter
1 cup thinly sliced carrot
1 tablespoon chopped fresh parsley
½ teaspoon freshly ground black pepper
¼ teaspoon salt

❶ Prepare rice according to package directions.
❷ Melt butter in a large nonstick skillet over medium heat. Add carrot; cook 8 minutes or until tender, stirring frequently. Stir in rice, parsley, pepper, and salt; cook 1 minute.

SERVES 4 (serving size: ½ cup)

CALORIES 113; FAT 4.6g (sat 2.8g, mono 1.2g, poly 0.3g); PROTEIN 3g; CARB 16g; FIBER 2g; CHOL 11mg; IRON 1mg; SODIUM 173mg; CALC 16mg

Wild Rice Dressing with Roasted Chestnuts and Cranberries

HANDS-ON TIME: 17 MIN. | **TOTAL TIME:** 1 HR. 17 MIN.

2 cups uncooked wild rice
2 cups fat-free, lower-sodium chicken broth
2 cups water
½ teaspoon kosher salt, divided
1½ cups whole roasted bottled chestnuts
1 cup sweetened dried cranberries
1½ tablespoons unsalted butter
1½ cups halved lengthwise and thinly sliced carrot
1½ cups chopped yellow onion
1¼ cups thinly sliced celery
½ cup minced fresh flat-leaf parsley
2 tablespoons minced fresh sage
1 tablespoon thyme leaves
¼ teaspoon freshly ground black pepper
Cooking spray

❶ Combine rice, broth, 2 cups water, and ¼ teaspoon salt in a saucepan; bring to a boil. Partially cover, reduce heat, and simmer 40 minutes or until rice is tender, stirring occasionally. (Do not drain.) Place rice in a large bowl; cover.

❷ Preheat oven to 400°

❸ Arrange chestnuts on a baking sheet. Bake at 400° for 15 minutes. Cool slightly; cut chestnuts into quarters.

❹ Place cranberries in a small bowl; cover with hot water. Let stand 20 minutes or until soft. Drain and add to rice.

❺ Melt butter in a large nonstick skillet over medium heat. Add carrot, onion, and celery; cook 15 minutes or until vegetables are tender, stirring occasionally. Stir in herbs; remove from heat. Add to rice mixture. Stir in ¼ teaspoon salt, chestnuts, and pepper.

❻ Spoon rice mixture into a 13 x 9–inch glass or ceramic baking dish coated with cooking spray. Cover and bake at 400° for 10 minutes or until thoroughly heated.

SERVES 12 (serving size: about ¾ cup)

CALORIES 213; **FAT** 2.4g (sat 1.1g, mono 0.6g, poly 0.5g); **PROTEIN** 6g; **CARB** 44g; **FIBER** 5g; **CHOL** 4mg; **IRON** 1mg; **SODIUM** 182mg; **CALC** 31mg

Prep Pointer

With grains like wild rice, it's best to cook them to al dente first before assembling the dressing to bake. If you're worried about mushiness, start with a pilaf method: Sauté the grains in a few teaspoons of oil for a minute or two.

Multigrain Risotto

HANDS-ON TIME: 40 MIN. | **TOTAL TIME:** 1 HR. 45 MIN.

3 cups cubed peeled butternut squash

2 tablespoons extra-virgin olive oil, divided

⅓ cup uncooked pearl barley

3½ cups water

⅓ cup uncooked long-grain brown rice

⅓ cup uncooked wild rice

4 cups thinly sliced shiitake mushroom caps (about 11 ounces)

¾ cup chopped leek

⅓ cup chopped carrot

⅓ cup chopped celery

2 garlic cloves, minced

½ cup dry white wine

1 cup chopped tomato

½ cup chopped fresh chives

½ cup chopped fresh parsley

1 tablespoon chopped fresh thyme

2 teaspoons chopped fresh sage

1 cup frozen petite green peas, thawed

2 ounces shredded fontina cheese (about ½ cup)

½ teaspoon salt

¼ teaspoon freshly ground black pepper

¼ cup unsalted pumpkinseed kernels, toasted

❶ Preheat oven to 450°.

❷ Place squash and 1 tablespoon oil in a large bowl; toss gently to coat. Arrange squash in a single layer on a large baking sheet. Bake at 450° for 35 minutes or until tender and browned. Cool 20 minutes.

❸ While squash cools, place barley in a large nonstick skillet; cook over medium heat 4 minutes or until toasted.

❹ Bring 3½ cups water to a boil in a large saucepan. Add brown rice and wild rice; cover, reduce heat, and simmer 10 minutes. Stir in toasted barley; cover and simmer 30 minutes or until grains are tender. Drain any remaining liquid.

❺ Heat a skillet over medium-high heat. Add 1 tablespoon oil to pan; swirl to coat. Add mushrooms and next 4 ingredients (through garlic); sauté 5 minutes or until vegetables are tender. Stir in wine; cook 4 minutes or until liquid evaporates. Stir in rice mixture, tomato, and next 4 ingredients (through sage); cook 4 minutes or until thoroughly heated. Remove from heat; stir in squash, peas, and next 3 ingredients (through pepper). Sprinkle with pumpkinseed kernels.

SERVES 8 (serving size: about ¾ cup)

CALORIES 236; **FAT** 8.4g (sat 2.4g, mono 3.9g, poly 1.7g); **PROTEIN** 8g; **CARB** 35g; **FIBER** 5g; **CHOL** 8mg; **IRON** 3mg; **SODIUM** 191mg; **CALC** 111mg

Did You Know?

The earthy, umami flavor of the mushrooms enhances the nutty taste of the barley and brown rice, and the toasted pumpkinseed kernels add a crunchy texture to the dish.

Black Bean–Cilantro Rice

HANDS-ON TIME: 12 MIN. | **TOTAL TIME:** 12 MIN.

1 (3.5-ounce) bag boil-in-bag brown rice
$^3/_4$ cup chopped red onion
5 garlic cloves, thinly sliced
$^1/_4$ teaspoon ground cumin
$^1/_2$ jalapeño pepper, seeded and minced
1 tablespoon olive oil
1 (15-ounce) can unsalted black beans, rinsed and drained
1 cup unsalted chicken stock (such as Swanson)
$^1/_4$ teaspoon kosher salt
2 tablespoons queso fresco
$^1/_4$ cup cilantro leaves

❶ Cook rice according to package directions. Sauté onion, garlic, cumin, and jalapeño pepper in olive oil over medium-high heat 2 minutes. Add beans, chicken stock, and salt. Cook 6 minutes. Lightly mash with a fork. Top rice with bean mixture, queso fresco, and cilantro.

SERVES 4 (serving size: $^1/_3$ cup rice and $^2/_3$ cup bean mixture)

CALORIES 205; **FAT** 5.1g (sat 1g, mono 2.7g, poly 0.4g); **PROTEIN** 8g; **CARB** 33g; **FIBER** 5g; **CHOL** 3mg; **IRON** 1mg; **SODIUM** 191mg; **CALC** 72mg

Prep Pointer

Brown rice is easy to make ahead and reheat for a quick side dish. Cook a large batch of rice and refrigerate for up to 3 days or freeze for up to 3 months.

Fiesta Rice

HANDS-ON TIME: 24 MIN. | **TOTAL TIME:** 1 HR. 19 MIN.

2 teaspoons olive oil
1 (10-ounce) package frozen whole-kernel corn, thawed
1 tablespoon butter
1 cup chopped green onions
1½ cups uncooked brown rice
1 teaspoon ground cumin
1 teaspoon minced fresh garlic
2 cups fat-free, lower-sodium chicken broth
⅛ teaspoon freshly ground black pepper
1 (14.5-ounce) can diced tomatoes with chiles, undrained
1 (15-ounce) can unsalted black beans, rinsed and drained
½ cup chopped fresh cilantro
1 tablespoon fresh lime juice

❶ Heat oil in a medium saucepan over medium-high heat. Add corn to pan; cook 10 minutes or until corn starts to brown, stirring occasionally. Remove from pan. Set aside.

❷ Melt butter in pan. Add onions; sauté 5 minutes or until tender. Stir in rice, cumin, and garlic; cook 1 minute. Add broth, black pepper, and diced tomatoes to pan; bring to a boil. Cover, reduce heat, and simmer 45 minutes, stirring occasionally. Remove from heat; stir in reserved corn and beans. Cover and let stand 10 minutes. Stir in cilantro and juice.

SERVES 12 (serving size: about ⅔ cup)

CALORIES 158; FAT 3.7g (sat 1.1g, mono 1.4g, poly 1.1g); PROTEIN 5g; CARB 27g; FIBER 3g; CHOL 3mg; IRON 1mg; SODIUM 237mg; CALC 39mg

Spicy Brown Rice

HANDS-ON TIME: 12 MIN. | **TOTAL TIME:** 12 MIN.

2 cups cooked brown rice
1 teaspoon chile paste with garlic
1 teaspoon sesame oil
¼ cup chopped green onions
¼ teaspoon kosher salt

❶ Combine all ingredients in a medium bowl.

SERVES 4 (serving size: about ½ cup)

CALORIES 120; FAT 2g (sat 0.3g, mono 0.8g, poly 0.8g); PROTEIN 3g; CARB 23g; FIBER 2g; CHOL 0mg; IRON 1mg; SODIUM 153mg; CALC 14mg

Multigrain Pilaf with Sunflower Seeds

HANDS-ON TIME: 11 MIN. | **TOTAL TIME:** 67 MIN.

4 teaspoons canola oil, divided
1/3 cup sunflower seed kernels
1/2 teaspoon salt, divided
2 teaspoons butter
1 cup thinly sliced leek (about 1 large)
2 1/2 cups water
1 1/2 cups fat-free, lower-sodium chicken broth
1/2 cup uncooked pearl barley
1/2 cup uncooked brown rice blend (such as Lundberg) or brown rice
1/2 cup dried currants
1/4 cup uncooked bulgur
1/4 cup chopped fresh parsley
1/4 teaspoon freshly ground black pepper

❶ Heat a Dutch oven over medium-high heat. Add 2 teaspoons oil, sunflower seeds, and 1/4 teaspoon salt; sauté 2 minutes or until lightly browned. Remove from pan; set aside.

❷ Heat pan over medium heat; add 2 teaspoons oil and butter. Add leek; cook 4 minutes or until tender, stirring frequently. Add 2 1/2 cups water and next 3 ingredients (through rice); bring to a boil. Cover, reduce heat, and simmer 35 minutes. Stir in currants and bulgur; cover and simmer 10 minutes or until grains are tender. Remove from heat; stir in 1/4 teaspoon salt, sunflower seeds, parsley, and pepper. Serve immediately.

SERVES 8 (serving size: 1/2 cup)

CALORIES 198; FAT 6.6g (sat 1.1g, mono 2.2g, poly 2.6g); PROTEIN 5g; CARB 33g; FIBER 5g; CHOL 3mg; IRON 2mg; SODIUM 266mg; CALC 26mg

Simple Swap

This recipe calls for long-cooking barley and brown rice, but if you're in a hurry, substitute instant brown rice and quick-cooking barley. Just be sure to adjust cooking times according to the package directions.

Did You Know?

Sunflower seeds and brown rice pack a double nutrition punch, enhancing this side dish with both vitamin E and niacin.

Barley and Butternut Risotto

HANDS-ON TIME: 65 MIN. | **TOTAL TIME:** 65 MIN.

2 pounds butternut squash, peeled,
  seeded, and cut into ½-inch cubes
Cooking spray
4 cups unsalted chicken stock
  (such as Swanson)
1 cup water
2 teaspoons olive oil
1 cup chopped onion
¼ teaspoon salt
¼ teaspoon freshly ground black pepper
1¼ cups uncooked pearl barley
3 garlic cloves, minced
1.5 ounces shaved Parmesan cheese
  (about ⅓ cup), divided
1 teaspoon dried sage

❶ Preheat oven to 425°.
❷ Place squash on a jelly-roll pan coated with cooking spray. Bake at 425° for 25 minutes.
❸ Bring stock and 1 cup water to a simmer in a saucepan. Keep warm.
❹ Heat a large saucepan over medium-high heat. Add oil to pan; swirl to coat. Add onion, salt, and pepper; cook 4 minutes. Add barley and garlic; cook 2 minutes. Stir in ½ cup stock mixture; cook 4 minutes, stirring frequently. Reduce heat to medium-low. Reserve ¼ cup stock. Add remaining stock, ½ cup at a time, stirring frequently until each portion is absorbed. Remove from heat. Stir in reserved ¼ cup stock and 1 ounce cheese. Fold in squash. Sprinkle with remaining cheese and sage.

SERVES 7 (serving size: about ¾ cup)

CALORIES 241; FAT 3.6g (sat 1.2g, mono 1.5g, poly 0.5g);
**PROTEIN 10g; CARB 45g; FIBER 8g; CHOL 5mg; IRON 2mg;
SODIUM 250mg; CALC 150mg**

Did You Know?

This ancient grain is perfect in modern cooking. Pearl barley offers fiber plus a bevy of nutrients.

Prep Pointer

As a general rule, use 2½ parts water to 1 part barley, but grains aren't delicate: You can add more water during the cooking process, or if they're done before all liquid is absorbed, drain the excess off.

Lemon-Rosemary Barley

HANDS-ON TIME: 6 MIN. | **TOTAL TIME:** 66 MIN.

¾ cup uncooked pearl barley
3 cups water
4 teaspoons extra-virgin olive oil, divided
¾ cup chopped onion
1 teaspoon chopped fresh rosemary
½ teaspoon grated lemon rind
⅜ teaspoon kosher salt

❶ Combine barley and water in a saucepan; bring to a boil. Cover, reduce heat, and cook 50 minutes. Drain.
❷ Heat a skillet over medium heat. Add 2 teaspoons olive oil. Add onion and rosemary; cook, stirring frequently, 5 minutes or until onion is lightly browned. Combine barley, onion mixture, 2 teaspoons olive oil, lemon rind, and salt.

SERVES 4 (serving size: about ¾ cup)

CALORIES 184; FAT 5g (sat 0.7g mono 3.4g, poly 0.7g); PROTEIN 4g; CARB 32g; FIBER 6g; CHOL 0mg; IRON 1mg; SODIUM 185mg; CALC 19mg

Fresh Vegetable Barley

HANDS-ON TIME: 15 MIN. | **TOTAL TIME:** 55 MIN.

1 teaspoon olive oil
¾ cup chopped onion (about 1 small)
1 garlic clove, minced
¾ cup uncooked pearl barley
1¾ cups unsalted chicken stock (such as Swanson)
1½ cups chopped zucchini (about 1)
1½ cups halved cherry tomatoes
¼ teaspoon kosher salt
¼ teaspoon freshly ground black pepper
2 tablespoons crumbled feta cheese
Chopped fresh parsley (optional)

❶ Heat oil in a large saucepan over medium-high heat. Add onion and garlic; sauté 2 minutes. Add barley; cook 1 minute. Stir in chicken stock; bring to a boil. Cover, reduce heat, and simmer 30 minutes.
❷ Stir in zucchini, tomatoes, salt, and pepper; cover and cook 5 minutes. Ladle 1 cup barley mixture into each of 4 bowls. Top each serving with 1½ teaspoons feta and parsley, if desired.

SERVES 4

CALORIES 177; FAT 3.3g (sat 0.9g, mono 1.1g, poly 0.3g); PROTEIN 6g; CARB 31g; FIBER 8g; CHOL 5mg; IRON 2mg; SODIUM 187mg; CALC 64mg

Sorghum with Summer Corn, Tomatoes, and Tarragon

HANDS-ON TIME: 18 MIN. | **TOTAL TIME:** 1 HR. 30 MIN.

3 cups unsalted chicken stock
1 cup uncooked sorghum
8 teaspoons olive oil
1 tablespoon chopped fresh tarragon
2 tablespoons vinegar
1 teaspoon Dijon mustard
1 teaspoon minced fresh garlic
½ teaspoon kosher salt
¼ teaspoon freshly ground black pepper
8 ounces roasted sliced asparagus
2 cups halved cherry tomatoes
1½ cups fresh corn kernels

❶ Combine stock and sorghum in a medium saucepan. Bring to a boil; cover, reduce heat to low, and simmer 1 hour and 10 minutes or until tender. Drain; cool.

❷ Combine olive oil, tarragon, vinegar, Dijon mustard, garlic, salt, and pepper in a large bowl, stirring well with a whisk. Add cooked sorghum, asparagus, tomatoes, and corn kernels; toss.

SERVES 6 (serving size: 1 cup)

CALORIES 234; FAT 8.6g (sat 1.2g, mono 5.4g, poly 1.4g); PROTEIN 9g; CARB 35g; FIBER 4g; CHOL 0mg; IRON 3mg; SODIUM 256mg; CALC 38mg

Did You Know?

Sorghum is mild and slightly sweet, like a chewier version of Israeli couscous when cooked. It needs at least an hour to simmer. It's great to make in batches and freeze.

Toasted Millet with Cilantro Vinaigrette

HANDS-ON TIME: 30 MIN. | **TOTAL TIME:** 40 MIN.

3 tablespoons olive oil, divided
½ cup chopped onion
1 cup uncooked millet
1 tablespoon minced fresh garlic
1 cup unsalted chicken stock
   (such as Swanson)
1 cup water
½ teaspoon kosher salt, divided
½ cup chopped fresh cilantro
2 tablespoons fresh lime juice
1 teaspoon honey
½ teaspoon cumin
¼ teaspoon freshly ground black pepper
1 cup chopped red bell pepper
¾ cup diced avocado
1½ cups canned unsalted black beans,
   rinsed and drained
2 ounces crumbled feta cheese

❶ Heat 1½ teaspoons oil in a saucepan over medium heat. Add onion; sauté 3 minutes. Add millet and garlic to pan; cook 2 minutes. Stir in stock, 1 cup water, and ¼ teaspoon salt; bring to a boil. Cover, reduce heat, and simmer 25 minutes or until liquid is absorbed.

❷ Combine 2½ tablespoons oil, ¼ teaspoon salt, cilantro, lime juice, honey, cumin, and black pepper in a bowl. Add millet mixture, bell pepper, avocado, and beans; toss to coat. Sprinkle with feta.

SERVES 8 (serving size: ¾ cup)

CALORIES 225; **FAT** 9.8g (sat 2.3g, mono 5.6g, poly 1.4g); **PROTEIN** 7g; **CARB** 28g; **FIBER** 5g; **CHOL** 6mg; **IRON** 2mg; **SODIUM** 223mg; **CALC** 65mg

Mint and Pistachio Tabbouleh

HANDS-ON TIME: 10 MIN. | **TOTAL TIME:** 10 MIN.

1 cup cooked bulgur
1 cup chopped stemmed kale
½ cup chopped cucumber
½ cup halved grape tomatoes
¼ cup chopped red onion
¼ cup chopped fresh mint
¼ cup shelled pistachios
1 tablespoon fresh lemon juice
2 teaspoons olive oil
¼ teaspoon kosher salt
¼ teaspoon freshly ground black pepper
Dash of allspice

❶ Combine cooked bulgur, kale, cucumber, tomatoes, onion, mint, and pistachios in a large bowl. Combine lemon juice, olive oil, kosher salt, black pepper, and allspice in a bowl, stirring with a whisk. Add lemon juice mixture to kale mixture; toss to coat.

SERVES 6 (serving size: about ⅔ cup)

CALORIES 81; **FAT** 4g (sat 0.5g, mono 2.3g, poly 0.9g); **PROTEIN** 3g; **CARB** 10g; **FIBER** 3g; **CHOL** 0mg; **IRON** 1mg; **SODIUM** 88mg; **CALC** 32mg

Grits-Style Bulgur with Corn-Basil Relish

HANDS-ON TIME: 15 MIN. | **TOTAL TIME:** 15 MIN.

2¼ cups water
1 cup uncooked bulgur
2 ounces shredded extra-sharp cheddar cheese
¼ teaspoon salt, divided
1 cup fresh corn kernels
¼ cup finely chopped fresh basil
1 tablespoon minced shallots
1 tablespoon white wine vinegar

❶ Bring 2¼ cups water and bulgur to a boil in a small saucepan. Cover, reduce heat, and cook 8 minutes. Stir in cheese and ⅛ teaspoon salt.
❷ Combine corn kernels, basil, shallots, vinegar, and ⅛ teaspoon salt in a small bowl. Top bulgur mixture with corn mixture.

SERVES 4 (serving size: ⅔ cup bulgur and ¼ cup corn relish)

CALORIES 209; **FAT** 5.5g (sat 3.2g, mono 0.2g, poly 0.4g); **PROTEIN** 9g; **CARB** 34g; **FIBER** 7g; **CHOL** 13mg; **IRON** 1mg; **SODIUM** 250mg; **CALC** 120mg

Did You Know?

Bulgur is wheat that's been parboiled, dried, and cracked. It cooks fast and tastes good. Boil a big batch, and store in the refrigerator for up to 1 week, or divide into manageable portions and freeze.

Farro Stuffing with Butternut Squash, Red Onion, and Almonds

HANDS-ON TIME: 15 MIN. | **TOTAL TIME:** 40 MIN.

4 cups unsalted chicken stock
(such as Swanson)
2 cups uncooked farro
2 tablespoons olive oil
2 cups diced peeled butternut squash
1 cup chopped red onion
1 cup thinly sliced carrot
¾ cup thinly sliced celery
¾ cup almonds, toasted and coarsely
chopped
¾ cup chopped fresh flat-leaf parsley
1 tablespoon thyme leaves
1 tablespoon minced fresh sage
1¼ teaspoons kosher salt
½ teaspoon freshly ground black pepper

❶ Bring stock and farro to a boil in a large saucepan; cover, reduce heat, and simmer 25 minutes or until farro is al dente. Drain in a colander over a bowl, reserving cooking liquid.
❷ Heat a large nonstick skillet over medium heat. Add oil; swirl to coat. Add squash, onion, carrot, and celery; sauté 5 minutes. Stir in ¼ cup reserved cooking liquid. Reduce heat to low; cover and cook 7 minutes or until vegetables are tender. Stir squash mixture into farro mixture. Stir in almonds, parsley, thyme, sage, salt, and pepper.
❸ Spoon into an 11 x 7–inch glass or ceramic baking dish. Cover and keep warm until ready to serve. Stir in additional reserved cooking liquid as needed just before serving.

SERVES 12 (serving size: ³⁄₄ cup)

CALORIES 216; FAT 7.5g (sat 0.7g, mono 4.4g, poly 1.4g); PROTEIN 9g; CARB 31g; FIBER 6g; CHOL 0mg; IRON 2mg; SODIUM 259mg; CALC 71mg

Prep Pointer

You can assemble up to 2 days ahead. Take out of the fridge, let stand at room temperature 45 minutes, and bake at 350° for 25 minutes or until thoroughly heated.

Prep Pointer

The trick with farro is not to overcook it. You can serve this as soon as the tomatoes and farro are cooled and combined, but it benefits from a couple of hours in the fridge.

Farro with Honey-Garlic Roasted Tomatoes

HANDS-ON TIME: 15 MIN. | **TOTAL TIME:** 60 MIN.

1½ tablespoons olive oil

1 tablespoon honey

3 garlic cloves, minced

1 pound cherry or grape tomatoes, halved lengthwise

¾ cup uncooked farro

1½ teaspoons sherry vinegar

⅝ teaspoon kosher salt

3 tablespoons toasted walnuts, coarsely chopped

2 ounces feta cheese, crumbled (about ½ cup)

2 teaspoons chopped fresh thyme

❶ Preheat oven to 375°.

❷ Combine oil, honey, and garlic in a large bowl. Add tomatoes; gently, with your hands, toss until thoroughly coated. Pour tomatoes onto a jelly-roll pan; turn tomatoes until they're all cut side down. Draw tomatoes together until they're cozy and touching. If there's any honey mixture left, drizzle over tomatoes. Bake at 375° for 20 to 25 minutes or until wrinkled and soft but not mushy; do not brown. (Grape tomatoes may take less time than cherry tomatoes.) Remove tomatoes from oven; cool to room temperature.

❸ While tomatoes cook, place farro in a medium saucepan; cover with water to 2 inches above farro. Bring to a boil. Cover, reduce heat, and simmer 15 minutes or until nicely chewy and not puffed open and starchy. Drain and rinse with cold water; drain.

❹ Combine farro, tomato mixture, vinegar, and salt in a large bowl; toss gently to combine. Top with walnuts and feta; sprinkle with thyme. Serve immediately, or let the flavors marry in the fridge for an hour or 2.

SERVES 6 (serving size: about ½ cup)

CALORIES 191; **FAT** 8.4g (sat 2.1g, mono 3.3g, poly 2.2g); **PROTEIN** 6g; **CARB** 25g; **FIBER** 4g; **CHOL** 8mg; **IRON** 2mg; **SODIUM** 310mg; **CALC** 73mg

Creamy Gorgonzola Teff with Roasted Tomatoes

HANDS-ON TIME: 15 MIN. | **TOTAL TIME:** 30 MIN.

1½ cups unsalted chicken stock
(such as Swanson)
1½ cups 2% reduced-fat milk
1 cup uncooked teff
½ teaspoon kosher salt
2 ounces crumbled Gorgonzola cheese
¼ cup fat-free sour cream
¼ teaspoon freshly ground black pepper
¼ cup oven-roasted cherry tomatoes
Chopped fresh thyme

❶ Combine chicken stock and milk in a medium saucepan; bring to a boil. Stir in teff and salt. Cover and simmer 20 minutes or until liquid is absorbed, stirring occasionally.
❷ Remove pan from heat; stir in crumbled Gorgonzola, sour cream, and pepper. Divide teff mixture evenly among 6 plates. Top each with tomatoes; sprinkle with fresh thyme.

SERVES 6 (serving size: about ½ cup teff and about ¼ cup tomato mixture)

CALORIES 219; FAT 7g (sat 3.1g, mono 2g, poly 0.4g); PROTEIN 10g; CARB 30g; FIBER 5g; CHOL 0mg; IRON 0mg; SODIUM 375mg; CALC 0mg

Balsamic and Grape Quinoa

HANDS-ON TIME: 17 MIN. | **TOTAL TIME:** 17 MIN.

1⅔ cups water
1 cup uncooked red quinoa
2 tablespoons chopped fresh flat-leaf
parsley
1 tablespoon white balsamic vinegar
2 teaspoons extra-virgin olive oil
¼ teaspoon kosher salt
20 seedless red grapes, halved

❶ Bring 1⅔ cups water and quinoa to a boil in a medium saucepan. Reduce heat to low, and simmer 12 minutes or until quinoa is tender; drain. Place quinoa in a bowl. Add parsley, vinegar, olive oil, kosher salt, and grapes, stirring to combine.

SERVES 4 (serving size: about ¾ cup)

CALORIES 201; FAT 4.8g (sat 0.3g, mono 1.7g, poly 0.3g); PROTEIN 6g; CARB 34g; FIBER 2g; CHOL 0mg; IRON 3mg; SODIUM 133mg; CALC 26mg

Simple Swap

We love the color and texture of red quinoa, but regular quinoa also works well.

◄ *Nutty Almond-Sesame Red Quinoa*

HANDS-ON TIME: 17 MIN. | **TOTAL TIME:** 17 MIN.

1²⁄₃ cups water
1 cup uncooked red quinoa
¼ cup sliced almonds, toasted
2 tablespoons fresh lemon juice
2 teaspoons olive oil
2 teaspoons dark sesame oil
¼ teaspoon kosher salt
3 green onions, thinly sliced

❶ Bring 1²⁄₃ cups water and quinoa to a boil in a medium saucepan. Reduce heat to low, and simmer 12 minutes or until quinoa is tender; drain. Stir in almonds, juice, oils, salt, and onions.

SERVES 4 (serving size: about ¹⁄₂ cup)

CALORIES 238; **FAT** 10g (sat 0.9g, mono 4.4g, poly 1.9g); **PROTEIN** 8g; **CARB** 32g; **FIBER** 3g; **CHOL** 0mg; **IRON** 3mg; **SODIUM** 132mg; **CALC** 44mg

Lemon–Snap Pea Quinoa

HANDS-ON TIME: 17 MIN. | **TOTAL TIME:** 17 MIN.

1²⁄₃ cups water
1 cup uncooked red quinoa
1 cup diagonally halved sugar snap peas
¼ cup fresh lemon juice
1 tablespoon extra-virgin olive oil
1 teaspoon chopped fresh thyme
¼ teaspoon kosher salt
¼ teaspoon freshly ground black pepper

❶ Bring 1²⁄₃ cups water and quinoa to a boil in a medium saucepan. Reduce heat to low, and simmer 12 minutes or until quinoa is tender; drain. Add sugar snap peas and remaining ingredients, stirring to combine.

SERVES 4 (serving size: about ²⁄₃ cup)

CALORIES 201; **FAT** 6g (sat 0.5g, mono 2.5g, poly 0.4g); **PROTEIN** 7g; **CARB** 31g; **FIBER** 3g; **CHOL** 0mg; **IRON** 3mg; **SODIUM** 131mg; **CALC** 29mg

Prep Pointer

Quinoa is done when liquid is absorbed and tiny curly tails emerge from the seeds.

Superfast

Ready in 15
minutes or less!

Simple Swap

You can substitute
1 teaspoon of crushed
red pepper flakes for
the chile paste.

Kale, Brown Rice, and Quinoa Pilaf

HANDS-ON TIME: 15 MIN. | **TOTAL TIME:** 15 MIN.

2 teaspoons canola oil
½ cup chopped onion
½ cup thinly sliced carrot
½ cup chopped red bell pepper
2 garlic cloves, minced
2 teaspoons curry powder
1 teaspoon chile paste with garlic
½ teaspoon grated peeled fresh ginger
6 cups torn kale
2 cups cooked brown rice
1 cup cooked quinoa
2 tablespoons minced fresh cilantro
2 tablespoons lower-sodium soy sauce
1 (15-ounce) can chickpeas
(garbanzo beans), rinsed and drained

❶ Heat oil in a large nonstick skillet over medium heat. Add onion, carrot, bell pepper, and garlic; sauté 2 minutes. Add curry, chile paste, and ginger; sauté 1 minute. Add remaining ingredients; cook 3 minutes or until thoroughly heated, stirring occasionally. Serve at room temperature.

SERVES 8 (serving size: ¾ cup)

CALORIES 163; FAT 2.9g (sat 0.2g, mono 0.9g, poly 0.7g); PROTEIN 6g; CARB 30g; FIBER 4g; CHOL 0mg; IRON 2mg; SODIUM 231mg; CALC 92mg

Prep Pointer

To avoid lumps, bring the broth to a simmer and constantly whisk as the polenta grains slowly trickle in.

Two-Corn Polenta with Tomato, Basil, and Cheese

HANDS-ON TIME: 27 MIN. | **TOTAL TIME:** 32 MIN.

2 teaspoons olive oil
2 cups chopped onion (2 medium)
4 cups fat-free, lower-sodium chicken broth
2 cups fresh corn kernels (about 2 ears)
2 garlic cloves, chopped
1 cup instant dry polenta
2 ounces grated fresh Parmesan cheese (about $\frac{1}{2}$ cup)
$\frac{1}{4}$ teaspoon salt
$\frac{1}{8}$ teaspoon freshly ground black pepper
1 cup chopped tomato
$\frac{1}{2}$ cup chopped fresh basil

❶ Heat oil in a Dutch oven over medium heat. Add onion to pan; cook 8 minutes or until tender, stirring occasionally. Stir in broth, corn, and garlic; bring to a boil. Cover, reduce heat, and simmer 5 minutes.

❷ Slowly add polenta, stirring with a whisk until polenta is thick (about 5 minutes). Add cheese, stirring to melt. Stir in salt and pepper. Remove from heat; sprinkle with tomato and basil. Serve immediately.

SERVES 10 (serving size: about $\frac{3}{4}$ cup)

CALORIES 136; **FAT** 3g (sat 1.1g, mono 1.3g, poly 0.3g); **PROTEIN** 6g; **CARB** 22g; **FIBER** 3g; **CHOL** 4mg; **IRON** 4mg; **SODIUM** 262mg; **CALC** 94mg

Goat Cheese and Basil Polenta

HANDS-ON TIME: 18 MIN. | **TOTAL TIME:** 18 MIN.

3 cups water
1 cup instant dry polenta
3 ounces goat cheese
1 tablespoon chopped fresh basil
$\frac{1}{4}$ teaspoon freshly ground black pepper
$\frac{1}{4}$ teaspoon kosher salt

❶ Bring 3 cups water to a boil in a medium saucepan. Gradually add polenta, stirring constantly with a whisk. Reduce heat to low; cook 7 minutes, stirring occasionally. Remove from heat; stir in goat cheese, basil, pepper, and salt.

SERVES 4 (serving size: $\frac{3}{4}$ cup)

CALORIES 204; **FAT** 4.5g (sat 3.1g, mono 1g, poly 0.1g); **PROTEIN** 7g; **CARB** 32g; **FIBER** 1g; **CHOL** 10mg; **IRON** 2mg; **SODIUM** 198mg; **CALC** 32mg

Polenta-Sausage Triangles

HANDS-ON TIME: 25 MIN. | **TOTAL TIME:** 4 HR. 40 MIN.

Cooking spray
8 ounces reduced-fat pork sausage
  (such as Jimmy Dean)
3/4 cup finely chopped yellow onion
3/4 cup finely chopped celery
3 garlic cloves, minced
1 1/2 cups water
1 1/4 cups 1% low-fat milk
1 cup instant dry polenta
1/4 teaspoon kosher salt
2 tablespoons olive oil, divided

❶ Heat a large saucepan over medium-high heat. Coat pan with cooking spray. Add sausage; cook 2 minutes or until sausage begins to brown, stirring to crumble. Add onion, celery, and garlic; sauté 8 minutes or until vegetables are tender.

❷ Add 1 1/2 cups water and milk to sausage mixture in pan, and bring to a boil. Gradually add polenta, stirring constantly with a whisk. Stir in salt. Cook 3 minutes or until thick, stirring constantly. Spoon polenta into an 11 x 7–inch glass or ceramic baking dish coated with cooking spray. Cool to room temperature; cover and refrigerate at least 4 hours.

❸ Cut chilled polenta into 8 squares, and cut each polenta square diagonally into triangles. Heat a large nonstick skillet over medium-high heat. Add 1 tablespoon oil to pan; swirl to coat. Place 8 triangles in pan; cook 2 minutes on each side or until browned. Repeat procedure with remaining oil and polenta triangles.

SERVES 8 (serving size: 2 triangles)

CALORIES 190; FAT 9g (sat 2.5g, mono 2.6g, poly 0.4g); PROTEIN 8g; CARB 15g; FIBER 2g; CHOL 22mg; IRON 1mg; SODIUM 265mg; CALC 55mg

Prep Pointer

Prepare the polenta through step 2 up to 2 days ahead. Before serving, let the dish stand at room temperature 1 hour, cut polenta into triangles, and toast them at mealtime.

◄ *Awendaw*

HANDS-ON TIME: 20 MIN. | **TOTAL TIME:** 1 HR. 20 MIN.

3 cups water
¾ teaspoon salt
¾ cup uncooked regular grits
3 large eggs, lightly beaten
1 tablespoon butter
1 cup 1% low-fat milk
½ cup yellow cornmeal
Cooking spray

❶ Preheat oven to 375°.
❷ Combine 3 cups water and salt in a medium saucepan; bring to a boil. Gradually add grits, stirring constantly. Reduce heat to low, and simmer 12 minutes or until grits are tender and thick, stirring constantly. Remove from heat.
❸ Place eggs in a bowl; gradually add 1 cup hot grits to eggs, stirring constantly with a whisk. Return grits mixture to pan. Add butter, stirring until butter melts. Stir in milk and cornmeal. Pour batter into a 2-quart soufflé dish coated with cooking spray. Bake at 375° for 1 hour or until set.

SERVES 10 (serving size: about ⅔ cup)

CALORIES 96; FAT 3g (sat 1.3g, mono 1g, poly 0.3g); PROTEIN 5g; CARB 12g; FIBER 1g; CHOL 70mg; IRON 3mg; SODIUM 218mg; CALC 70mg

Creamy Grits

HANDS-ON TIME: 13 MIN. | **TOTAL TIME:** 13 MIN.

2 cups 1% low-fat milk
1 cup water
¾ cup uncooked quick-cooking grits
¼ teaspoon salt
¼ teaspoon freshly ground black pepper
1 tablespoon butter

❶ Bring milk and 1 cup water to a boil in a medium saucepan. Gradually add grits, stirring constantly with a whisk. Cook 5 minutes or until thick, stirring frequently. Remove from heat; stir in salt. Sprinkle with pepper; top each serving with butter.

SERVES 4 (serving size: about ¾ cup grits and ¾ teaspoon butter)

CALORIES 186; FAT 4.4g (sat 2.6g, mono 1.2g, poly 0.3g); PROTEIN 7g; CARB 30g; FIBER 1g; CHOL 14mg; IRON 1mg; SODIUM 222mg; CALC 147mg

Did You Know?

This classic spoon bread, named for an Indian settlement located north of Charleston, is typically served hot from the oven with butter and lots of shrimp.

Superfast

Ready in 15 minutes or less!

Corn Bread, Chorizo, and Jalapeño Dressing

HANDS-ON TIME: 40 MIN. | **TOTAL TIME:** 2 HR.

4.5 ounces all-purpose flour (about 1 cup)
1¼ cups low-fat buttermilk
1 cup yellow cornmeal
2 tablespoons sugar
2 tablespoons unsalted butter, melted
1 tablespoon baking powder
2 large eggs, lightly beaten
¾ cup shredded reduced-fat sharp cheddar cheese
Cooking spray
1 jalapeño pepper, halved
1 teaspoon olive oil
3 ounces Mexican pork chorizo, casing removed and crumbled
1¼ cups diced red bell pepper (1 large)
1 cup thinly sliced green onions
2 cups (½-inch) cubed French bread baguette (crusts removed)
¼ cup chopped fresh cilantro
2 large egg whites, lightly beaten
1 (14.5-ounce) can fat-free, lower-sodium chicken broth
1 lime, cut into wedges

❶ Preheat oven to 350°. Place a 10-inch cast-iron skillet in oven as it preheats.

❷ Weigh or lightly spoon flour into a dry measuring cup; level with a knife. Combine flour and next 6 ingredients (through eggs) in a large bowl; fold in cheese.

❸ Remove skillet from oven. Coat pan with cooking spray. Pour batter into hot skillet. Bake at 350° for 35 minutes or until edges are lightly browned and a wooden pick inserted in center comes out clean. Cool completely on a wire rack. Crumble corn bread into a large bowl.

❹ Remove seeds and membrane from half of jalapeño. Coarsely chop both jalapeño halves. Heat a large skillet over medium-high heat. Add oil to pan; swirl to coat. Add chorizo; sauté 2 minutes. Add jalapeño, bell pepper, and onions; sauté 3 minutes. Remove from heat. Add chorizo mixture to crumbled corn bread; stir in baguette, cilantro, egg whites, and broth, stirring until bread is moist.

❺ Spoon corn bread mixture into a 13 x 9–inch glass or ceramic baking dish coated with cooking spray. Bake at 350° for 45 minutes or until lightly browned. Serve with lime wedges.

SERVES 12 (serving size: ¾ cup)

CALORIES 218; FAT 8.1g (sat 3.6g, mono 3g, poly 0.7g); PROTEIN 9g; CARB 28g; FIBER 2g; CHOL 53mg; IRON 2mg; SODIUM 374mg; CALC 232mg

Mushroom and Leek Stuffing

HANDS-ON TIME: 23 MIN. | **TOTAL TIME:** 68 MIN.

9 cups (½-inch) cubed Italian bread
   (about 12 ounces)
3 tablespoons olive oil
2½ cups chopped leek (about 2 medium)
1½ cups chopped celery
1 cup chopped carrot
2 tablespoons minced fresh sage
1 tablespoon chopped fresh thyme
4 garlic cloves, minced
1 pound sliced cremini mushrooms
1 cup unsalted chicken stock (such
   as Swanson)
1 cup water
½ teaspoon freshly ground black pepper
¼ teaspoon kosher salt
2 large eggs, lightly beaten
Cooking spray

❶ Preheat oven to 350°.
❷ Arrange bread cubes in a single layer on a large baking sheet or jelly-roll pan. Bake at 350° for 18 minutes or until golden. Cool slightly.
❸ Heat a large nonstick skillet over medium-high heat. Add oil to pan; swirl to coat. Add leek and next 5 ingredients (through garlic); sauté 10 minutes or until leek begins to brown, stirring occasionally. Stir in mushrooms; sauté 8 minutes or until mushrooms are tender, stirring occasionally. Place mushroom mixture in a large bowl. Add toasted bread cubes, chicken stock, and remaining ingredients except cooking spray. Toss mixture gently to combine. Spoon mixture into an 11 x 7–inch glass or ceramic baking dish coated with cooking spray. Bake at 350° for 45 minutes or until top of stuffing is browned.

SERVES 10 (serving size: about ¾ cup)

CALORIES 179; FAT 6.6g (sat 1.2g, mono 3.6g, poly 1.2g); PROTEIN 7g; CARB 24g; FIBER 2g; CHOL 42mg; IRON 2mg; SODIUM 302mg; CALC 65mg

Simple Swap

If you don't have leeks on hand, shallots, yellow onion, or any mild onion makes a satisfying substitution.

◄ *Chestnut, Cranberry, and Leek Stuffing*

HANDS-ON TIME: 10 MIN. | **TOTAL TIME:** 1 HR. 15 MIN.

1½ cups unsalted chicken stock
(such as Swanson)

2 large eggs

12 ounces toasted sourdough bread cubes

7.4 ounces jarred roasted chestnuts,
quartered

½ cup dried cranberries

2 cups sliced leek

1 tablespoon butter

¼ teaspoon salt

¼ teaspoon pepper

Cooking spray

❶ Preheat oven to 350°.

❷ Combine stock and eggs. Add bread cubes.

❸ Bake chestnuts at 350° for 20 minutes. Cover dried cranberries with boiling water. Let stand 20 minutes; drain. Sauté leek in butter over medium heat 5 minutes. Add chestnuts, cranberries, leeks, salt, and pepper to bread mixture.

❹ Spoon mixture into an 11 x 7–inch glass or ceramic baking dish coated with cooking spray. Bake stuffing at 350° for 45 minutes.

SERVES 12

CALORIES 162; FAT 2.8g (sat 1.1g, mono 0.8g, poly 0.6g), PROTEIN 6g; CARB 29g; FIBER 1g; CHOL 34mg; IRON 2mg; SODIUM 298mg; CALC 38mg

Prep Pointer

Use toasted rather than day-old bread. Oven-dried bread absorbs liquid better and gives stuffing a crisp-moist texture that's not tough like stale bread.

◄ *Ham, Gruyère, and Onion Stuffing*

HANDS-ON TIME: 10 MIN. | **TOTAL TIME:** 1 HR. 15 MIN.

1½ cups unsalted chicken stock
(such as Swanson)

2 large eggs

12 ounces toasted sourdough bread cubes

1 tablespoon olive oil

2 cups finely chopped onion

2 ounces finely chopped lower-sodium
ham (about ⅔ cup)

2 ounces diced Gruyère cheese

¼ cup chopped fresh flat-leaf parsley

Cooking spray

❶ Combine stock and eggs. Add bread cubes.

❷ Heat a nonstick skillet over medium-high heat. Add oil; swirl. Add onion; sauté 2 minutes. Reduce heat to low; cook 30 minutes. Cool slightly. Add onion, ham, cheese, and parsley to bread mixture.

❸ Preheat oven to 350°.

❹ Spoon mixture into an 11 x 7–inch glass or ceramic baking dish coated with cooking spray. Bake stuffing at 350° for 45 minutes.

SERVES 12

CALORIES 153; FAT 4.4g (sat 1.6g, mono 1.8g, poly 0.6g); PROTEIN 8g; CARB 20g; FIBER 1g; CHOL 39mg; IRON 2mg; SODIUM 296mg; CALC 77mg

Prep Pointer

If your stuffing comes out too wet, pop it back in the oven, uncovered, for a few minutes until the top crisps up.

Sausage and Apple Stuffing

HANDS-ON TIME: 45 MIN. | **TOTAL TIME:** 1 HR. 30 MIN.

8 cups (1-inch) cubed sourdough bread (about 12 ounces)
6 ounces mild Italian breakfast sausage
1½ cups chopped onion
1¼ cups chopped fennel bulb
1 cup chopped celery
3 cups chopped peeled Golden Delicious apple (about 2 medium)
6 garlic cloves, minced
3 tablespoons chopped fresh sage
⅓ cup chopped fresh flat-leaf parsley
1¼ cups unsalted chicken stock (such as Swanson)
¼ cup unfiltered apple cider
2 large eggs, lightly beaten
½ teaspoon freshly ground black pepper
Cooking spray

❶ Preheat oven to 350°.

❷ Arrange bread cubes in a single layer on a large baking sheet or jelly-roll pan. Bake at 350° for 20 minutes or until golden. Cool slightly. Place in a large bowl.

❸ Heat a large nonstick skillet over medium-high heat. Add sausage to pan, and cook 5 minutes or until browned, stirring frequently to crumble. Add sausage to bread in bowl.

❹ Return pan to medium-high heat. Add onion, fennel, and celery to pan; sauté 7 minutes or until crisp-tender, stirring occasionally. Stir in apple and garlic; sauté 5 minutes or until vegetables are tender. Add sage to pan; cook 1 minute, stirring occasionally. Remove from heat; stir in parsley. Add onion mixture to bread mixture; toss well to combine.

❺ Combine chicken stock, apple cider, eggs, and black pepper in a medium bowl, stirring with a whisk. Add egg mixture to bread mixture, stirring gently to combine. Spoon bread mixture into an 11 x 7–inch glass or ceramic baking dish coated with cooking spray. Bake at 350° for 45 minutes or until top of stuffing is browned.

SERVES 12 (serving size: about ¾ cup)

CALORIES 166; **FAT** 6g (sat 1.8g, mono 2.7g, poly 0.9g); **PROTEIN** 7g; **CARB** 22g; **FIBER** 2g; **CHOL** 41mg; **IRON** 2mg; **SODIUM** 310mg; **CALC** 62mg

Greek-Style Stuffing

HANDS-ON TIME: 15 MIN. | **TOTAL TIME:** 60 MIN.

1½ cups unsalted chicken stock
(such as Swanson)

2 large eggs

12 ounces toasted sourdough bread
cubes

2 ounces coarsely chopped pitted
kalamata olives

2 ounces chopped drained sun-dried
tomatoes

3 tablespoons chopped fresh oregano

½ teaspoon crushed red pepper

Cooking spray

2 ounces crumbled goat cheese

❶ Preheat oven to 350°.

❷ Combine stock and eggs. Add bread cubes. Add olives, sun-dried tomatoes, oregano, and red pepper to bread mixture; toss well.

❸ Spoon mixture into an 11 x 7–inch glass or ceramic baking dish coated with cooking spray; sprinkle with goat cheese. Bake at 350° for 45 minutes.

SERVES 12

CALORIES 151; FAT 4.1g (sat 1.5g, mono 1.7g, poly 0.6g); PROTEIN 7g; CARB 21g; FIBER 2g; CHOL 35mg; IRON 2mg; SODIUM 339mg; CALC 41mg

Simple Swap

If you find sourdough too acidic, substitute French bread.

◄ *Tri-Pepper–Chorizo Stuffing*

HANDS-ON TIME: 13 MIN. | **TOTAL TIME:** 58 MIN.

1½ cups unsalted chicken stock
2 large eggs
12 ounces toasted sourdough bread
  cubes
2 teaspoons canola oil
1 cup diced poblano pepper
1 cup diced red bell pepper
½ cup diced onion
3 ounces Mexican pork chorizo
1 jalapeño pepper, minced
Cooking spray

❶ Preheat oven to 350°.
❷ Combine stock and eggs. Add bread cubes.
❸ Heat a skillet over medium-high heat. Add canola oil; swirl. Add diced poblano, diced red bell pepper, diced onion, pork chorizo, and minced jalapeño; sauté 5 minutes. Stir into bread mixture.
❹ Spoon mixture into an 11 x 7–inch glass or ceramic baking dish coated with cooking spray. Bake stuffing at 350° for 45 minutes.

SERVES 12

CALORIES 148; FAT 4.7g (sat 1.7g, mono 2.3g, poly 0.9g); PROTEIN 7g; CARB 20g; FIBER 1g; CHOL 41mg; IRON 1mg; SODIUM 291mg; CALC 23mg

◄ *Simply Herby Stuffing*

HANDS-ON TIME: 7 MIN. | **TOTAL TIME:** 57 MIN.

1½ cups unsalted chicken stock
2 large eggs
12 ounces toasted sourdough bread
  cubes
5 garlic cloves, minced
2 tablespoons olive oil
½ cup chopped fresh parsley
2 tablespoons chopped fresh thyme
1 tablespoon chopped fresh sage
½ teaspoon salt
½ teaspoon black pepper
Cooking spray

❶ Preheat oven to 350°.
❷ Combine stock and eggs. Add bread cubes.
❸ Sauté minced garlic in olive oil. Stir garlic mixture, parsley, thyme, sage, salt, and pepper into bread mixture. Let stand 5 minutes.
❹ Spoon mixture into an 11 x 7–inch glass or ceramic baking dish coated with cooking spray. Bake stuffing at 350° for 45 minutes.

SERVES 12

CALORIES 129; FAT 3.7g (sat 0.7g, mono 2.1g, poly 0.6g); PROTEIN 6g; CARB 19g; FIBER 1g; CHOL 31mg; IRON 2mg; SODIUM 332mg; CALC 29mg

Prep Pointer

Be sure to cut off the white ribs inside the peppers before chopping them, as they can be bitter and change the flavor of the dish.

Fresh Peas
with Spicy
Pepper Relish,
p. 127

Edamame
Succotash,
p. 150

Split Pea–Spinach
Dal with Cauliflower,
p. 144

beans, lentils, and peas

Beans, lentils, and peas may be the most nutritious foods going. Nothing else in the vegetable kingdom packs as much satisfying protein and fiber. Not only that, but they are easy to cook and are some of the most wallet-friendly ingredients in your pantry arsenal. Filling and full of flavor, sides made from these versatile legumes win raves from vegetarians and meat lovers alike.

Know Your Legumes

Legumes such as lentils, beans, and peas are high in protein and fiber, low in fat, and cholesterol free. You can buy them fresh, canned, dried, or frozen. Canned beans are a busy cook's go-to pantry staple, and you can easily find organic and unsalted varieties that are lower in sodium. Dried beans and peas often taste better than canned, but they usually require lengthier cooking times.

Borlotti
(cranberry beans)

Creamy texture; earthy flavor; thin skin.

Chickpeas
(garbanzo beans)

Nutty flavor. Their firm texture holds well when cooking.

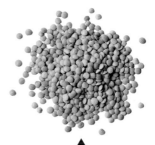

Lentils

Because of their small size and thin skins, lentils require no soaking and cook quickly. All legumes have folate, but lentils take the prize.

Cannellini beans
(white navy beans)

Versatile with a delicate flavor and texture. Cook gently to avoid mushiness. Navy beans edge out black beans and pintos in fiber content.

Corona beans

Slightly mealy texture and meaty taste. Best in recipes that call for long, slow cooking.

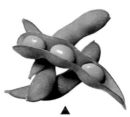

Soybeans

These "super beans" have almost twice the iron of other beans and are one of the few complete proteins the plant world has to offer.

How to Prepare

If you can boil water, you can cook beans. Depending on the type of bean, preparation times may vary.

FRESH FAVA BEANS

❶ Remove beans from their pods.
❷ Cook shelled beans in boiling water for 1 minute. Drain and plunge beans into ice water; drain.
❸ Remove the tough outer skins from beans by pinching the outer skin between your thumb and forefinger; discard skins. The beans are ready to use in any recipe.

DRIED BEANS

❶ Choose the quantity you want to cook, keeping in mind that the beans will expand when soaked.
❷ Place in a large bowl, and fill with water; soak overnight (6 to 8 hours). Presoaking the beans shortens the cooking time and promotes even cooking. Rinse; toss out shriveled or discolored beans.
❸ Add new water to a large pot; bring beans to a boil. (If cooking kidney beans, boil for at least 10 minutes; they contain a toxin that is neutralized by high temperature.)
❹ After boiling, reduce heat, cover pot, and simmer until beans have reached the desired texture; this can take up to a few hours.

LENTILS

❶ Combine the water and lentils in a large saucepan—3 cups of water for 1 cup of dried lentils is a good ratio.
❷ Bring to a boil.
❸ Cover, reduce the heat, and simmer 30 minutes.
❹ Uncover, increase the heat to medium-high, and, if desired, stir in any cooked vegetables or seasonings; cook for 2 minutes or until the liquid almost evaporates.
❺ Cover with a kitchen towel, and cool slightly.

Prep Pointer

Lentils cook quickly and don't require soaking like other dried beans.

This dish is a winner for barbecues because it can be made the day before and reheated the day of the party. Canned beans make this easy to toss together.

The Ultimate Baked Beans

HANDS-ON TIME: 38 MIN. | **TOTAL TIME:** 1 HR. 23 MIN.

1 (16-ounce) can unsalted cannellini beans or other white beans, undrained
1 (16-ounce) can unsalted chickpeas (garbanzo beans), undrained
1 (16-ounce) can unsalted kidney beans, undrained
1 (16-ounce) can lima beans, undrained
1 (16-ounce) can baked beans, undrained
6 bacon slices
2 cups chopped onion
½ cup packed brown sugar
½ cup cider vinegar
1 teaspoon dry mustard
1 garlic clove, crushed
Cooking spray

❶ Preheat oven to 350°.
❷ Drain beans in a colander over a bowl, reserving 1 cup liquid. Set beans and liquid aside.
❸ Cook bacon in a large nonstick skillet over medium heat until crisp. Remove bacon from pan, reserving 3 tablespoons drippings in pan. Crumble bacon.
❹ Add onion to drippings in pan, and cook 10 minutes over medium heat or until golden brown, stirring frequently. Stir in bacon, sugar, and remaining ingredients except cooking spray; cook over medium-low heat until thick and bubbly (about 15 minutes), stirring occasionally.
❺ Combine beans, reserved bean liquid, and onion mixture in a 3-quart glass or ceramic baking dish coated with cooking spray. Cover and bake at 350° for 45 minutes, stirring every 15 minutes.

SERVES 15 (serving size: ½ cup)

CALORIES 170; FAT 4.6g (sat 1.5g, mono 1.8g, poly 0.4g); PROTEIN 6g; CARB 26g; FIBER 5g; CHOL 6mg; IRON 1mg; SODIUM 251mg; CALC 50mg

Santa Fe Black Beans

HANDS-ON TIME: 23 MIN. | **TOTAL TIME:** 11 HR. 23 MIN.

1 (1-pound) package dried black beans
3 cups fat-free, lower-sodium chicken broth
2 cups finely chopped onion (about 1 large)
1 tablespoon chopped chipotle chile, canned in adobo sauce
½ teaspoon salt
4 garlic cloves, minced
1 tablespoon fresh lime juice
4 ounces crumbled queso fresco (about 1 cup)
½ cup chopped fresh cilantro
½ cup unsalted pumpkinseed kernels

❶ Sort and wash beans; place in a large Dutch oven. Cover with water to 2 inches above beans; bring to a boil. Cook 2 minutes; remove from heat. Cover and let stand 1 hour. Drain beans.

❷ Place beans in a 3-quart electric slow cooker. Stir in broth and next 4 ingredients (through garlic). Cover and cook on LOW 10 hours or until beans are tender.

❸ Stir in lime juice. Mash bean mixture with a potato masher until slightly thick. Sprinkle with queso fresco, cilantro, and pumpkinseed kernels.

SERVES 14 (serving size: ½ cup beans, about 1 tablespoon cheese, about 1½ teaspoons cilantro, and about 1½ teaspoons pumpkinseed kernels)

CALORIES 165; **FAT** 4.4g (sat 1.8g, mono 1.2g, poly 0.9g); **PROTEIN** 10g; **CARB** 23g; **FIBER** 4g; **CHOL** 6mg; **IRON** 2mg; **SODIUM** 263mg; **CALC** 9mg

Prep Pointer

You can mash the beans as much or as little as you like to create a consistency that suits your texture preferences.

Spicy Black Beans ▶

HANDS-ON TIME: 12 MIN. | **TOTAL TIME:** 12 MIN.

2 teaspoons canola oil
1 cup chopped red bell pepper
1 jalapeño pepper, minced
2 tablespoons fresh lime juice
1/4 teaspoon salt
1 (15-ounce) can organic unsalted
 black beans, rinsed and drained
1 tablespoon chopped fresh cilantro

❶ Heat a large nonstick skillet over medium-high heat. Add oil to pan; swirl to coat. Add bell pepper and jalapeño; sauté 4 minutes. Add lime juice, salt, and beans. Cook 3 minutes or until thoroughly heated. Sprinkle with chopped cilantro.

SERVES 4 (serving size: about 1/2 cup)

CALORIES 83; FAT 2.4g (sat 0.2g, mono 1.5g, poly 0.7g);
PROTEIN 4g; CARB 12g; FIBER 4g; CHOL 0mg; IRON 1mg;
SODIUM 157mg; CALC 34mg

Simple Black Beans

HANDS-ON TIME: 15 MIN. | **TOTAL TIME:** 45 MIN.

1 1/2 tablespoons canola oil
1 cup chopped onion
3/4 cup finely chopped red bell pepper
1/2 teaspoon brown sugar
1 1/2 teaspoons minced fresh garlic
1/4 teaspoon freshly ground black pepper
1/4 teaspoon ground cumin
1 cup water
2 (15-ounce) cans 50%-less-sodium
 black beans, undrained
1 teaspoon white wine vinegar

❶ Heat oil in a large Dutch oven over medium heat. Add onion and bell pepper to pan; cook 5 minutes or until tender, stirring occasionally. ❷ Stir in sugar, garlic, black pepper, and cumin; cook 1 minute, stirring constantly. Stir in 1 cup water and beans; bring to a boil. Partially cover, reduce heat, and simmer 30 minutes or until slightly thick, stirring frequently. Remove from heat, and stir in vinegar.

SERVES 6 (serving size: 2/3 cup)

CALORIES 128; FAT 3.6g (sat 0.3g, mono 2.1g, poly 1.1g);
PROTEIN 6g; CARB 23g; FIBER 8g; CHOL 0mg; IRON 2mg;
SODIUM 294mg; CALC 58mg

Black Bean Cakes with Ginger-Cilantro Cream

HANDS-ON TIME: 23 MIN. | **TOTAL TIME:** 23 MIN.

2 tablespoons butter, divided
½ cup finely chopped onion
1 tablespoon minced fresh garlic
¾ teaspoon ground cumin
½ teaspoon kosher salt, divided
½ teaspoon ground coriander
½ teaspoon crushed red pepper
½ teaspoon freshly ground black
  pepper, divided
¼ cup panko (Japanese breadcrumbs)
1 tablespoon fresh lime juice
1 (14.5-ounce) can unsalted black beans,
  rinsed and drained
2 large eggs, lightly beaten
¼ cup reduced-fat sour cream
2 tablespoons finely chopped fresh
  cilantro
1 teaspoon grated peeled fresh ginger

❶ Heat a medium skillet over medium heat. Add 1 tablespoon butter to pan; swirl until butter melts. Add onion and garlic; cook 4 minutes, stirring occasionally. Stir in cumin, ¼ teaspoon salt, coriander, red pepper, and ¼ teaspoon black pepper; cook 30 seconds, stirring. Remove from heat. Stir in panko and lime juice.

❷ Place beans in a bowl; coarsely mash with a fork. Stir in eggs. Stir in onion mixture. Divide bean mixture into 4 portions, gently shaping each into a ½-inch-thick patty. Heat pan over medium-high heat. Add 1 tablespoon butter to pan; swirl until butter melts. Add patties to pan; cook 3 minutes on each side or until browned.

❸ Combine ¼ teaspoon salt, ¼ teaspoon black pepper, sour cream, cilantro, and ginger. Serve with patties.

SERVES 4 (serving size: 1 patty and about ¼ cup sauce)

CALORIES 192; FAT 10.3g (sat 5.6g, mono 2.4g, poly 0.7g); PROTEIN 9g; CARB 16g; FIBER 4g; CHOL 116mg; IRON 2mg; SODIUM 356mg; CALC 86mg

Prep Pointer

Turn cakes gently, as they may fall apart. If they do, don't worry; you can press them back together.

Prep Pointer

This can be frozen for up to 3 months. After spooning into casserole dish, cover and freeze. Thaw in refrigerator; bake as directed.

Barbecued Beans and Greens

HANDS-ON TIME: 12 MIN. | **TOTAL TIME:** 57 MIN.

2 teaspoons olive oil
1 cup chopped onion
4 garlic cloves, minced
8 cups chopped kale (about ¾ pound)
½ cup water
½ cup hickory barbecue sauce
    (such as Kraft Hickory Smoke)
2 tablespoons Dijon mustard
1 tablespoon cider vinegar
1 teaspoon hot sauce
2 (16-ounce) cans unsalted kidney
    beans, rinsed and drained

❶ Preheat oven to 350°.
❷ Heat a large nonstick skillet over medium heat. Add oil to pan; swirl to coat. Add onion and garlic; sauté 5 minutes or until onion is tender. Add kale; cook 3 to 4 minutes or until kale wilts, stirring occasionally. Stir in ½ cup water and remaining ingredients.
❸ Spoon mixture into a 2-quart glass or ceramic baking dish. Cover and bake at 350° for 30 minutes. Uncover and bake an additional 15 minutes.

SERVES 9 (serving size: about ½ cup)

CALORIES 124; FAT 1.9g (sat 0.2g, mono 0.8g, poly 0.3g); PROTEIN 5g; CARB 23g; FIBER 4g; CHOL 0mg; IRON 2mg; SODIUM 240mg; CALC 106mg

Quick Classic Baked Beans

HANDS-ON TIME: 21 MIN. | **TOTAL TIME:** 31 MIN.

6 center-cut bacon slices, chopped
1 cup finely chopped onion
3 thyme sprigs
4 garlic cloves, minced
½ cup fat-free, lower-sodium chicken broth
⅓ cup packed dark brown sugar
1 tablespoon prepared mustard
½ teaspoon kosher salt
½ teaspoon smoked paprika
⅛ teaspoon ground red pepper
3 (15-ounce) cans organic navy beans, rinsed and drained
1 (8-ounce) can unsalted tomato sauce

❶ Preheat broiler to high.
❷ Cook bacon in a 10-inch cast-iron skillet over medium-high heat until crisp. Remove bacon with a slotted spoon, reserving drippings. Add onion and thyme sprigs to drippings in pan; sauté 3 minutes. Add garlic; sauté 1 minute. Stir in broth and remaining ingredients; reduce heat to medium and cook, uncovered, 10 minutes or until slightly thick, stirring occasionally. Discard thyme.
❸ Remove from heat; stir in bacon. Broil 4 minutes or until bubbly and edges are crusty.

SERVES 8 (serving size: about ½ cup)

CALORIES 158; **FAT** 2.1g (sat 0.8g, mono 0.6g, poly 0.4g); **PROTEIN** 8g; **CARB** 29g; **FIBER** 6g; **CHOL** 6mg; **IRON** 3mg; **SODIUM** 296mg; **CALC** 81mg

Prep Pointer

If you want extra herby flavor, garnish with fresh thyme leaves.

Fiery Chipotle Baked Beans

HANDS-ON TIME: 17 MIN. | **TOTAL TIME:** 1 HR. 17 MIN.

4 ounces Spanish chorizo, thinly sliced
2½ cups chopped onion
1 cup fat-free, lower-sodium chicken broth
⅓ cup packed brown sugar
⅓ cup cider vinegar
⅓ cup dark molasses
2 tablespoons bottled chili sauce
2 teaspoons dry mustard
2 teaspoons chipotle chile powder
¼ teaspoon salt
¼ teaspoon ground cloves
¼ teaspoon ground allspice
1 (15-ounce) can unsalted black beans, rinsed and drained
1 (15-ounce) can unsalted kidney beans, rinsed and drained
1 (15-ounce) can unsalted pinto beans, rinsed and drained

❶ Preheat oven to 325°.
❷ Heat a Dutch oven over medium-high heat. Add chorizo; sauté 2 minutes. Add onion; sauté 5 minutes, stirring occasionally. Stir in broth and remaining ingredients; bake, uncovered, at 325° for 1 hour.

SERVES 10 (serving size: ½ cup)

CALORIES 198; FAT 4.8g (sat 1.7g, mono 2.1g, poly 0.4g); PROTEIN 8g; CARB 32g; FIBER 4g; CHOL 10mg; IRON 3mg; SODIUM 334mg; CALC 107mg

Did You Know?

Yankee-style baked beans date back to America's earliest days, when Native Americans showed settlers how to cook beans flavored with maple sugar and bear fat. Here, the classic dish is updated with molasses and chipotle chile to incorporate old and new flavors.

Be sure to use firm dry-cured Spanish chorizo and not soft, raw Mexican chorizo for this recipe.

Smoky Baked Beans with Chorizo

HANDS-ON TIME: 20 MIN. | **TOTAL TIME:** 10 HR. 30 MIN.

1 pound dried Great Northern beans (2½ cups)
1 cup diced dry-cured Spanish chorizo
4 cups chopped onion
8 garlic cloves, thinly sliced
4 cups water
2 tablespoons chopped fresh oregano
2 tablespoons chopped fresh thyme
1½ teaspoons salt
1 teaspoon ground cumin
½ teaspoon smoked paprika
½ teaspoon paprika
2 bay leaves
2 tablespoons brown sugar
3 tablespoons unsalted tomato paste
3 tablespoons molasses
¼ teaspoon crushed red pepper
2½ tablespoons red wine vinegar
¼ teaspoon freshly ground black pepper
⅛ teaspoon ground red pepper
½ cup chopped green onions
2 tablespoons chopped fresh flat-leaf parsley

❶ Sort and wash beans; place in a large Dutch oven. Cover with water to 2 inches above beans. Cover; let stand 8 hours. Drain.

❷ Heat Dutch oven over medium heat. Add chorizo; cook 4 minutes or until fat begins to render. Add onion and garlic; sauté 10 minutes or until tender. Add beans, 4 cups water, and next 7 ingredients (through bay leaves); bring to a boil. Cover, reduce heat, and simmer 45 minutes or until beans are just tender.

❸ Preheat oven to 350°.

❹ Stir brown sugar and next 3 ingredients (through crushed red pepper) into bean mixture; bring to a simmer. Cover; bake at 350° for 1½ hours or until beans are very tender and sauce is thick. Remove from oven; stir in vinegar, black pepper, and ground red pepper. Discard bay leaves; sprinkle with green onions and parsley.

SERVES 12 (serving size: ⅔ cup)

CALORIES 184; FAT 2.9g (sat 1g, mono 1.2g, poly 0.5g); PROTEIN 11g; CARB 30g; FIBER 8g; CHOL 0mg; IRON 3mg; SODIUM 306mg; CALC 98mg

Simmered Pinto Beans with Chipotle Sour Cream

HANDS-ON TIME: 5 MIN. | **TOTAL TIME:** 15 MIN.

2 teaspoons olive oil
½ cup chopped onion
½ cup chopped red bell pepper
½ teaspoon ground cumin
2 garlic cloves, minced
½ cup unsalted chicken stock
   (such as Swanson)
⅛ teaspoon kosher salt
⅛ teaspoon freshly ground black pepper
1 (15-ounce) can unsalted pinto beans,
   rinsed and drained
1 tablespoon fresh lemon juice
2 tablespoons chopped fresh flat-leaf
   parsley
¾ cup reduced-fat sour cream
3 tablespoons low-fat buttermilk
1½ teaspoons minced chipotle chiles,
   canned in adobo sauce

❶ Heat a saucepan over medium-high heat. Add oil; swirl to coat. Add onion, bell pepper, cumin, and garlic; sauté 2 minutes. Add stock, salt, black pepper, and beans; simmer 7 minutes. Stir in juice and parsley.
❷ Combine remaining ingredients; serve with beans.

SERVES 6 (serving size: about ¼ cup beans and 2 tablespoons cream)

CALORIES 128; **FAT** 5.4g (sat 2.6g, mono 1.1g, poly 0.2g); **PROTEIN** 5g; **CARB** 14g; **FIBER** 4g; **CHOL** 16mg; **IRON** 1mg; **SODIUM** 100mg; **CALC** 99mg

Smoky Refried Beans

HANDS-ON TIME: 11 MIN. | **TOTAL TIME:** 11 MIN.

¼ cup water
2 (15-ounce) cans unsalted pinto
   beans, rinsed and drained
1 (7-ounce) can chipotle chiles in adobo
   sauce
2 teaspoons fresh lime juice
¼ teaspoon ground cumin
¼ teaspoon salt
Chopped fresh cilantro (optional)

❶ Place ¼ cup water and beans in a medium saucepan; bring to a simmer.
❷ Remove 2 chiles and 1 teaspoon adobo sauce from can of chiles; reserve remaining chiles and sauce for another use. Finely chop chiles; stir chiles and adobo sauce into beans; return to a simmer. Remove from heat; stir in juice, cumin, and salt. Mash with a potato masher to desired consistency; add additional water, if necessary. Sprinkle with cilantro, if desired.

SERVES 4 (serving size: about ⅔ cup)

CALORIES 102; **FAT** 0.1g (sat 0g, mono 0.1g, poly 0g); **PROTEIN** 6g; **CARB** 19g; **FIBER** 6g; **CHOL** 0mg; **IRON** 2mg; **SODIUM** 224mg; **CALC** 60mg

Louisiana Red Beans

HANDS-ON TIME: 23 MIN. | **TOTAL TIME:** 23 MIN.

1 ounce diced andouille sausage
½ cup sliced celery
¼ cup diced onion
¼ cup diced green bell pepper
1 teaspoon salt-free Creole seasoning
1 bay leaf
1 thyme sprig
2 garlic cloves, minced
2 (15-ounce) cans unsalted red kidney
   beans, rinsed and drained
1 cup unsalted chicken stock
   (such as Swanson)
1 tablespoon chopped fresh parsley

❶ Sauté sausage in a skillet over medium heat 2 minutes. Add celery and next 6 ingredients (through garlic); sauté 5 minutes. Add beans and stock. Bring to a boil; simmer 5 minutes. Stir in parsley.

SERVES 4 (serving size: about ¾ cup)

CALORIES 120; **FAT** 1.3g (sat 0.5g, mono 0.3g, poly 0.2g); **PROTEIN** 10g; **CARB** 19g; **FIBER** 9g; **CHOL** 5mg; **IRON** 2mg; **SODIUM** 207mg; **CALC** 57mg

◄ *White Beans with Prosciutto*

HANDS-ON TIME: 15 MIN. | **TOTAL TIME:** 15 MIN.

2 teaspoons extra-virgin olive oil
¼ cup finely chopped red onion
2 teaspoons minced fresh garlic
½ teaspoon minced fresh rosemary
2 tablespoons dry white wine
3 tablespoons fat-free, lower-sodium
   chicken broth
¼ teaspoon freshly ground black pepper
1 (15-ounce) can cannellini beans, rinsed
   and drained
2 tablespoons chopped fresh parsley
1 ounce thinly sliced prosciutto, chopped
   (about ¼ cup)

❶ Heat a large skillet over medium heat. Add oil to pan; swirl to coat. Add onion; sauté 2 minutes. Add garlic and rosemary; sauté 30 seconds. Add wine; cook until liquid evaporates. Add broth, pepper, and beans; cook 3 minutes or until beans are thoroughly heated. Stir in parsley and prosciutto.

SERVES 4 (serving size: about ⅓ cup)

CALORIES 94; FAT 3.1g (sat 0.6g, mono 1.7g, poly 0.3g); PROTEIN 6g; CARB 11g; FIBER 3g; CHOL 6mg; IRON 1mg; SODIUM 356mg; CALC 35mg

Prep Pointer

Canned beans are incredibly versatile and filling. Look for organic beans, which are low in sodium. Cook gently to avoid mushiness.

Escarole and Bean Sauté

HANDS-ON TIME: 10 MIN. | **TOTAL TIME:** 10 MIN.

2 teaspoons extra-virgin olive oil
1 (1-pound) bag chopped escarole
¼ cup water
4 teaspoons minced fresh garlic
½ teaspoon crushed red pepper
¼ teaspoon salt
1 (15-ounce) can cannellini beans, rinsed
   and drained
1 teaspoon grated lemon rind
2 teaspoons fresh lemon juice
¼ teaspoon freshly ground black pepper

❶ Heat oil in a Dutch oven over medium-high heat. Gradually add escarole, and cook 1 minute. Add ¼ cup water; cover. Cook 30 seconds, and uncover. Add garlic, red pepper, salt, and beans; cook 2 minutes. Add lemon rind, lemon juice, and black pepper.

SERVES 6 (serving size: about ⅔ cup)

CALORIES 71; FAT 1.8g (sat 0.3g, mono 1.2g, poly 0.2g); PROTEIN 4g; CARB 11g; FIBER 5g; CHOL 0mg; IRON 1mg; SODIUM 238mg; CALC 66mg

Prep Pointer

Give the sliced fennel a head start by roasting at a high temperature until caramelized and crisp-tender.

Warm White Beans with Roasted Fennel

HANDS-ON TIME: 14 MIN. | **TOTAL TIME:** 34 MIN.

4 cups thinly sliced fennel bulb

3 tablespoons olive oil, divided

3/4 teaspoon freshly ground black pepper, divided

1/2 teaspoon salt, divided

1/4 teaspoon ground red pepper

2 garlic cloves, minced

Cooking spray

3 tablespoons grated Parmigiano-Reggiano cheese

2 (15.8-ounce) cans Great Northern beans, rinsed and drained

4 cups fresh baby spinach

❶ Preheat oven to 450°.

❷ Combine fennel, 1 tablespoon oil, 1/2 teaspoon black pepper, 1/4 teaspoon salt, red pepper, and garlic in a large bowl; toss to coat fennel. Arrange fennel mixture in a single layer on a baking sheet coated with cooking spray. Bake at 450° for 15 minutes or until fennel begins to brown. Stir; sprinkle cheese evenly over fennel mixture. Bake 5 minutes or until golden brown.

❸ Heat a large nonstick skillet over medium heat; add 2 tablespoons oil. Add beans; cook 2 minutes or until heated. Add fennel mixture, spinach, 1/4 teaspoon black pepper, and 1/4 teaspoon salt. Cook 2 minutes; serve immediately.

SERVES 6 (serving size: about 2/3 cup)

CALORIES 140; FAT 6.1g (sat 1.1g, mono 3.9g, poly 0.7g); PROTEIN 6g; CARB 17g; FIBER 5g; CHOL 2mg; IRON 2mg; SODIUM 231mg; CALC 90mg

Tuscan White Beans

HANDS-ON TIME: 10 MIN. | TOTAL TIME: 40 MIN.

½ cup chopped onion
½ cup chopped celery
½ cup chopped carrot
⅓ cup chopped fresh parsley
1 tablespoon grated lemon rind
⅓ cup fresh lemon juice
2 tablespoons chopped fresh sage
2 tablespoons extra-virgin olive oil
½ teaspoon salt
¼ teaspoon crushed red pepper
3 (15.5-ounce) cans cannellini beans or other white beans, rinsed and drained
2 garlic cloves, minced

❶ Combine all ingredients in a large bowl. Let stand at room temperature at least 30 minutes before serving.

SERVES 10 (serving size: about ⅔ cup)

CALORIES 114; FAT 3.2g (sat 0.4g, mono 2g, poly 0.7g); PROTEIN 4g; CARB 17g; FIBER 4g; CHOL 0mg; IRON 2mg; SODIUM 341mg; CALC 45mg

Lemony White Bean Mash

HANDS-ON TIME: 7 MIN. | **TOTAL TIME:** 7 MIN.

1 (15-ounce) can cannellini beans, rinsed
  and drained
3 tablespoons chopped celery
2 tablespoons chopped fresh parsley
1 tablespoon fresh lemon juice
2 teaspoons olive oil
¼ teaspoon kosher salt

❶ Place beans in a bowl; mash with a fork.
Add celery, parsley, lemon juice, oil, and salt;
stir to combine.

SERVES 4 (serving size: ½ cup)

CALORIES 65; FAT 2.7g (sat 0.3g, mono 1.7g, poly 0.2g);
PROTEIN 3g; CARB 8g; FIBER 2g; CHOL 0mg; IRON 1mg;
SODIUM 142mg; CALC 22mg

Fresh Cranberry Beans with Lemon and Olive Oil

HANDS-ON TIME: 8 MIN. | **TOTAL TIME:** 25 MIN.

4 cups water
2 teaspoons sea salt
3 pounds fresh shelled cranberry beans
  (about 7¾ cups)
¼ cup fresh lemon juice
2 tablespoons chopped fresh cilantro
2 tablespoons extra-virgin olive oil
½ teaspoon freshly ground black pepper

❶ Bring 4 cups water and salt to a boil in
a stockpot. Add beans. Reduce heat, and simmer
15 minutes or until beans are tender. Drain.
❷ Combine lemon juice and remaining ingredients in a small bowl; stir well with a whisk.
Combine juice mixture and beans, tossing to
coat. Serve at room temperature or chilled.

SERVES 10 (serving size: about ¾ cup)

CALORIES 211; FAT 3.4g (sat 0.6g, mono 2.1g, poly 0.5g);
PROTEIN 13g; CARB 34g; FIBER 6g; CHOL 0mg; IRON 3mg;
SODIUM 232mg; CALC 70mg

Simple Swap

Pureed canned beans
are an alternative to
mashed potatoes.

Did You Know?

Fresh cranberry
beans are generally
available at farmers'
markets and farm
stands in the late
summer and fall.
Once shelled, they
freeze well. Just
blanch them briefly
in boiling water, drain,
cool, and freeze in
zip-top plastic bags.
If you can't find them
in your area, substitute
another fresh shelled
bean, such as fava or
baby lima beans.

Prep Pointer

These creamy, fresh-from-the-pod cranberry beans are delicious alongside grilled pork or lamb.

Cranberry Beans with Parsley Pesto

HANDS-ON TIME: 28 MIN. | **TOTAL TIME:** 1 HR. 8 MIN.

2 quarts water
4 cups shelled fresh cranberry beans (about 2¼ pounds unshelled beans)
1 teaspoon salt
1¼ cups chopped seeded plum tomato (about 2 large)
½ cup finely chopped red onion
¾ cup parsley leaves
½ cup basil leaves
2 tablespoons grated fresh Parmesan cheese
2 tablespoons chopped walnuts, toasted
3 tablespoons extra-virgin olive oil
2 tablespoons water
1 tablespoon fresh lemon juice
½ teaspoon salt
⅛ teaspoon freshly ground black pepper
1 garlic clove

❶ Bring 2 quarts water to a boil in a large saucepan; stir in beans and 1 teaspoon salt. Reduce heat, and simmer, uncovered, 40 minutes or until beans are tender. Drain beans; place in a large bowl. Stir in tomato and onion.

❷ Place parsley and remaining ingredients in a food processor; process until finely chopped, scraping sides of bowl occasionally. Add herb mixture to bean mixture; toss to combine. Serve at room temperature.

SERVES 8 (serving size: about ¾ cup)

CALORIES 193; FAT 7.1g (sat 1.2g, mono 4g, poly 1.6g); PROTEIN 10g; CARB 24g; FIBER 10g; CHOL 1mg; IRON 3mg; SODIUM 246mg; CALC 77mg

Fresh Peas with Spicy Pepper Relish

HANDS-ON TIME: 17 MIN. | **TOTAL TIME:** 37 MIN.

1 cup diced red bell pepper
½ cup diced onion
2 tablespoons chopped fresh parsley
1 tablespoon cider vinegar
2 teaspoons minced seeded jalapeño pepper
½ teaspoon sugar
¼ teaspoon dry mustard
⅛ teaspoon salt
3 cups shelled fresh black-eyed peas
2 teaspoons olive oil
1 cup chopped onion
¼ teaspoon minced fresh garlic
2½ cups organic vegetable broth
½ teaspoon ground cumin
½ teaspoon Spanish smoked paprika
¼ teaspoon ground red pepper
⅛ teaspoon salt
1 bay leaf

❶ Combine first 8 ingredients in a bowl. Cover and chill.

❷ Sort and wash peas; set aside. Heat a medium saucepan over medium-high heat. Add oil to pan; swirl to coat. Add 1 cup onion and garlic to pan; sauté 5 minutes. Stir in peas, broth, and remaining ingredients; bring to a boil. Cover, reduce heat, and simmer 20 minutes or until peas are tender. Discard bay leaf. Serve with relish.

SERVES 6 (serving size: ²/₃ cup peas and 2 tablespoons relish)

CALORIES 113; FAT 2g (sat 0.3g, mono 1.2g, poly 0.3g); PROTEIN 3g; CARB 21g; FIBER 5g; CHOL 0mg; IRON 1mg; SODIUM 343mg; CALC 106mg

Prep Pointer

The lightly pickled relish will keep up to 2 days in the refrigerator.

Prep Pointer

Freeze your summer bounty of black-eyed peas for fresh flavor in the fall. Fill a heavy-duty zip-top plastic bag with unrinsed peas, and freeze for up to 3 months.

Spicy Black-Eyed Peas

HANDS-ON TIME: 10 MIN. | **TOTAL TIME:** 8 HR. 10 MIN.

3 cups shelled fresh black-eyed peas
2 cups fat-free, lower-sodium chicken broth
2 cups chopped sweet onion
2 tablespoons finely chopped jalapeño pepper
½ teaspoon dried thyme
¼ teaspoon salt
¼ teaspoon freshly ground black pepper
4 garlic cloves, minced
1 (12-ounce) smoked turkey leg
1 bay leaf
Hot sauce (optional)

❶ Place first 10 ingredients in a 3-quart electric slow cooker; stir well. Cover and cook on LOW 8 hours or until peas are tender. Discard bay leaf and turkey leg. Serve peas with a slotted spoon, and sprinkle with hot sauce, if desired.

SERVES 7 (serving size: ½ cup)

CALORIES 135; **FAT** 2.8g (sat 1g, mono 0.7g, poly 0.8g); **PROTEIN** 10g; **CARB** 17g; **FIBER** 4g; **CHOL** 22mg; **IRON** 2mg; **SODIUM** 287mg; **CALC** 101mg

Black-Eyed Peas with Swiss Chard

HANDS-ON TIME: 39 MIN. | **TOTAL TIME:** 1 HR.

1 pound Swiss chard
1½ cups dried black-eyed peas
1 teaspoon olive oil
1 cup finely chopped onion
1½ tablespoons tomato paste
2 garlic cloves, minced
2 cups fat-free, lower-sodium chicken broth
4 ounces crumbled feta cheese (about 1 cup)
1 tablespoon chopped fresh oregano
¼ teaspoon freshly ground black pepper
¼ cup fresh lemon juice

❶ Wash Swiss chard thoroughly. Remove and chop stems. Slice leaves into (1-inch) strips.
❷ Place peas in a large Dutch oven; cover with water to 2 inches above beans. Bring to a boil; cook 5 minutes. Drain peas; set aside. Wipe pan with a paper towel.
❸ Heat pan over medium-high heat. Add oil to pan; swirl to coat. Add onion; sauté 2 minutes. Add tomato paste and garlic; cook 1 minute, stirring constantly. Stir in peas and broth; bring to a boil. Cover, reduce heat, and simmer 20 minutes or until peas are tender. Stir in chard stems and cheese; cover and cook 4 minutes. Stir in chard leaves, oregano, and pepper; cover and cook 2 minutes. Stir in lemon juice.

SERVES 12 (serving size: ½ cup)

CALORIES 118; FAT 2.7g (sat 1.5g, mono 0.7g, poly 0.3g); PROTEIN 8g; CARB 17g; FIBER 3g; CHOL 9mg; IRON 3mg; SODIUM 261mg; CALC 95mg

Prep Pointer

To easily remove the stems, fold each Swiss chard leaf in half lengthwise, and cut out the hard stems.

Prep Pointer

This side dish can be made a day ahead and is, in fact, better after the flavors have had a chance to meld.

Hoppin' John's Cousin

HANDS-ON TIME: 32 MIN. | **TOTAL TIME:** 9 HR. 32 MIN.

1 cup dried black-eyed peas
2 teaspoons olive oil
1 cup chopped onion
$\frac{1}{2}$ cup finely chopped red bell pepper
$\frac{1}{2}$ cup finely chopped green bell pepper
3 garlic cloves, minced
1 jalapeño pepper, seeded and minced
$\frac{1}{2}$ teaspoon paprika
$\frac{1}{2}$ teaspoon ground cumin
2 cups water, divided
$1\frac{1}{2}$ cups fat-free, lower-sodium chicken
  broth
$1\frac{1}{2}$ teaspoons chopped fresh thyme
$\frac{1}{2}$ teaspoon freshly ground black pepper
$\frac{1}{4}$ teaspoon salt
$\frac{1}{4}$ teaspoon hot pepper sauce
  (such as Tabasco)
3 ounces andouille sausage, cut into
  $\frac{1}{4}$-inch cubes
1 (14.5-ounce) can diced tomatoes,
  drained
1 bay leaf
$\frac{1}{2}$ cup uncooked long-grain white rice
$\frac{1}{4}$ cup thinly sliced green onions
  (optional)

❶ Sort and wash black-eyed peas; place in a large bowl. Cover with water to 2 inches above peas; soak 8 hours or overnight. Drain.

❷ Heat oil in a Dutch oven over medium-high heat. Add onion and next 4 ingredients (through jalapeño); sauté 7 minutes or until vegetables are tender. Stir in paprika and cumin; sauté 1 minute. Add peas, 1 cup water, and next 8 ingredients (through bay leaf), stirring to combine. Bring to a boil; cover, reduce heat, and simmer 50 minutes or until peas are tender. Discard bay leaf.

❸ Combine 1 cup water and rice in a small saucepan, and bring to a boil. Cover, reduce heat, and simmer 12 minutes or until rice is tender and water is absorbed. Fluff rice with a fork, and stir into pea mixture. Top with green onions, if desired.

SERVES 8 (serving size: about $\frac{3}{4}$ cup)

CALORIES 112; FAT 2.6g (sat 0.6g, mono 0.9g, poly 0.2g); PROTEIN 4g; CARB 18g; FIBER 3g; CHOL 11mg; IRON 1mg; SODIUM 294mg; CALC 45mg

Simple Swap

Peeled frozen beans can be used in place of fresh, with slightly increased cooking time.

Fava Beans with Tomato and Onion

HANDS-ON TIME: 37 MIN. | **TOTAL TIME:** 57 MIN.

4½ pounds unshelled fresh fava beans (about 2¼ cups shelled)
2 cups sliced, halved plum tomatoes (about 4)
1 cup vertically sliced sweet onion
1 tablespoon red wine vinegar
2 teaspoons extra-virgin olive oil
1 teaspoon minced fresh garlic
¼ teaspoon salt
¼ teaspoon freshly ground black pepper
Cooking spray
½ teaspoon sugar
½ teaspoon red wine vinegar
⅛ teaspoon salt

❶ Preheat oven to 425°.
❷ Remove beans from pods; discard pods. Cook beans in boiling water 1 minute. Remove beans with a slotted spoon. Plunge beans into ice water; drain. Remove tough outer skins from beans; discard skins.
❸ Combine beans, tomatoes, and next 6 ingredients (through black pepper) in a 13 x 9–inch glass or ceramic baking dish coated with cooking spray, tossing well. Bake at 425° for 20 minutes, stirring once.
❹ Combine sugar, ½ teaspoon vinegar, and ⅛ teaspoon salt in a small bowl, stirring until sugar dissolves. Drizzle over bean mixture, tossing gently to coat.

SERVES 5 (serving size: ½ cup)

CALORIES 123; FAT 2.2g (sat 0.3g, mono 1.4g, poly 0.4g); PROTEIN 7g; CARB 20g; FIBER 5g; CHOL 0mg; IRON 1mg; SODIUM 182mg; CALC 39mg

Simple Garlicky Lima Beans

HANDS-ON TIME: 13 MIN. | **TOTAL TIME:** 33 MIN.

4 cups shelled fresh lima beans
2½ cups water
1 tablespoon olive oil
2 garlic cloves, crushed
3 thyme sprigs
1 bay leaf
½ teaspoon sea salt
¼ teaspoon freshly ground black pepper

❶ Sort and wash beans; drain. Combine beans and next 5 ingredients (through bay leaf) in a medium saucepan. Bring to a boil. Cover, reduce heat, and simmer 20 minutes or until tender. Discard thyme sprigs and bay leaf. Stir in salt and pepper.

SERVES 8 (serving size: ½ cup)

CALORIES 105; FAT 2.4g (sat 0.4g, mono 1.3g, poly 0.5g); PROTEIN 5g; CARB 16g; FIBER 4g; CHOL 0mg; IRON 3mg; SODIUM 152mg; CALC 30mg

Fresh Lima Beans

HANDS-ON TIME: 7 MIN. | **TOTAL TIME:** 30 MIN.

2 cups shelled fresh lima beans
1 tablespoon olive oil
2 teaspoons red wine vinegar
⅛ teaspoon salt
½ cup quartered grape tomatoes
¼ cup sliced kalamata olives
2 tablespoons chopped fresh parsley

❶ Cook lima beans in simmering water to cover 20 minutes or until tender. Rinse with cold water; drain. Combine oil, vinegar, and salt in a large bowl. Add beans, grape tomatoes, olives, and parsley; toss well.

SERVES 4 (serving size: ½ cup)

CALORIES 140; FAT 4.6g (sat 0.7g, mono 3.2g, poly 0.6g); PROTEIN 6g; CARB 19g; FIBER 6g; CHOL 0mg; IRON 2mg; SODIUM 164mg; CALC 39mg

Simple Swap

This is a basic way to cook any kind of fresh shell bean or pea. For another variation, drizzle with olive oil and lemon juice, and sprinkle with crushed red pepper or a few shavings of Parmesan cheese.

Mom's Pennsylvania Dutch Beans

HANDS-ON TIME: 45 MIN. | **TOTAL TIME:** 3 HR.

1 pound dried baby lima beans
4 cups water
1½ teaspoons salt, divided
Cooking spray
1 cup chopped yellow onion
1 teaspoon minced fresh garlic
½ cup fat-free, lower-sodium chicken broth
⅓ cup packed light brown sugar
3 tablespoons butter, cut into pieces
1 tablespoon molasses
2 teaspoons dry mustard
1 cup light sour cream (such as Daisy)

❶ Sort and wash beans; place in a large Dutch oven. Cover with water to 2 inches above beans; bring to a boil. Cook 2 minutes; remove from heat. Cover and let stand 1 hour. Drain beans; return to pan. Add 4 cups water and 1 teaspoon salt; bring to a boil. Reduce heat, and simmer 1 hour. Drain and set aside.

❷ Preheat oven to 350°.

❸ Wipe pan dry with paper towel. Heat pan over medium-high heat. Coat pan with cooking spray. Add onion to pan; sauté 5 minutes or until tender. Add garlic to pan; sauté 30 seconds. Combine beans, ½ teaspoon salt, onion mixture, broth, and next 4 ingredients (through mustard) in a 13 x 9–inch glass or ceramic baking dish coated with cooking spray. Bake at 350° for 1 hour. Remove from oven; stir in sour cream. Serve immediately.

SERVES 10 (serving size: about ⅔ cup)

CALORIES 241; FAT 6g (sat 3.9g, mono 0.9g, poly 0.3g); PROTEIN 11g; CARB 37g; FIBER 9g; CHOL 9mg; IRON 3mg; SODIUM 213mg; CALC 49mg

Did You Know?

Many Pennsylvania Dutch dishes, including this bean bake, trace their origins to the 17th century German immigrants who farmed the southeast part of the state.

Lady Pea Salad

HANDS-ON TIME: 15 MIN. | **TOTAL TIME:** 1 HR. 15 MIN.

4 cups shelled fresh lady peas
4 cups water
½ teaspoon kosher salt
2 thyme sprigs
1 small onion, trimmed and quartered
1 teaspoon fennel seeds
3 tablespoons extra-virgin olive oil
2 tablespoons white balsamic vinegar
2 tablespoons whole-grain Dijon
   mustard
¼ teaspoon freshly ground black pepper
¼ cup chopped fresh chives

❶ Combine first 5 ingredients in a saucepan; bring to a boil. Partially cover, reduce heat, and simmer 30 minutes. Drain. Discard onion and thyme. Place peas on a jelly-roll pan; cool 30 minutes.
❷ Heat a small skillet over medium heat. Add fennel seeds; cook 3 minutes or until toasted, stirring occasionally. Combine fennel seeds, oil, vinegar, mustard, and pepper in a medium bowl, stirring with a whisk. Add peas; toss to coat. Stir in chives.

SERVES 8 (serving size: about ⅔ cup)

CALORIES 58; FAT 5.2g (sat 0.7g, mono 3.7g, poly 0.6g); PROTEIN 1g; CARB 3g; FIBER 0g; CHOL 0mg; IRON 1mg; SODIUM 237mg; CALC 17mg

Field Pea and Basil Succotash ▶

HANDS-ON TIME: 45 MIN. | **TOTAL TIME:** 1 HR. 12 MIN.

1½ ounces sliced pancetta, finely
   chopped
1 cup chopped onion
3 garlic cloves, minced
1½ cups shelled fresh purple-hull peas
¼ teaspoon freshly ground black pepper
Dash of kosher salt
½ cup water
1 cup fresh corn kernels
⅓ cup Castelvetrano olives, pitted and
   quartered
¼ cup torn Round Midnight basil leaves
   or fresh basil leaves

❶ Heat a medium saucepan over medium-high heat. Add pancetta; cook 3 minutes or until crisp. Remove pancetta from pan with a slotted spoon; set aside.
❷ Add onion to drippings in pan; cook 5 minutes or until tender. Stir in garlic; cook 1 minute. Add peas, pepper, and salt; cook 30 seconds. Add ½ cup water to pan; bring to a simmer. Cover and simmer 25 minutes or until peas are tender. Add corn and olives; simmer, covered, 2 minutes. Sprinkle evenly with reserved pancetta and basil.

SERVES 4 (serving size: ¾ cup)

CALORIES 147; FAT 5.4g (sat 1.9g, mono 1.1g, poly 0.4g); PROTEIN 6g; CARB 20g; FIBER 5g; CHOL 8mg; IRON 2mg; SODIUM 297mg; CALC 43mg

Simple Swap

You can substitute chopped yellow onion for the shallots in a pinch.

Buttery Lentils with Shallots

HANDS-ON TIME: 20 MIN. | **TOTAL TIME:** 40 MIN.

²/₃ cup dried petite green lentils
1 tablespoon butter
½ cup chopped shallots
2 tablespoons chopped fresh flat-leaf parsley
1 teaspoon chopped fresh thyme
¼ teaspoon kosher salt
¼ teaspoon black pepper

❶ Place lentils in a medium saucepan. Cover with water to 3 inches above lentils; bring to a boil. Reduce heat, and simmer 20 minutes or until lentils are tender. Drain. Melt butter in a large skillet over medium heat. Sauté shallots 2 minutes. Add lentils, parsley, thyme, salt, and pepper; toss.

SERVES 4 (serving size: about ½ cup)

CALORIES 154; FAT 3.3g (sat 1.9g, mono 0.8g, poly 0.3g); PROTEIN 9g; CARB 23g; FIBER 11g; CHOL 8mg; IRON 3mg; SODIUM 151mg; CALC 30mg

Lentils with Carrots

HANDS-ON TIME: 10 MIN. | **TOTAL TIME:** 35 MIN.

3 cups water
3 cups finely diced carrot
1 cup dried small black, green, or brown lentils
¼ cup minced fresh onion
½ teaspoon salt
1 bay leaf
1 tablespoon butter

❶ Combine first 6 ingredients in a saucepan; bring to a boil. Reduce heat, and simmer 25 minutes. Drain. Stir in butter. Discard bay leaf.

SERVES 6 (serving size: ½ cup)

CALORIES 150; FAT 2.3g (sat 1.3g, mono 0.6g, poly 0.3g); PROTEIN 10g; CARB 24g; FIBER 6g; CHOL 5mg; IRON 3mg; SODIUM 140mg; CALC 33mg

Warm Spiced Lentils

HANDS-ON TIME: 40 MIN. | **TOTAL TIME:** 2 HR. 50 MIN.

1 tablespoon olive oil

2 cups chopped onion

1 tablespoon finely chopped peeled
   fresh ginger

¾ teaspoon salt

¾ teaspoon freshly ground black
   pepper, divided

2 tablespoons minced fresh garlic

2 teaspoons ground cumin

2 teaspoons curry powder

1 teaspoon ground coriander

2½ cups water

2 cups fat-free, lower-sodium chicken
   broth

2 cups dried lentils

3 bay leaves

1 cup plain whole-milk yogurt

¾ cup tomato puree

❶ Heat olive oil in a Dutch oven over medium heat. Add chopped onion, ginger, salt, and ½ teaspoon pepper; cover and cook 10 minutes or until soft, stirring occasionally. Stir in minced garlic, cumin, curry powder, and ground coriander; cook 1 minute. Stir in 2½ cups water, chicken broth, lentils, and bay leaves; bring to a boil. Reduce heat; cover and simmer 2 hours or until tender. ❷ Uncover and cook 5 minutes or until most of liquid is absorbed. Remove from heat; cool slightly. Discard bay leaves. Gradually stir in ¼ teaspoon pepper, yogurt, and tomato puree; cook over low heat 5 minutes or until thoroughly heated.

SERVES 12 (serving size: ½ cup)

CALORIES 160; **FAT** 2.4g (sat 0.6g, mono 1.1g, poly 0.3g); **PROTEIN** 11g; **CARB** 25g; **FIBER** 11g; **CHOL** 3mg; **IRON** 4mg; **SODIUM** 244mg; **CALC** 60mg

Prep Pointer

To keep the whole-milk yogurt from curdling, allow the lentils to cool slightly before stirring. You can make the lentils a day ahead and refrigerate; then warm them over low heat.

Fragrant Red Lentils with Rice

HANDS-ON TIME: 25 MIN. | **TOTAL TIME:** 1 HR. 10 MIN.

1½ cups water
¾ cup uncooked brown basmati or
  whole-grain brown rice
1 tablespoon canola oil
1 cup diced onion
1 teaspoon grated peeled fresh ginger
1 teaspoon ground coriander
1 teaspoon ground cumin
½ teaspoon ground turmeric
2 garlic cloves, minced
2 bay leaves
3 cups water
1½ cups dried small red lentils
¾ teaspoon salt
2 tablespoons butter
¾ cup chopped green onions
1 tablespoon minced seeded jalapeño
  pepper
2 tablespoons minced fresh cilantro
3 tablespoons fresh lime juice
1 teaspoon garam masala
5 tablespoons plain low-fat yogurt

❶ Bring 1½ cups water to a boil in a medium saucepan; add rice. Cover, reduce heat, and simmer 45 minutes or until liquid is absorbed.

❷ While rice cooks, heat oil in a large saucepan over medium-high heat. Add onion, and sauté 6 minutes or until lightly browned. Stir in ginger and next 5 ingredients (though bay leaves); sauté 1 minute. Add 3 cups water, lentils, and salt; bring to a boil. Cover, reduce heat, and simmer 25 minutes or until lentils are tender, adding additional water as needed. Discard bay leaves.

❸ Melt butter in a small skillet over medium heat. Add green onions and jalapeño pepper; sauté 5 minutes. Add to lentil mixture; stir in cilantro, lime juice, and garam masala.

❹ Divide cooked rice among 10 shallow bowls; top with lentil mixture and yogurt.

SERVES 10 (serving size: ¼ cup rice, about ⅓ cup lentil mixture, and ½ tablespoon yogurt)

CALORIES 205; FAT 4.7g (sat 1.9g, mono 1.4g, poly 1.1g); PROTEIN 10g; CARB 32g; FIBER 5g; CHOL 7mg; IRON 3mg; SODIUM 214mg; CALC 52mg

Prep Pointer

Because jalapeño peppers can vary in heat intensity, you may wish to adjust the amount used based on your own preference for hot and spicy foods.

Did You Know?

Garam masala is an Indian blend of dry-roasted, ground spices that includes up to a dozen different flavors ranging from cinnamon to fennel to black pepper; it can be found with other spices in many large supermarkets or specialty food shops.

Prep Pointer

Cumin and turmeric provide slightly bitter notes, but this dish has an overall salty-savory flavor. For a thinner version, decrease the final simmering time.

Split Pea–Spinach Dal with Cauliflower

HANDS-ON TIME: 46 MIN. | **TOTAL TIME:** 1 HR. 56 MIN.

$3\frac{1}{2}$ cups water, divided
1 cup dried yellow split peas
1 bay leaf
2 cups chopped cauliflower florets
$\frac{1}{2}$ teaspoon salt
1 tablespoon butter
1 teaspoon canola oil
1 cup chopped onion
$1\frac{1}{2}$ teaspoons minced peeled fresh ginger
2 garlic cloves, minced
1 tablespoon cumin seeds
1 tablespoon brown mustard seeds
$1\frac{1}{2}$ teaspoons ground coriander
1 teaspoon ground turmeric
$\frac{1}{2}$ teaspoon ground red pepper
$\frac{1}{8}$ teaspoon ground cloves
4 cups torn fresh spinach

❶ Combine $2\frac{1}{2}$ cups water, peas, and bay leaf in a large saucepan; bring to a boil. Reduce heat, and simmer, partially covered, 50 minutes or until tender. Add 1 cup water, cauliflower, and salt, and bring to a boil. Reduce heat, and simmer, uncovered, 20 minutes or until cauliflower is very tender, stirring occasionally. Remove from heat; discard bay leaf.

❷ Heat butter and oil in a small skillet over medium-high heat until butter melts. Add onion, ginger, and garlic; sauté 3 minutes. Add cumin and next 5 ingredients (through cloves); cook over low heat 2 minutes, stirring frequently. Add onion mixture to pea mixture. Simmer, uncovered, 15 minutes or until thick. Stir in spinach; cook 3 minutes or until spinach wilts.

SERVES 6 (serving size: $\frac{2}{3}$ cup)

CALORIES 171; FAT 4.2g (sat 1.4g, mono 1.2g, poly 0.5g); PROTEIN 9g; CARB 26g; FIBER 12g; CHOL 5mg; IRON 2mg; SODIUM 242mg; CALC 55mg

Rotate zucchini slices once on each side as you grill to get crosshatch grill marks on both sides.

Chickpea and Red Pepper Zucchini

HANDS-ON TIME: 16 MIN. | **TOTAL TIME:** 16 MIN.

2 medium zucchini, sliced
Cooking spray
½ cup canned unsalted chickpeas, rinsed, drained, and chopped
¼ cup chopped fresh parsley
¼ cup chopped bottled roasted red bell peppers
2 tablespoons finely chopped red onion
2 tablespoons crumbled feta cheese
1 tablespoon olive oil
1 tablespoon fresh lemon juice
¼ teaspoon kosher salt
¼ teaspoon freshly ground black pepper

❶ Preheat grill to medium-high heat. Place zucchini on grill rack coated with cooking spray. Grill zucchini 3 to 4 minutes on each side.
❷ Combine chickpeas and remaining ingredients in a bowl. Spoon chickpea mixture over zucchini.

SERVES 4 (serving size: 4 zucchini slices and ¼ cup chickpea mixture)

CALORIES 99; FAT 5.1g (sat 1.3g, mono 2.7g, poly 0.5g); PROTEIN 4g; CARB 10g; FIBER 2g; CHOL 4mg; IRON 1mg; SODIUM 210mg; CALC 59mg

Chana Masala

HANDS-ON TIME: 38 MIN. | **TOTAL TIME:** 38 MIN.

1½ cups fresh chickpeas (garbanzo beans)
2 teaspoons olive oil
1 cup chopped onion
1 tablespoon minced peeled fresh ginger
1 garlic clove, minced
⅛ teaspoon salt
⅛ teaspoon ground cumin
⅛ teaspoon ground red pepper
¾ cup organic vegetable broth (such as Swanson Certified Organic)
½ cup chopped seeded tomato
2 tablespoons chopped fresh cilantro
⅛ teaspoon garam masala

❶ Sort and wash chickpeas; place in a large saucepan. Cover with water to 2 inches above chickpeas; bring to a boil. Cook 5 minutes. Drain.
❷ Heat oil in a large nonstick skillet over medium heat. Add onion, ginger, and garlic; cook 5 minutes, stirring occasionally. Stir in salt, cumin, and pepper; cook 1 minute. Add chickpeas, broth, and tomato; cook 5 minutes or until liquid almost evaporates. Remove from heat; stir in cilantro and garam masala.

SERVES 4 (serving size: ½ cup)

CALORIES 146; FAT 3.1g (sat 0.3g, mono 1.7g, poly 0.3g); PROTEIN 6g; CARB 23g; FIBER 5g; CHOL 0mg; IRON 1mg; SODIUM 228mg; CALC 51mg

Tomato-Chickpea Curry

HANDS-ON TIME: 27 MIN. | **TOTAL TIME:** 62 MIN.

1 tablespoon canola oil
1 cup chopped onion (1 small onion)
1 tablespoon minced peeled fresh ginger
1 garlic clove, minced
2 teaspoons garam masala
1½ teaspoons brown mustard seeds
¼ to ½ teaspoon ground red pepper
½ cup light coconut milk
1 tablespoon chopped seeded jalapeño
   pepper
1 teaspoon sugar
½ teaspoon ground turmeric
2 (15½-ounce) cans chickpeas
   (garbanzo beans), rinsed and drained
1 (28-ounce) can diced tomatoes,
   undrained
1 (8-ounce) can unsalted tomato sauce
3 tablespoons chopped fresh cilantro

❶ Heat oil in a large nonstick skillet over medium heat. Add onion, ginger, and garlic; cook 5 minutes. Stir in garam masala, mustard seeds, and red pepper; cook 2 minutes, stirring frequently. Stir in coconut milk and remaining ingredients except cilantro; bring to a boil.

❷ Reduce heat, and simmer 35 minutes, stirring occasionally. Remove from heat; stir in cilantro.

SERVES 12 (serving size: ½ cup)

CALORIES 107; FAT 3.1g (sat 0.6g, mono 1.2g, poly 1.1g); PROTEIN 4g; CARB 17g; FIBER 5g; CHOL 0mg; IRON 2mg; SODIUM 230mg; CALC 41mg

Simple Swap

Substitute yellow mustard seeds for the brown, or stir in 1½ teaspoons dry mustard with the chickpeas if you don't have mustard seeds.

Spinach with Chickpeas and Spices

HANDS-ON TIME: 20 MIN. | **TOTAL TIME:** 20 MIN.

1 tablespoon olive oil
1½ cups chopped onion
¼ teaspoon crushed red pepper
4 garlic cloves, minced
¾ teaspoon ground cumin
1½ cups water
¼ cup dry breadcrumbs
2 tablespoons dry sherry
¼ teaspoon saffron threads, crushed
2 (15½-ounce) cans chickpeas
   (garbanzo beans), rinsed and drained
2 (10-ounce) packages fresh spinach
1 tablespoon chopped fresh parsley
1 tablespoon fresh lemon juice
½ teaspoon salt
½ teaspoon freshly ground black
   pepper

❶ Heat oil in a Dutch oven over medium-high heat. Add onion; sauté 4 minutes. Add red pepper and garlic; sauté 1 minute. Add cumin, and cook 30 seconds, stirring constantly. Stir in 1½ cups water and next 4 ingredients (through chickpeas); cook 2 minutes or until slightly thick, stirring frequently. Add half of spinach; cook 3 minutes or until spinach wilts. Repeat procedure with remaining spinach. Remove from heat. Stir in parsley and remaining ingredients.

SERVES 12 (serving size: about ½ cup)

CALORIES 94; FAT 2.6g (sat 0.2g, mono 1.3g, poly 0.9g); PROTEIN 4g; CARB 15g; FIBER 4g; CHOL 0mg; IRON 3mg; SODIUM 279mg; CALC 77mg

Did You Know?

This is a popular dish from southern Spain's Andalusia region, where it is often served as tapas with crostini. The breadcrumbs help thicken the liquid to coat the spinach and chickpeas.

Simple Swap

If you can't find frozen shelled edamame, substitute the more traditional lima beans.

Edamame Succotash ▶

HANDS-ON TIME: 28 MIN. | **TOTAL TIME:** 28 MIN.

1 center-cut bacon slice
1 tablespoon butter
2 cups chopped sweet onion
2 cups fresh corn kernels (about 3 ears)
1 (16-ounce) bag frozen shelled
   edamame, thawed
2 tablespoons red wine vinegar
½ teaspoon salt
½ teaspoon freshly ground black pepper
½ teaspoon sugar
3 plum tomatoes, coarsely chopped
1 red bell pepper, seeded and coarsely
   chopped
3 tablespoons torn basil

❶ Cook bacon in a nonstick skillet over medium heat until crisp. Remove bacon from pan, reserving 2 teaspoons drippings in pan; coarsely chop bacon.
❷ Increase heat to medium-high. Melt butter in drippings in pan. Add onion; sauté 3 minutes, stirring occasionally. Add corn kernels; sauté 3 minutes or until lightly charred. Add edamame, and sauté 3 minutes, stirring occasionally. Stir in vinegar and next 5 ingredients (through bell pepper); cook 30 seconds, stirring occasionally. Sprinkle with bacon and basil.

SERVES 8 (serving size: ⅔ cup)

CALORIES 150; **FAT** 6.1g (sat 1.7g, mono 1.7g, poly 1.8g); **PROTEIN** 9g; **CARB** 19g; **FIBER** 5g; **CHOL** 5mg; **IRON** 0mg; **SODIUM** 193mg; **CALC** 14mg

Edamame with Lime-Sesame Salt

HANDS-ON TIME: 5 MIN. | **TOTAL TIME:** 5 MIN.

2 tablespoons toasted sesame seeds
2 tablespoons grated lime rind
⅜ teaspoon kosher salt
2 cups cooked shelled edamame

❶ Combine sesame seeds, rind, and salt on a cutting board; rock knife over mixture to crush some of the sesame seeds. Toss sesame mixture with edamame.

SERVES 4 (serving size: ½ cup)

CALORIES 127; **FAT** 5.2g (sat 0.3g, mono 0.8g, poly 1g); **PROTEIN** 9g; **CARB** 10g; **FIBER** 5g; **CHOL** 0mg; **IRON** 2mg; **SODIUM** 211mg; **CALC** 94mg

Edamame Salad with Tart Cherries

HANDS-ON TIME: 17 MIN. | **TOTAL TIME:** 17 MIN.

3 tablespoons canola oil

1 cup coarsely chopped shiitake mushroom caps

1½ tablespoons minced peeled fresh ginger

5 garlic cloves, minced

1 jalapeño pepper, seeded and minced

2 cups fresh or frozen shelled edamame (green soybeans), thawed

1 cup frozen whole-kernel corn

½ cup fat-free soy milk or milk

1 tablespoon rice vinegar

1 small English cucumber, quartered lengthwise and sliced

1 cup dried tart cherries

¼ teaspoon salt

⅛ teaspoon white pepper

2 tablespoons black sesame seeds, toasted (optional)

❶ Heat a large nonstick skillet over medium-high heat. Add oil to pan; swirl to coat. Add mushrooms, ginger, garlic, and jalapeño; stir-fry 2 minutes. Add edamame; stir-fry 1 minute. Stir in corn, soy milk, and vinegar; cook until liquid almost evaporates (about 3 minutes). Remove from heat, and stir in cucumber, cherries, salt, and white pepper. Garnish with sesame seeds, if desired.

SERVES 8

CALORIES 186; FAT 7.1g (sat 0.4g, mono 3.4g, poly 1.6g); PROTEIN 6g; CARB 24g; FIBER 7g; CHOL 0mg; IRON 1mg; SODIUM 96mg; CALC 59mg

Prep Pointer

Fresh ginger has very thin skin, and it will peel off easily when scraped with the edge of a metal spoon.

Fig and Tomato Salad, p. 185

Cucumber, Black Olive, and Mint Salad, p. 180

Jalapeño-Lime Slaw, p. 179

salads
and
slaws

Salads are easy, adaptable sides that can set the tone of a meal as a first course or round out an entrée with seasonal produce. We've compiled our best vegetable and green salad recipes as well as bean salads, pasta and grain salads, and potato salads. Experiment with cutting food into different shapes or customize your salads by trying different combinations of texture, crunch, and flavors.

Know Your Salads

Whether you are making a green salad or a grain salad, it is important to combine a range of flavors and textures. Grains offer a satisfying chew; fresh fruits and vegetables add juiciness, crunch, and sweet or tart flavor; and nuts and seeds give a savory note and high-quality protein. When you make a tossed salad, first choose the lettuce or salad greens you'll use. Many choices are available, so it helps to know what flavor and texture to expect and what type of dressing works best.

Mild lettuces
This group includes butter lettuces, such as Boston and Bibb, as well as spinach, leafy green and red lettuce, and mâche. All of these are mild in flavor and tend to be delicate, so pair them with tart vinaigrettes and bolder flavors.

Hearty lettuces
Lettuces such as romaine and iceberg are good choices for heavier, thick-and-creamy dressings, such as Caesar and blue cheese.

Peppery greens
This category includes arugula and watercress. These lettuces pack a spicy punch, so they can stand up to other strong flavors. These are also great mixed with milder lettuces.

Bitter greens
These include radicchio, escarole, endive, and frisée. These lettuces have a pleasantly bitter flavor. Balance the bitterness with fatty ingredients such as nuts, olives, and good-quality oil, or sweet ingredients like fruits.

Bean salads
Because beans are heartier than salad greens, they require bold dressings. Bright citrus dressings or rich mayo vinaigrettes are two examples. Beans can be soft and bland, so it is best to pair them with crunchy foods that have some bite.

Grain salads
Whole grains can lend substance and subtle earthiness to almost any salad combination. Make sure to cook the grains properly, and toss with your favorite chopped fresh herbs and a tangy vinaigrette. Fresh chopped raw vegetables add crunch, while shaved or crumbled cheese gives more richness.

How to Prepare a Basic Vinaigrette

A good vinaigrette is easy to prepare and can take plain greens and veggies from bland to bold. The building blocks of any vinaigrette are an acid, an oil, a base, and a seasoning. The acid (vinegar or lemon, lime, or orange juice) wakes up the palate. The oil coats the vegetables and helps you absorb nutrients in the salad. The base (honey, mustard, or mayo) emulsifies the dressing, and spices and fresh herbs round it out. Combine your acid, base, and spices first; then gradually whisk in the oil. If you are using fresh herbs, add them at the very end.

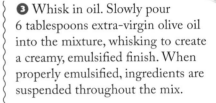

❶ Build a flavor base. Finely mince 2 tablespoons shallots so pieces will incorporate easily and spread throughout your dressing. Place in a bowl with 1 teaspoon Dijon mustard.

❷ Add an acid. Pour 2 tablespoons sherry vinegar into the mixture with ¼ teaspoon kosher salt and ¼ teaspoon freshly ground black pepper; stir with a whisk to combine.

❸ Whisk in oil. Slowly pour 6 tablespoons extra-virgin olive oil into the mixture, whisking to create a creamy, emulsified finish. When properly emulsified, ingredients are suspended throughout the mix.

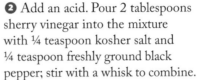

Simple Salad with Lemon Dressing ▶

HANDS-ON TIME: 5 MIN. | **TOTAL TIME:** 5 MIN.

1½ tablespoons fresh lemon juice
1½ tablespoons extra-virgin olive oil
¼ teaspoon freshly ground black pepper
⅛ teaspoon kosher salt
6 cups mixed greens
1 cup halved cherry tomatoes
½ cup thinly sliced radishes

❶ Combine lemon juice, olive oil, pepper, and salt in a large bowl, stirring with a whisk. Add mixed greens, cherry tomatoes, and radishes; toss to coat.

SERVES 4 (serving size: 1½ cups)

CALORIES 71; FAT 5.2g (sat 0.7g, mono 3.7g, poly 0.6g); PROTEIN 1g; CARB 6g; FIBER 3g; CHOL 0mg; IRON 1mg; SODIUM 98mg; CALC 8mg

Autumn Salad with Red Wine Vinaigrette

HANDS-ON TIME: 15 MIN. | **TOTAL TIME:** 15 MIN.

2 tablespoons extra-virgin olive oil
2 tablespoons red wine vinegar
½ teaspoon sugar
½ teaspoon minced fresh garlic
¼ teaspoon paprika
¼ teaspoon dry mustard
⅛ teaspoon salt
Pinch of dried basil
Pinch of ground red pepper
5 cups mixed greens
4 cups torn romaine lettuce
2½ cups cubed Asian pear
   (about 1 large)
2 cups chopped Granny Smith apple
   (about 1 large)
½ cup thinly sliced red onion
1 ounce crumbled goat cheese
   (about ¼ cup)

❶ Combine first 9 ingredients in a bowl, stirring with a whisk.
❷ Combine mixed greens, romaine lettuce, cubed pear, chopped apple, and onion in a large bowl. Drizzle with vinaigrette, and toss well to coat. Sprinkle with crumbled goat cheese.

SERVES 12 (serving size: about 1 cup salad mixture and 1 teaspoon crumbled cheese)

CALORIES 48; FAT 3.2g (sat 0.8g, mono 2g, poly 0.3g); PROTEIN 1g; CARB 5g; FIBER 1g; CHOL 2mg; IRON 0mg; SODIUM 40mg; CALC 19mg

Mixed Lettuce, Pear, and Goat Cheese Salad

HANDS-ON TIME: 10 MIN. | **TOTAL TIME:** 10 MIN.

1 tablespoon finely chopped shallots
1 teaspoon Dijon mustard
¼ cup fresh orange juice
4 teaspoons fresh Meyer lemon juice
¼ teaspoon kosher salt
⅛ teaspoon freshly ground black pepper
4 teaspoons extra-virgin olive oil
2 tablespoons fresh orange juice
2 firm ripe Bosc pears, cored and thinly
   sliced
6 cups mixed baby lettuces
1 head Boston or butter lettuce, torn
   (about 2 cups)
3 ounces crumbled goat cheese
   (about ¾ cup)

❶ Combine shallots and mustard in a medium bowl, stirring with a whisk. Stir in ¼ cup orange juice and next 3 ingredients (through pepper). Gradually add oil, stirring constantly with a whisk.
❷ Combine 2 tablespoons orange juice and pears, tossing to coat. Combine lettuces in a large bowl. Drizzle with dressing; toss gently to coat. Arrange about 1 cup lettuce mixture on each of 8 salad plates. Top each serving with about ¼ cup pear and 1½ tablespoons cheese.

SERVES 8

CALORIES 100; FAT 5.6g (sat 2.5g, mono 2.4g, poly 0.4g); PROTEIN 4g; CARB 10g; FIBER 3g; CHOL 8mg; IRON 1mg; SODIUM 141mg; CALC 67mg

Simple Swap

If you can't find Meyer lemons, use regular lemon juice and add a pinch of sugar to approximate the flavor.

Superfast

Ready in 15 minutes or less!

Prep Pointer

Using a pasteurized egg yolk is important since you aren't cooking it. Pasteurized eggs have been heated in their shells to kill bacteria like salmonella.

Grilled Caesar Salad

HANDS-ON TIME: 25 MIN. | **TOTAL TIME:** 25 MIN.

10 ($\frac{1}{2}$-ounce) slices diagonally cut French bread (about $\frac{1}{4}$ inch thick)
Cooking spray
3 garlic cloves, divided
7 canned anchovy fillets, rinsed, drained and divided
$\frac{1}{4}$ cup fresh lemon juice
1 teaspoon Dijon mustard
$\frac{1}{2}$ teaspoon freshly ground black pepper
1 large pasteurized egg yolk
$\frac{1}{4}$ cup extra-virgin olive oil
3 romaine lettuce hearts, cut in half lengthwise (about 24 ounces)
$\frac{1}{2}$ ounce Parmigiano-Reggiano cheese, shaved (about $\frac{1}{3}$ cup)

❶ Preheat grill to high.

❷ Coat bread slices with cooking spray. Place bread on grill rack coated with cooking spray; grill 1 minute or until golden, turning once. Remove bread from grill. Cut 1 garlic clove in half; rub both sides of bread with cut sides of garlic clove. Discard clove.

❸ Pat anchovy fillets dry with a paper towel. Place 2 garlic cloves, 2 anchovy fillets, juice, mustard, pepper, and egg yolk in a blender; process until smooth. With blender on, add oil, 1 tablespoon at a time; process until smooth.

❹ Place lettuce, cut sides down, on grill rack coated with cooking spray; grill 2 minutes. Turn; grill 1 minute. Remove from heat; coarsely chop lettuce. Place lettuce in a large bowl; drizzle with dressing, tossing gently to coat.

❺ Cut remaining 5 anchovy fillets in half lengthwise. Arrange about $\frac{3}{4}$ cup salad on each of 10 plates; top each serving with 1 bread slice and 1 anchovy half. Sprinkle each serving with about $1\frac{1}{2}$ teaspoons Parmigiano-Reggiano.

SERVES 10

CALORIES 118; FAT 7g (sat 1.2g, mono 4.4g, poly 0.7g); PROTEIN 4g; CARB 11g; FIBER 1g; CHOL 25mg; IRON 2mg; SODIUM 232mg; CALC 66mg

Mixed Greens Salad with Hoisin-Sesame Vinaigrette

HANDS-ON TIME: 15 MIN. | **TOTAL TIME:** 15 MIN.

Superfast

Ready in 15
minutes or less!

2 tablespoons extra-virgin olive oil

1 tablespoon rice vinegar

2 teaspoons finely chopped green onions

2 teaspoons fresh lemon juice

2 teaspoons hoisin sauce

1 teaspoon dark sesame oil

½ teaspoon minced fresh garlic

¼ teaspoon freshly ground white pepper

⅛ teaspoon kosher salt

6 cups torn romaine lettuce leaves

1 cup trimmed snow peas, sliced diagonally

1 cup thinly sliced red bell pepper

½ cup fresh cilantro

1 tablespoon toasted sesame seeds

❶ Combine first 9 ingredients in a large bowl, and stir with a whisk. Add lettuce, peas, bell pepper, and cilantro; toss. Top with sesame seeds.

SERVES 4 (serving size: about 1½ cups)

CALORIES 114; **FAT** 9.2g (sat 1.3g, mono 5.8g, poly 1.8g); **PROTEIN** 2g; **CARB** 7g; **FIBER** 3g; **CHOL** 0mg; **IRON** 1mg; **SODIUM** 158mg; **CALC** 36mg

Superfast

Ready in 15
minutes or less!

Lemony Kale Salad

HANDS-ON TIME: 11 MIN. | **TOTAL TIME:** 15 MIN.

1 tablespoon fresh lemon juice
1 tablespoon olive oil
½ teaspoon sugar
½ teaspoon freshly ground black pepper
¼ teaspoon kosher salt
4 cups torn kale leaves
2 cups torn Swiss chard leaves
4 teaspoons unsalted pumpkinseed
  kernels
¼ cup sliced green onions (about 2)
1 ounce shaved pecorino
  Romano cheese

❶ Combine first 5 ingredients in a large bowl, stirring until sugar dissolves. Add kale and Swiss chard; toss. Let stand 10 minutes.
❷ While kale mixture stands, heat a skillet over medium heat. Add pumpkinseeds; cook 5 minutes or until brown, stirring frequently. Add pumpkinseeds, onions, and cheese to greens; toss.

SERVES 6 (serving size: 1 cup)

CALORIES 65; FAT 4g (sat 0.8g, mono 2g, poly 0.8g); PROTEIN 3g; CARB 6g; FIBER 1g; CHOL 2mg; IRON 1mg; SODIUM 234mg; CALC 87mg

Spicy Soy-Kale Salad ▶

HANDS-ON TIME: 8 MIN. | **TOTAL TIME:** 16 MIN.

1 tablespoon rice vinegar
1 tablespoon lower-sodium soy sauce
2 teaspoons dark sesame oil
½ teaspoon brown sugar
¼ teaspoon chili garlic sauce
4 cups torn kale leaves
2 cups torn Savoy cabbage leaves
1 cup shredded carrot
1 cup sliced red bell pepper
½ cup sliced radishes
¼ cup chopped fresh cilantro

❶ Combine rice vinegar, soy sauce, sesame oil, brown sugar, and chili garlic sauce in a large bowl. Add kale, cabbage, carrot, bell pepper, radish, and cilantro; toss. Let stand 8 minutes.

SERVES 6 (serving size: 1 cup)

CALORIES 60; FAT 2g (sat 0.3g, mono 0.6g, poly 0.8g); PROTEIN 2g; CARB 10g; FIBER 3g; CHOL 0mg; IRON 1mg; SODIUM 136mg; CALC 79mg

Fizz Kale Salad with Roasted Garlic–Bacon Dressing and Beets

HANDS-ON TIME: 20 MIN. | **TOTAL TIME:** 1 HR. 20 MIN.

1 whole garlic head
6 ounces baby yellow beets
6 ounces baby red beets
6 ounces baby striped beets
   (such as Chioggia)
3 tablespoons extra-virgin olive oil
1 tablespoon water
1 tablespoon heavy cream
1½ teaspoons fresh lemon juice
1 teaspoon red wine vinegar
¼ teaspoon kosher salt
¼ teaspoon freshly ground black pepper
4 cups Fizz kale, torn
4 cups Lacinato kale, torn
1 thick applewood-smoked bacon slice,
   chopped

❶ Preheat oven to 350°.
❷ Remove white papery skin from garlic head (do not peel or separate cloves). Wrap head in foil. Arrange yellow beets on a large sheet of foil; wrap tightly. Repeat procedure with red and striped beets. Bake garlic and beets at 350° for 1 hour or until beets are tender; cool 10 minutes. Separate garlic cloves; squeeze to extract garlic pulp. Discard skins. Combine garlic pulp, oil, and next 6 ingredients (through pepper) in a small bowl, stirring with a whisk. Place kale in a large bowl.
❸ Heat a medium skillet over medium heat; add chopped bacon. Cook 5 minutes or until crisp, stirring occasionally. Increase heat to high. Stir in garlic mixture; remove from heat. Pour hot bacon mixture over kale, tossing to coat.
❹ Peel beets; discard skins. Cut beets in half. Arrange over kale mixture.

SERVES 6 (serving size: 1 cup)

CALORIES 149; **FAT** 9.2g (sat 1.9g, mono 5.3g, poly 1.1g); **PROTEIN** 4.6g; **CARB** 15g; **FIBER** 3.1g; **CHOL** 5mg; **IRON** 2mg; **SODIUM** 189mg; **CALC** 140mg

Simple Swap

If Fizz kale is unavailable, the salad will still be delicious using Lacinato, which is more widely available.

Spinach with Garlic Vinaigrette ▶

HANDS-ON TIME: 5 MIN. | **TOTAL TIME:** 5 MIN.

1½ tablespoons extra-virgin olive oil
1 tablespoon white wine vinegar
½ teaspoon Dijon mustard
¼ teaspoon freshly ground black pepper
⅛ teaspoon salt
2 garlic cloves, minced
6 cups baby spinach (about 6 ounces)
¼ cup vertically sliced red onion

❶ Combine first 6 ingredients in a large bowl, stirring well with a whisk. Add spinach and red onion; toss to coat.

SERVES 4 (serving size: 1¾ cups)

CALORIES 66; FAT 5.1g (sat 0.7g, mono 3.7g, poly 0.5g); PROTEIN 1g; CARB 5g; FIBER 2g; CHOL 0mg; IRON 1mg; SODIUM 147mg; CALC 31mg

Mixed Greens with Cherries, Goat Cheese, and Pistachios

HANDS-ON TIME: 15 MIN. | **TOTAL TIME:** 15 MIN.

4 cups arugula
2 cups baby spinach
⅓ cup thinly vertically sliced red onion
1½ tablespoons fresh lemon juice
½ teaspoon Dijon mustard
½ teaspoon honey
¼ teaspoon salt
¼ teaspoon freshly ground black pepper
1 small garlic clove, minced
2 tablespoons extra-virgin olive oil
1 cup Rainier cherries, pitted and halved
1 ounce goat cheese, crumbled
    (about ¼ cup)
¼ cup salted, dry-roasted pistachios

❶ Combine arugula, spinach, and onion in a large bowl. Combine juice and next 5 ingredients (through garlic) in a medium bowl, stirring with a whisk. Gradually drizzle in olive oil, stirring constantly with a whisk.
❷ Drizzle dressing over salad, and toss gently to coat. Arrange 1½ cups salad on each of 4 plates. Top each with ¼ cup cherries, 1 tablespoon cheese, and 1 tablespoon nuts.

SERVES 4

CALORIES 173; FAT 12.6g (sat 2.9g, mono 7.3g, poly 1.9g); PROTEIN 5g; CARB 13g; FIBER 3g; CHOL 6mg; IRON 1mg; SODIUM 256mg; CALC 80mg

Prep Pointer

Remove the hard vein from the center of each leaf of Swiss chard before chopping.

Lemon-Garlic Swiss Chard

HANDS-ON TIME: 20 MIN. | **TOTAL TIME:** 20 MIN.

1 tablespoon extra-virgin olive oil
1 tablespoon minced fresh garlic
12 cups Swiss chard, chopped (about 10 ounces)
2 tablespoons water
1½ teaspoons fresh lemon juice
⅛ teaspoon freshly ground black pepper
4 teaspoons shaved fresh Parmesan cheese

❶ Heat a large skillet over medium-high heat. Add oil to pan; swirl to coat. Add garlic; sauté 2 minutes or until garlic begins to brown. Add Swiss chard and 2 tablespoons water to pan; cook 3 minutes or until chard wilts. Stir in lemon juice and pepper. Sprinkle with cheese.

SERVES 4 (serving size: about ½ cup)

CALORIES 61; FAT 4.1g (sat 0.8g, mono 2.7g, poly 0.5g); PROTEIN 3g; CARB 5g; FIBER 2g; CHOL 1mg; IRON 2mg; SODIUM 256mg; CALC 78mg

Chopped Chard Salad with Apricot Vinaigrette

HANDS-ON TIME: 20 MIN. | **TOTAL TIME:** 20 MIN.

¼ cup thinly sliced shallots
2 tablespoons extra-virgin olive oil
2 tablespoons white wine vinegar
1½ tablespoons apricot preserves
1 teaspoon whole-grain Dijon mustard
6 cups chopped Swiss chard
1 (15.5-ounce) can chickpeas
   (garbanzo beans), rinsed and drained
2 tablespoons walnuts, toasted
1 tablespoon chopped green onions
1 teaspoon freshly ground black pepper
½ ounce goat cheese, crumbled

❶ Combine first 5 ingredients in a large bowl, stirring with a whisk. Let stand 10 minutes. Set aside half of shallot mixture. Add chard to bowl; toss to coat. Place chard mixture on a serving platter.
❷ Return reserved half of shallot mixture to bowl. Add chickpeas; toss to coat. Top chard mixture with chickpea mixture. Sprinkle evenly with walnuts and remaining ingredients.

SERVES 6 (serving size: about 1 cup)

CALORIES 147; FAT 8.6g (sat 2.1g, mono 3.7g, poly 2.1g); PROTEIN 5g; CARB 13g; FIBER 3g; CHOL 6mg; IRON 1mg; SODIUM 261mg; CALC 51mg

Spinach-and-Watermelon Salad

HANDS-ON TIME: 22 MIN. | **TOTAL TIME:** 22 MIN.

1 tablespoon honey
1 tablespoon balsamic vinegar
1 tablespoon water
1½ teaspoons olive oil
½ teaspoon fresh lemon juice
⅛ teaspoon dried tarragon
Dash of salt
4 cups torn spinach
4 cups thinly sliced romaine lettuce
2 cups (1-inch) watermelon balls
1 cup sliced strawberries
½ cup sliced cucumber
¼ cup thinly sliced onion

❶ Combine first 7 ingredients in a bowl; stir well with a whisk. Set aside.
❷ Combine spinach and remaining ingredients in a large bowl. Drizzle dressing over salad, and toss gently to coat. Serve immediately.

SERVES 5 (serving size: 2 cups)

CALORIES 72; FAT 1.8g (sat 0.4g, mono 0.8g, poly 0.4g); PROTEIN 3g; CARB 12g; FIBER 4g; CHOL 0mg; IRON 2mg; SODIUM 46mg; CALC 74mg

Prep Pointer

If you don't have a melon baller, use a small, rounded measuring spoon or coffee scoop.

Beet and Arugula Salad with Kefalotyri ▶

HANDS-ON TIME: 15 MIN. | **TOTAL TIME:** 2 HR. 40 MIN.

3 beets (about 1 pound)
2 tablespoons red wine vinegar
1 teaspoon extra-virgin olive oil
½ teaspoon salt
½ teaspoon freshly ground black pepper
6 cups arugula (about 6 ounces)
1 ounce shaved fresh kefalotyri cheese (about ¼ cup)

❶ Preheat oven to 425°.
❷ Leave root and 1 inch stem on beets; scrub with a brush. Place beets in a baking dish; bake at 425° for 1 hour and 10 minutes or until tender. Cool; peel and cut into ¼-inch slices.
❸ Combine vinegar, oil, salt, and pepper, stirring with a whisk. Arrange beet slices in a single layer on a platter; drizzle with half of vinegar mixture.
❹ Combine remaining vinegar mixture and arugula in a bowl. Top beets with arugula mixture. Sprinkle with cheese.

SERVES 8 (serving size: about ½ cup beets, ¾ cup arugula, and 1½ teaspoons cheese)

CALORIES 50; **FAT** 1.8g (sat 0.7g, mono 0.7g, poly 0.2g); **PROTEIN** 3g; **CARB** 6g; **FIBER** 2g; **CHOL** 3mg; **IRON** 1mg; **SODIUM** 250mg; **CALC** 73mg

Arugula Salad with Parmesan Vinaigrette

HANDS-ON TIME: 8 MIN. | **TOTAL TIME:** 8 MIN.

4 teaspoons fresh lemon juice
4 teaspoons olive oil
3 tablespoons grated Parmesan cheese
1 green onion, chopped
4 cups arugula
½ cup thinly sliced fennel bulb
⅛ teaspoon kosher salt
⅛ teaspoon freshly ground black pepper

❶ Combine juice, oil, Parmesan, and onion in a large bowl, stirring with a whisk. Add arugula, fennel, salt, and pepper; toss gently to coat.

SERVES 4 (serving size: about 1 cup)

CALORIES 67; **FAT** 5.8g (sat 1.3g, mono 3.6g, poly 0.6g); **PROTEIN** 2g; **CARB** 2g; **FIBER** 1g; **CHOL** 3mg; **IRON** 1mg; **SODIUM** 129mg; **CALC** 82mg

Bitter Greens Salad
with Spiced Mirin Dressing

HANDS-ON TIME: 5 MIN. | **TOTAL TIME:** 15 MIN.

Superfast

Ready in 15
minutes or less!

2 dried red Thai chiles
4 cups baby arugula
2 cups torn radicchio
1 cup sliced Belgian endive
2 tablespoons extra-virgin olive oil
2 teaspoons minced fresh garlic
½ teaspoon fennel seeds (optional)
6 tablespoons mirin (sweet rice wine)
½ teaspoon salt

❶ Soak chiles in warm water 10 minutes; drain.
❷ Place arugula, radicchio, and endive in a large bowl; toss gently to combine.
❸ Heat a large skillet or wok over medium-high heat. Add oil to pan; swirl to coat. Add garlic, fennel seeds, if desired, and chiles; stir constantly 30 seconds. Reduce heat to low; cook 1 minute. Stir in mirin and salt; increase heat to high. Bring to a boil; boil 15 seconds. Remove chiles from mixture. Drizzle hot dressing over greens; toss gently to coat. Serve salad immediately.

SERVES 6 (serving size: about 1 cup)

CALORIES 84; FAT 4.7g (sat 0.7g, mono 3.3g, poly 0.5g); PROTEIN 1g; CARB 7g; FIBER 1g; CHOL 0mg; IRON 0mg; SODIUM 204mg; CALC 32mg

Radicchio Caesar Salad

HANDS-ON TIME: 8 MIN. | **TOTAL TIME:** 8 MIN.

3 tablespoons canola mayonnaise
1½ tablespoons fresh lemon juice
½ teaspoon black pepper
2 garlic cloves, minced
1 anchovy fillet, minced
2½ cups very thinly sliced, cored radicchio
2½ cups baby spinach
5 teaspoons grated Parmesan cheese

❶ Combine first 5 ingredients in a large bowl. Add radicchio and spinach; toss to coat. Top with cheese.

SERVES 4 (serving size: about 1 cup)

CALORIES 55; FAT 3.6g (sat 0.4g, mono 2g, poly 1.1g); PROTEIN 2g; CARB 4g; FIBER 1g; CHOL 3mg; IRON 1mg; SODIUM 179mg; CALC 45mg

Winter Citrus, Escarole, and Endive Salad ▶

HANDS-ON TIME: 35 MIN. | **TOTAL TIME:** 35 MIN.

6 cups torn escarole
2 cups thinly sliced Belgian endive (about 2 heads)
1 cup thinly sliced radicchio
1 cup pink grapefruit sections
1 cup navel orange sections
¾ cup blood orange sections
¼ cup minced shallots
2 tablespoons extra-virgin olive oil
2 tablespoons fresh orange juice
1 tablespoon white wine vinegar or champagne vinegar
1½ teaspoons honey
½ teaspoon kosher salt
¼ teaspoon freshly ground black pepper
½ cup pomegranate arils
2 tablespoons pistachios, toasted

❶ Combine first 3 ingredients in a large bowl. Add grapefruit, orange, and blood orange sections; toss gently.
❷ Combine shallots and next 6 ingredients (through pepper) in a small bowl, stirring well with a whisk. Drizzle dressing over salad; toss gently to coat. Divide salad evenly among 6 plates. Divide pomegranate arils and toasted pistachios evenly among servings.

SERVES 6 (serving size: about 1¼ cups)

CALORIES 159; FAT 6.3g (sat 0.9g, mono 3.9g, poly 1.1g); PROTEIN 5g; CARB 24g; FIBER 10g; CHOL 0mg; IRON 3mg; SODIUM 220mg; CALC 164mg

Jalapeño-Lime Slaw

HANDS-ON TIME: 7 MIN. | **TOTAL TIME:** 67 MIN.

⅓ cup fresh lime juice
1 teaspoon sugar
¾ teaspoon kosher salt
¼ teaspoon freshly ground black pepper
3 tablespoons olive oil
½ cup thinly vertically sliced red onion
½ cup coarsely chopped fresh cilantro
1 (16-ounce) package cabbage-and-carrot coleslaw
4 jalapeño peppers, halved crosswise

❶ Combine first 4 ingredients in a large bowl, stirring with a whisk. Gradually add olive oil, stirring constantly with a whisk. Add onion, cilantro, and coleslaw. Thinly slice 1 jalapeño half crosswise (keeping seeds), and remove seeds from remaining jalapeño halves. Cut remaining halves into thin crosswise slices. Add jalapeños to onion mixture, and toss well to coat. Cover and chill at least 1 hour.

SERVES 8 (serving size: about ¾ cup)

CALORIES 71; FAT 5.2g (sat 0.7g, mono 3.7g, poly 0.6g); PROTEIN 1g; CARB 6g; FIBER 2g; CHOL 0mg; IRON 0mg; SODIUM 198mg; CALC 26mg

Waldorf Coleslaw

HANDS-ON TIME: 13 MIN. | **TOTAL TIME:** 2 HR. 13 MIN.

3 cups shredded cabbage
3 cups diced Granny Smith apple
6 tablespoons raisins
3 tablespoons coarsely chopped walnuts
3 tablespoons plain fat-free yogurt
2 tablespoons fat-free mayonnaise
1 tablespoon honey
1 teaspoon prepared horseradish
¼ teaspoon salt
¼ teaspoon black pepper

❶ Combine first 4 ingredients in a medium bowl. Combine yogurt and remaining ingredients, stirring well with a whisk. Pour over cabbage mixture; toss well. Cover and chill 2 hours.

SERVES 10 (serving size: ½ cup)

CALORIES 69; FAT 1.8g (sat 0.2g, mono 0.2g, poly 1.1g); PROTEIN 1g; CARB 14g; FIBER 2g; CHOL 1mg; IRON 1mg; SODIUM 91mg; CALC 27mg

Did You Know?

The word "coleslaw" comes from the Dutch word "koolsla," which means cabbage salad.

Herby Cucumber Salad

HANDS-ON TIME: 12 MIN. | **TOTAL TIME:** 12 MIN.

¼ cup plain low-fat yogurt
2 tablespoons coarsely chopped fresh dill
1 tablespoon coarsely chopped fresh parsley
2 tablespoons fresh lemon juice
1 tablespoon extra-virgin olive oil
1½ teaspoons coarsely chopped fresh mint
2 teaspoons Dijon mustard
¼ teaspoon sugar
¼ teaspoon salt
¼ teaspoon freshly ground black pepper
1 garlic clove
5½ cups thinly sliced cucumber (about 2 large)
2½ cups thinly sliced red onion

❶ Place first 11 ingredients in a food processor or a blender; process until well blended. Combine cucumber and onion in a large bowl. Drizzle with yogurt mixture, and toss to coat.

SERVES 6 (serving size: 1 cup)

CALORIES 65; **FAT** 2.6g (sat 0.5g, mono 1.7g, poly 0.3g); **PROTEIN** 2g; **CARB** 10g; **FIBER** 1g; **CHOL** 1mg; **IRON** 1mg; **SODIUM** 150mg; **CALC** 48mg

Cucumber, Black Olive, and Mint Salad

HANDS-ON TIME: 10 MIN. | **TOTAL TIME:** 10 MIN.

2 cups thinly sliced English cucumber
¼ cup chopped pitted kalamata olives
3 tablespoons chopped fresh mint
2 tablespoons fresh lemon juice
1 tablespoon olive oil
½ teaspoon freshly ground black pepper

❶ Combine all ingredients in a medium bowl.

SERVES 4 (serving size: about ½ cup)

CALORIES 70; **FAT** 6.1g (sat 0.8g, mono 4.5g, poly 0.7g); **PROTEIN** 1g; **CARB** 4g; **FIBER** 1g; **CHOL** 0mg; **IRON** 1mg; **SODIUM** 164mg; **CALC** 22mg

Sesame-Miso Cucumber Salad

HANDS-ON TIME: 15 MIN. | **TOTAL TIME:** 15 MIN.

1½ tablespoons sesame seeds, toasted

2 tablespoons white miso
   (soybean paste) or lower-sodium
   soy sauce

1 tablespoon rice vinegar

1 tablespoon honey

1 tablespoon hot water

1 teaspoon crushed red pepper

2 teaspoons dark sesame oil

4 cups thinly sliced seeded cucumber

❶ Combine first 7 ingredients in a large bowl, stirring with a whisk. Add cucumber; toss to coat.

SERVES 6 (serving size: ¾ cup)

CALORIES 60; **FAT** 2.7g (sat 0.2g, mono 0.6g, poly 0.7g); **PROTEIN** 2g; **CARB** 7g; **FIBER** 2g; **CHOL** 0mg; **IRON** 4mg; **SODIUM** 182mg; **CALC** 12mg

Superfast

Ready in 15 minutes or less!

Superfast

Ready in 15 minutes or less!

Prep Pointer

For the brightest taste and juiciest texture, store tomatoes in a single layer, stem side up, at room temperature. Refrigeration destroys their flavor.

Tomato, Fresh Mozzarella, and Basil Salad ▶

HANDS-ON TIME: 8 MIN. | **TOTAL TIME:** 8 MIN.

4 tomatoes, cut into 18 slices total
½ pound fresh mozzarella cheese, cut into 12 slices
¼ teaspoon kosher salt
¼ teaspoon freshly ground black pepper
1 tablespoon extra-virgin olive oil
½ cup basil leaves

❶ Arrange 3 tomato slices and 2 cheese slices on each of 6 salad plates. Sprinkle with salt and pepper; drizzle with oil. Top evenly with basil.

SERVES 6

CALORIES 150; FAT 10.7g (sat 5.8g, mono 1.9g, poly 0.4g); PROTEIN 8g; CARB 5g; FIBER 2g; CHOL 30mg; IRON 1mg; SODIUM 138mg; CALC 231mg

Summer Peach and Tomato Salad

HANDS-ON TIME: 15 MIN. | **TOTAL TIME:** 15 MIN.

¼ cup thinly vertically sliced red onion
½ pound ripe peaches, pitted and cut into wedges
¼ pound heirloom beefsteak tomatoes, cut into thick wedges
¼ pound heirloom cherry or pear tomatoes, halved
1 tablespoon sherry vinegar
1½ teaspoons extra-virgin olive oil
1 teaspoon honey
⅛ teaspoon salt
⅛ teaspoon freshly ground black pepper
1 ounce crumbled feta cheese (about ¼ cup)
2 tablespoons small basil leaves or torn basil

❶ Combine first 4 ingredients in a large bowl.
❷ Combine vinegar, olive oil, honey, salt, and pepper in a small bowl, stirring with a whisk. Drizzle vinegar mixture over peach mixture; toss well to coat. Sprinkle with cheese and basil.

SERVES 4 (serving size: 1 cup)

CALORIES 75; FAT 3.5g (sat 1.3g, mono 1.6g, poly 0.3g); PROTEIN 2g; CARB 10g; FIBER 2g; CHOL 6mg; IRON 0mg; SODIUM 156mg; CALC 47mg

◄ *Fig and Tomato Salad*

HANDS-ON TIME: 20 MIN. | **TOTAL TIME:** 20 MIN.

2 tablespoons red wine vinegar
2 teaspoons extra-virgin olive oil
1/4 teaspoon freshly ground black pepper
2 cups quartered fresh figs
(about 1/2 pound)
2 cups torn romaine lettuce
1 cup cherry tomatoes, halved
3/4 cup vertically sliced Vidalia or other
sweet onion
3 tablespoons chopped fresh mint
1 ounce crumbled feta cheese
(about 1/4 cup)

❶ Combine first 3 ingredients in a large bowl; stir well with a whisk. Add figs, lettuce, tomatoes, onion, and mint; toss gently to coat. Sprinkle with cheese.

SERVES 4 (serving size: 1 1/2 cups)

CALORIES 128; FAT 4.8g (sat 1.8g, mono 2.2g, poly 0.6g); PROTEIN 3g; CARB 20g; FIBER 4g; CHOL 8mg; IRON 2mg; SODIUM 114mg; CALC 105mg

Tomato and Grilled Bread Salad

HANDS-ON TIME: 20 MIN. | **TOTAL TIME:** 40 MIN.

4 (1-ounce) slices day-old country-style
bread
4 cups coarsely chopped tomato
(about 1 1/2 pounds)
1 cup finely chopped red onion
(about 1 medium)
3/4 cup chopped yellow bell pepper
3/4 cup chopped orange bell pepper
1/2 cup torn basil leaves
1 English cucumber, peeled and coarsely
chopped
1/4 cup red wine vinegar
1/2 teaspoon freshly ground black pepper
1/4 teaspoon salt
2 garlic cloves, minced
1/4 cup extra-virgin olive oil

❶ Preheat grill to medium-high heat.
❷ Place bread slices on grill rack; grill 1 minute on each side or until golden brown with grill marks. Remove from grill; tear bread into 1-inch pieces.
❸ Combine tomatoes, onion, bell peppers, basil, and cucumber in a large bowl. Add bread; toss gently.
❹ Combine vinegar, black pepper, salt, and garlic in a small bowl, stirring with a whisk. Gradually add oil, stirring constantly with a whisk. Drizzle dressing over salad; toss gently to coat. Cover and chill 20 minutes before serving.

SERVES 6 (serving size: 1 2/3 cups)

CALORIES 178; FAT 9.7g (sat 1.3g, mono 6.6g, poly 1g); PROTEIN 3.5g; CARB 19.5g; FIBER 3.1g; CHOL 0mg; IRON 1.6mg; SODIUM 237mg; CALC 43mg

Simple Swap

Try Walla Walla, Bermuda, Maui, or Sweet Imperial as a sweet-onion alternative to Vidalia.

Apple Salad with Mustard Dressing

HANDS-ON TIME: 10 MIN. | **TOTAL TIME:** 10 MIN.

1½ tablespoons extra-virgin olive oil
1½ tablespoons cider vinegar
1 tablespoon minced shallots
2 teaspoons whole-grain Dijon mustard
2 teaspoons honey
¼ teaspoon salt
¼ teaspoon freshly ground black pepper
2 cups thinly sliced Fuji apple
1 (5-ounce) package mixed spring
  greens

❶ Combine first 7 ingredients in a large bowl, stirring with a whisk. Add apple and greens; toss to coat.

SERVES 4 (serving size: about 1½ cups)

CALORIES 93; FAT 5.1g (sat 0.7g, mono 3.7g, poly 0.6g); PROTEIN 1g; CARB 13g; FIBER 2g; CHOL 0mg; IRON 0mg; SODIUM 221mg; CALC 5mg

Frisée Salad with Persimmons, Dates, and Almonds

HANDS-ON TIME: 15 MIN. | **TOTAL TIME:** 15 MIN.

1½ cups thinly sliced leek (about 1 large),
  divided
3 tablespoons water
2 tablespoons white wine vinegar
1 teaspoon extra-virgin olive oil
½ teaspoon kosher salt
1 ripe Fuyu persimmon, peeled and
  chopped (about 7 ounces)
6 cups frisée or bagged mâche salad
  greens
3 cups peeled and thinly sliced
  quartered ripe Fuyu persimmons
  (about 3)
3 tablespoons sliced almonds, toasted
8 pitted dates, chopped (about ¼ cup)

❶ Place 1 tablespoon leek in blender. Place 3 tablespoons water and next 4 ingredients (through the chopped persimmon) in blender; process until smooth.
❷ Combine frisée and remaining sliced leek in a large bowl; toss with dressing. Place 1 cup frisée mixture on each of 8 plates. Top each serving with about ⅓ cup sliced persimmon, about 1 teaspoon almonds, and 1½ teaspoons dates.

SERVES 8

CALORIES 157; FAT 2g (sat 0.2g, mono 1.2g, poly 0.5g); PROTEIN 2g; CARB 37g; FIBER 6g; CHOL 0mg; IRON 1mg; SODIUM 134mg; CALC 57mg

Tangerine and Avocado Salad with Pumpkinseeds

HANDS-ON TIME: 10 MIN. | **TOTAL TIME:** 10 MIN.

Superfast

Ready in 15 minutes or less!

2 tangerines, peeled
1 small ripe avocado, peeled and sliced
1 tablespoon fresh lime juice
1 teaspoon extra-virgin olive oil
3 tablespoons toasted pumpkinseed kernels
1/4 teaspoon chili powder
Dash of kosher salt

❶ Cut tangerines into rounds. Combine tangerines, avocado, lime juice, and olive oil; toss gently to coat. Sprinkle with pumpkinseeds, chili powder, and salt.

SERVES 4 (serving size: about 1/2 cup)

CALORIES 149; **FAT** 11.6g (sat 1.8g, mono 6.8g, poly 2.3g); **PROTEIN** 3g; **CARB** 11g; **FIBER** 5g; **CHOL** 0mg; **IRON** 1mg; **SODIUM** 38mg; **CALC** 26mg

Simple Avocado Salad

HANDS-ON TIME: 10 MIN. | **TOTAL TIME:** 10 MIN.

2 tablespoons chopped red onion
1 1/2 tablespoons fresh lime juice
1 1/2 tablespoons extra-virgin olive oil
1 large ripe avocado, peeled and diced
4 cups baby arugula
1/4 teaspoon salt
1/4 teaspoon freshly ground black pepper

❶ Combine onion, lime juice, and olive oil in a medium bowl, stirring with a whisk. Add avocado; toss gently to combine. Divide arugula among 4 salad plates; top evenly with avocado mixture. Sprinkle evenly with salt and pepper.

SERVES 4

CALORIES 134; **FAT** 12.6g (sat 1.8g, mono 8.6g, poly 1.5g); **PROTEIN** 2g; **CARB** 6g; **FIBER** 4g; **CHOL** 0mg; **IRON** 1mg; **SODIUM** 155mg; **CALC** 41mg

Simple Swap

You can use oranges
or tangerines instead
of the grapefruit,
and goat cheese
in place of feta.

Superfast

Ready in 15
minutes or less!

Grapefruit, Walnut, and Feta Salad ▶

HANDS-ON TIME: 13 MIN. | **TOTAL TIME:** 13 MIN.

1 small red grapefruit
2 tablespoons extra-virgin olive oil
½ teaspoon sugar
⅛ teaspoon salt
⅛ teaspoon freshly ground black pepper
4 cups torn butter lettuce
1 ounce crumbled feta cheese
    (about ¼ cup)
¼ cup chopped walnuts, toasted

❶ Peel and section grapefruit over a bowl; squeeze membranes to extract juice. Set grapefruit sections aside, and reserve 3 tablespoons juice. Discard membranes.
❷ Combine grapefruit juice, oil, sugar, salt, and pepper, stirring with a whisk. Divide lettuce evenly among 4 plates; sprinkle 1 tablespoon cheese and 1 tablespoon walnuts over each salad. Divide grapefruit sections evenly among salads; drizzle with vinaigrette.

SERVES 4

CALORIES 145; **FAT** 12.5g (sat 2.4g, mono 5.8g, poly 3.8g); **PROTEIN** 3g; **CARB** 7g; **FIBER** 1.6g; **CHOL** 6mg; **IRON** 1mg; **SODIUM** 156mg; **CALC** 67mg

Watermelon Salad

HANDS-ON TIME: 8 MIN. | **TOTAL TIME:** 18 MIN.

½ cup chopped red onion
3 tablespoons fresh lime juice
5 cups chopped seeded watermelon
¼ cup halved pitted kalamata olives
¼ cup finely chopped fresh parsley
¼ cup finely chopped fresh mint
3 ounces crumbled feta cheese
    (about ¾ cup)

❶ Combine red onion and lime juice in a medium bowl; let stand 10 minutes. Add watermelon, olives, parsley, and mint. Sprinkle with feta cheese.

SERVES 6 (serving size: about 1 cup salad and about 1 tablespoon feta cheese)

CALORIES 99; **FAT** 4.6g (sat 2.3g, mono 1.7g, poly 0.3g); **PROTEIN** 3g; **CARB** 13g; **FIBER** 1g; **CHOL** 13mg; **IRON** 1mg; **SODIUM** 243mg; **CALC** 91mg

Roasted Baby Beets and Blood Orange Salad with Blue Cheese

HANDS-ON TIME: 20 MIN. | **TOTAL TIME:** 1 HR. 15 MIN.

12 multicolored baby beets
4 medium blood oranges
1½ tablespoons balsamic vinegar
4 teaspoons extra-virgin olive oil
1 teaspoon Dijon mustard
⅛ teaspoon salt
⅛ teaspoon freshly ground black pepper
1 (5-ounce) package mixed baby greens
2 ounces blue cheese, crumbled (about ½ cup)
¼ cup chopped walnuts, toasted

❶ Preheat oven to 400°.

❷ Leave root and 1-inch stem on beets; scrub well with a brush. Cut an 18 x 12–inch sheet of foil. Place beets in center of foil. Gather edges of foil to form a pouch; tightly seal. Place pouch on a baking sheet. Bake at 400° for 45 minutes or until tender. Cool 20 minutes. Trim off beet roots; rub off skins. Cut beets into quarters.

❸ Grate 1 teaspoon orange rind. Peel and section oranges over a large bowl; squeeze membranes to extract juice. Set sections aside; reserve 3 table-spoons juice. Discard membranes. Combine rind, juice, vinegar, and next 4 ingredients (through pepper) in a small bowl; stir with a whisk.

❹ Divide greens evenly among 8 plates. Arrange beet quarters and orange sections on top of greens. Sprinkle each serving with 1 tablespoon blue cheese and 1½ teaspoons nuts. Drizzle each serving with about 2 teaspoons dressing.

SERVES 8

CALORIES 163; FAT 6.9g (sat 1.9g, mono 2.6g, poly 2.1g); PROTEIN 5g; CARB 22g; FIBER 6g; CHOL 5mg; IRON 1mg; SODIUM 255mg; CALC 92mg

Marinated Beet Salad

HANDS-ON TIME: 22 MIN. | **TOTAL TIME:** 1 HR. 45 MIN.

1 pound red baby beets, trimmed
½ cup water, divided
⅛ teaspoon kosher salt, divided
6 thyme sprigs, divided
2 rosemary sprigs, divided
1 pound gold baby beets, trimmed
1 medium leek, white and light green
    parts only, halved lengthwise
Cooking spray
1 teaspoon grated orange rind
3 tablespoons fresh orange juice
1 teaspoon grated lime rind
2 tablespoons fresh lime juice
2 tablespoons sherry vinegar
2 tablespoons olive oil
1 teaspoon thyme leaves
⅛ teaspoon kosher salt
6 cups herb salad mix
3 tablespoons plain fat-free Greek
    yogurt
1 tablespoon toasted unsalted sunflower
    seed kernels

❶ Preheat oven to 375°.
❷ Place red beets, ¼ cup water, a dash of salt, 3 thyme sprigs, and 1 rosemary sprig in an 11 x 7–inch glass baking dish; cover with foil. Repeat procedure with gold beets, ¼ cup water, dash of salt, 3 thyme sprigs, and 1 rosemary sprig. Roast at 375° for 1 hour and 15 minutes or until a knife inserted into center of a beet meets little resistance. Remove from oven; uncover. Let stand until cool enough to handle; rub skins from beets with a kitchen towel. Discard skins.
❸ Coat leek with cooking spray. Place leek, cut side down, on a foil-lined baking sheet. Roast at 375° for 25 minutes or until very tender. Cool slightly. Place leek, orange rind, and next 7 ingredients (through ⅛ teaspoon kosher salt) in a blender; process until smooth.
❹ Place beets in a large bowl with half of vinaigrette; toss to combine. Add salad mix and remaining vinaigrette; toss gently to coat. Place 1⅔ cups salad on each of 6 plates. Top each serving with 1½ teaspoons yogurt; sprinkle each with ½ teaspoon sunflower seeds.

SERVES 6

CALORIES 144; FAT 5.6g (sat 0.8g, mono 3.5g, poly 1g); PROTEIN 4g; CARB 21g; FIBER 6g; CHOL 0mg; IRON 2mg; SODIUM 233mg; CALC 45mg

Did You Know?

Beets are proven to boost stamina, purify the blood and liver, and lower blood pressure and could even help prevent cancer.

Marinated Asparagus-and-Carrot Salad

HANDS-ON TIME: 21 MIN. | **TOTAL TIME:** 4 HR. 21 MIN.

1 pound asparagus
½ cup balsamic vinegar
¼ cup olive oil
1 tablespoon chopped fresh parsley
½ teaspoon salt
½ teaspoon freshly ground black pepper
1 garlic clove, minced
4 cups julienne-cut carrot

❶ Snap off tough ends of asparagus. Cut into 2-inch pieces. Cook asparagus in boiling water to cover 3 minutes. Drain, and plunge asparagus into ice water; drain. Place vinegar and next 5 ingredients (through garlic) in a large heavy-duty zip-top plastic bag. Seal bag and shake to blend. Add asparagus to bag; seal bag and shake to coat. Chill 3 hours.

❷ Add carrot to bag; seal bag and shake to coat. Chill 1 hour.

SERVES 6 (serving size: 1 cup)

CALORIES 148; **FAT** 9.3g (sat 1.3g, mono 6.6g, poly 1.1g); **PROTEIN** 3g; **CARB** 15g; **FIBER** 4g; **CHOL** 0mg; **IRON** 2mg; **SODIUM** 260mg; **CALC** 53mg

Fennel Salad with Lemon

HANDS-ON TIME: 25 MIN. | **TOTAL TIME:** 1 HR. 25 MIN.

Simple Swap

If you don't have a Meyer lemon, try tangerine or ruby red grapefruit. Regular lemons would be too tart.

¼ cup coarsely chopped fresh parsley
2 fennel bulbs, trimmed, halved, and cut into thin vertical slices
1 shallot, halved and cut into thin vertical slices
2 tablespoons extra-virgin olive oil
1 teaspoon sugar
½ teaspoon kosher salt
¼ teaspoon freshly ground black pepper
⅔ cup Meyer lemon sections (about 3 lemons)
2 ounces goat cheese, cut into 6 slices

❶ Combine first 3 ingredients in a bowl. Drizzle mixture with oil; sprinkle with sugar, salt, and pepper. Toss. Add lemon sections; toss gently to combine. Cover and chill 1 hour. Top with cheese.

SERVES 6 (serving size: 1 cup salad and 1 cheese slice)

CALORIES 107; **FAT** 6.9g (sat 2.1g, mono 3.8g, poly 0.8g); **PROTEIN** 3g; **CARB** 11g; **FIBER** 3g; **CHOL** 4mg; **IRON** 1mg; **SODIUM** 238mg; **CALC** 65mg

Shaved Fennel with Orange and Olives

HANDS-ON TIME: 18 MIN. | **TOTAL TIME:** 18 MIN.

2 oranges
1 fennel bulb, trimmed
12 kalamata olives, pitted and coarsely chopped
¼ teaspoon freshly ground black pepper
Chopped fennel fronds (optional)

❶ Peel and section oranges over a bowl, reserving juices. Shave fennel bulb on a mandoline; toss with orange sections, juices, olives, and pepper. Sprinkle with chopped fennel fronds, if desired.

SERVES 4 (serving size: about ⅔ cup)

CALORIES 47; **FAT** 1.3g (sat 0g, mono 1.1g, poly 0.2g); **PROTEIN** 1g; **CARB** 9g; **FIBER** 2g; **CHOL** 0mg; **IRON** 0mg; **SODIUM** 145mg; **CALC** 43mg

Prep Pointer

Halve the fennel bulb and remove the core before shaving it.

Warm Brussels Sprouts Salad

HANDS-ON TIME: 26 MIN. | **TOTAL TIME:** 26 MIN.

1½ teaspoons extra-virgin olive oil, divided
1 garlic clove, minced
⅓ cup fresh breadcrumbs
¾ pound Brussels sprouts, trimmed and halved (about 8 cups)
¼ teaspoon salt
⅛ teaspoon freshly ground black pepper
1½ tablespoons finely chopped walnuts, toasted
½ ounce shaved Asiago cheese

❶ Heat 1 teaspoon oil in a large nonstick skillet over medium heat. Add garlic; cook 1 minute or just until golden, stirring constantly. Add breadcrumbs; cook 1 minute or until lightly browned, stirring constantly. Transfer garlic mixture to a small bowl.
❷ Separate leaves from Brussels sprouts; quarter cores. Heat ½ teaspoon oil over medium heat. Add leaves and cores to pan; cook 8 minutes or just until leaves wilt and cores are crisp-tender, stirring frequently. Remove from heat; toss with breadcrumb mixture, salt, and pepper. Top with walnuts and cheese.

SERVES 6 (serving size: ¾ cup)

CALORIES 71; **FAT** 3.1g (sat 0.6g, mono 1.1g, poly 1.1g); **PROTEIN** 4g; **CARB** 9g; **FIBER** 2g; **CHOL** 1mg; **IRON** 1mg; **SODIUM** 160mg; **CALC** 47mg

Did You Know?

Kohlrabi is a relative of the cabbage and is delicious in both raw and cooked forms. If its outermost layer is tough, remove it with a vegetable peeler before cooking or eating.

Honey-Glazed Kohlrabi with Onions and Herbs ▶

HANDS-ON TIME: 22 MIN. | **TOTAL TIME:** 1 HR. 25 MIN.

2 teaspoons olive oil
5 small green or red kohlrabi bulbs, cut lengthwise into wedges (about 1½ pounds)
1 teaspoon yellow mustard seeds
⅜ teaspoon kosher salt
¼ teaspoon freshly ground black pepper
½ cup water
2½ tablespoons honey
1 tablespoon white wine vinegar
2 teaspoons butter
1 medium sweet onion, vertically sliced into wedges
2 tablespoons chopped fresh flat-leaf parsley

❶ Preheat oven to 300°.
❷ Heat a large ovenproof skillet over medium-high heat. Add oil; swirl to coat. Add kohlrabi to pan; cook 2 minutes or until browned, stirring occasionally. Stir in mustard seeds, salt, and pepper; cook 1 minute. Add ½ cup water, honey, vinegar, butter, and onion; bring mixture to a boil.
❸ Cover and bake at 300° for 1 hour or until kohlrabi is tender. Uncover and remove kohlrabi from pan; place on a serving platter. Return pan to medium-high heat. Bring to a boil; cook 6 minutes or until syrupy. Drizzle kohlrabi with syrup; sprinkle evenly with chopped parsley.

SERVES 4 (serving size: about 1 cup)

CALORIES 155; FAT 4.7g (sat 1.6g, mono 2.2g, poly 0.4g); PROTEIN 4g; CARB 28g; FIBER 7g; CHOL 5mg; IRON 1mg; SODIUM 224mg; CALC 70mg

Zucchini Ribbons with Pecorino

HANDS-ON TIME: 15 MIN. | **TOTAL TIME:** 15 MIN.

2 zucchini
2 tablespoons fresh lemon juice
2 teaspoons olive oil
¼ teaspoon freshly ground black pepper
⅛ teaspoon kosher salt
3 tablespoons shaved pecorino Romano cheese

❶ Slice zucchini into thin ribbons using a vegetable peeler; toss with lemon juice, olive oil, pepper, and salt. Top with shaved pecorino Romano cheese.

SERVES 4 (serving size: about ½ cup)

CALORIES 59; FAT 4.3g (sat 1.7g, mono 1.7g, poly 0.3g); PROTEIN 3g; CARB 4g; FIBER 1g; CHOL 6mg; IRON 0mg; SODIUM 172mg; CALC 64mg

Grilled Corn, Poblano, and Black Bean Salad

HANDS-ON TIME: 40 MIN. | **TOTAL TIME:** 40 MIN.

2 ears shucked corn
2 tablespoons extra-virgin olive oil, divided
4 green onions
1 avocado, peeled, halved, and pitted
1 large red bell pepper
1 large poblano chile
Cooking spray
½ cup chopped fresh cilantro
3 tablespoons fresh lime juice
1 teaspoon ground cumin
¼ teaspoon salt
¼ teaspoon freshly ground black pepper
1 (15-ounce) can unsalted black beans, rinsed and drained

❶ Preheat grill to high heat.
❷ Brush corn with 2 teaspoons oil. Place green onions, avocado, bell pepper, poblano, and corn on grill rack coated with cooking spray. Grill onions 2 minutes on each side or until lightly browned. Grill avocado 2 minutes on each side or until well marked. Grill bell pepper 6 minutes on each side or until blackened; peel. Grill poblano 9 minutes on each side or until blackened; peel. Grill corn 12 minutes or until beginning to brown on all sides, turning occasionally.
❸ Cut kernels from ears of corn; place in a large bowl. Chop onions, bell pepper, and poblano; add to bowl. Add 4 teaspoons oil, cilantro, juice, cumin, salt, black pepper, and beans to bowl; toss well. Cut avocado into thin slices; place on top of salad.

SERVES 6 (serving size: ¾ cup)

CALORIES 167; **FAT** 9.9g (sat 1.4g, mono 6.7g, poly 1.3g); **PROTEIN** 5g; **CARB** 18g; **FIBER** 6g; **CHOL** 0mg; **IRON** 1mg; **SODIUM** 209mg; **CALC** 38mg

Prep Pointer

Pairing the sweet corn with more piquant ingredients like peppers, onions, and cilantro makes this salad pleasing and complex. Though served warm here, it's also tasty eaten chilled or at room temperature.

Simple Swap

Use Sriracha instead of the hot pepper sauce for a more garlicky, sweet flavor than Tabasco offers.

Curried Potato Salad ▶

HANDS-ON TIME: 20 MIN. | **TOTAL TIME:** 1 HR. 30 MIN.

2 pounds Red Bliss potatoes, cut into 1-inch pieces
3/4 cup plain 2% reduced-fat Greek yogurt
2 teaspoons Madras or regular curry powder
1 1/2 teaspoons hot pepper sauce (such as Tabasco)
3/4 teaspoon salt
3/4 cup shredded carrot
1/2 cup thinly sliced green onions, divided
1/3 cup thinly sliced celery
2 tablespoons unsalted cashews

❶ Place potatoes in a medium saucepan; cover with cold water. Bring to a boil. Reduce heat, and simmer 10 minutes or until tender. Drain and cool.
❷ Combine yogurt and next 3 ingredients (through salt), stirring with a whisk.
❸ Place cooled potatoes in a large bowl. Add carrot, 5 tablespoons green onions, celery, and yogurt mixture; toss gently to combine. Sprinkle with 3 tablespoons green onions and cashews. Serve chilled.

SERVES 8 (serving size: about 1 cup)

CALORIES 117; FAT 1.8g (sat 0.6g, mono 0.6g, poly 0.3g); PROTEIN 5g; CARB 22g; FIBER 3g; CHOL 1mg; IRON 1mg; SODIUM 275mg; CALC 48mg

Creamy Potato Salad

HANDS-ON TIME: 21 MIN. | **TOTAL TIME:** 21 MIN.

1 large egg
3/4 pound fingerling potatoes
2 tablespoons light mayonnaise
1 tablespoon plain nonfat Greek yogurt
1 1/2 teaspoons prepared mustard
1/3 cup prechopped celery
3 tablespoons prechopped red onion
1/4 teaspoon kosher salt
1/4 teaspoon freshly ground black pepper

❶ Place a saucepan filled two-thirds with water over high heat; add egg, and cover. Cut potatoes into 1-inch pieces. Add potatoes to pan; cover and bring to a boil. Reduce heat to medium-high; cook 5 minutes or until tender. Drain.
❷ Combine remaining ingredients in a medium bowl; add potatoes. Peel and coarsely chop egg; add to potatoes.

SERVES 6 (serving size: 1/2 cup)

CALORIES 74; FAT 2.5g (sat 0.5g, mono 0.8g, poly 1.1g); PROTEIN 3g; CARB 11g; FIBER 1g; CHOL 32mg; IRON 1mg; SODIUM 148mg; CALC 16mg

Blue potatoes are starchier than the others and tend to bleed, so cook them separately. You can prepare this dish a day ahead, but add the blue potatoes just before serving.

Red, White, and Blue Potato Salad

HANDS-ON TIME: 28 MIN. | **TOTAL TIME:** 38 MIN.

10 ounces fingerling potatoes, halved lengthwise (about 2 cups)
10 ounces small red potatoes, quartered (about 2 cups)
10 ounces blue potatoes, halved lengthwise (about 2 cups)
¼ cup finely chopped red onion
2 tablespoons chopped fresh parsley
1 tablespoon chopped fresh dill
1 tablespoon chopped fresh chives
3 hard-cooked large eggs, finely chopped
¼ cup red wine vinegar
2 tablespoons olive oil
½ teaspoon salt
2 teaspoons Dijon mustard
½ teaspoon freshly ground black pepper
1 garlic clove, minced

❶ Place fingerling and red potatoes in a large saucepan; cover with water. Bring to a boil. Reduce heat, and simmer 12 minutes or until tender. Drain and cool slightly.

❷ While fingerling and red potatoes cook, place blue potatoes in a medium saucepan; cover with water. Bring to a boil. Reduce heat, and simmer 8 minutes or until tender. Drain and cool slightly. Combine fingerling potatoes, red potatoes, and blue potatoes in a large bowl. Add onion and next 4 ingredients (through eggs) to potatoes; toss gently.

❸ Combine vinegar and next 5 ingredients (through garlic) in a small bowl. Pour over potato mixture, tossing gently to coat. Serve warm, at room temperature, or chilled.

SERVES 6 (serving size: about 1 cup)

CALORIES 250; **FAT** 7.5g (sat 1.5g, mono 4.4g, poly 0.9g); **PROTEIN** 7g; **CARB** 40g; **FIBER** 4g; **CHOL** 106mg; **IRON** 3mg; **SODIUM** 286mg; **CALC** 36mg

Roasted Potato Salad with Creamy Dijon Vinaigrette

HANDS-ON TIME: 10 MIN. | **TOTAL TIME:** 40 MIN.

2 pounds Yukon gold potatoes, cut into wedges
3 tablespoons extra-virgin olive oil, divided
2 tablespoons sliced garlic
1 teaspoon minced fresh thyme
3/4 teaspoon kosher salt, divided
3/4 teaspoon freshly ground black pepper, divided
1 1/2 tablespoons white wine vinegar
2 tablespoons minced shallots
2 teaspoons Dijon mustard
1 1/2 teaspoons chopped fresh tarragon

❶ Place a large heavy baking sheet in oven. Preheat oven to 400° (keep the baking sheet in oven as it preheats).

❷ Combine potatoes, 1 1/2 tablespoons oil, garlic, and thyme in a medium bowl; toss to coat. Arrange potato mixture on preheated baking sheet, and sprinkle with 1/2 teaspoon salt and 1/2 teaspoon black pepper. Bake at 400° for 30 minutes or until browned and tender, turning after 20 minutes.

❸ Combine 1 1/2 tablespoons oil, 1/4 teaspoon salt, 1/4 teaspoon pepper, vinegar, shallots, Dijon mustard, and tarragon in a small bowl, stirring well with a whisk. Drizzle dressing over potatoes.

SERVES 8 (serving size: about 3/4 cup potatoes and about 2 teaspoons dressing)

CALORIES 145; **FAT** 5g (sat 0.7g, mono 3.7g, poly 0.5g); **PROTEIN** 3g; **CARB** 22g; **FIBER** 2g; **CHOL** 0mg; **IRON** 1mg; **SODIUM** 218mg; **CALC** 7mg

Did You Know?

Preheating the baking sheet causes the potatoes to brown evenly and cook more quickly.

Zesty Three-Bean and Sautéed Corn Salad

HANDS-ON TIME: 33 MIN. | **TOTAL TIME:** 63 MIN.

Cooking spray
2½ cups (1-inch) cut green beans
    (about 1 pound)
¾ cup fresh corn kernels
    (about 2 medium ears)
¾ cup diced red bell pepper
½ cup minced red onion
¼ cup chopped fresh cilantro
1 tablespoon minced seeded jalapeño
1 (16-ounce) can cannellini beans or
    other white beans, rinsed and drained
1 (15-ounce) can black beans, rinsed and
    drained
¼ cup fresh lime juice
¼ cup red wine vinegar
1 tablespoon minced fresh garlic
1 tablespoon olive oil
2 teaspoons ground cumin
1 teaspoon chili powder
½ teaspoon salt
¼ teaspoon red chile sauce
    (such as Cholula)
Dash of ground red pepper
1 cup diced seeded tomato
    (about 2 medium)
1 cup diced avocado

❶ Heat a large nonstick skillet over medium-high heat. Coat pan with cooking spray. Add green beans and corn to pan; sauté 3 minutes or until lightly browned. Transfer green bean mixture to a large bowl. Add bell pepper and next 5 ingredients (through black beans) to bowl; toss well.
❷ Combine juice, vinegar, and next 7 ingredients (through red pepper) in a small bowl; stir with a whisk. Add juice mixture to bean mixture; toss well. Cover and chill 30 minutes. Gently stir in tomato and avocado. Serve immediately.

SERVES 10 (serving size: about 1 cup)

CALORIES 146; **FAT** 5.3g (sat 0.6g, mono 3g, poly 0.7g); **PROTEIN** 7g; **CARB** 23g; **FIBER** 7g; **CHOL** 0mg; **IRON** 2mg; **SODIUM** 233mg; **CALC** 64mg

Summer Bean Salad

HANDS-ON TIME: 35 MIN. | **TOTAL TIME:** 45 MIN.

3 tablespoons extra-virgin olive oil

1 teaspoon grated lemon rind

3½ tablespoons fresh lemon juice, divided

1 tablespoon chopped fresh thyme

¾ teaspoon freshly ground black pepper, divided

⅜ teaspoon kosher salt

8 cups water

8 ounces fresh yellow wax beans, cut into 1½-inch pieces (about 3 cups)

2 cups shelled and peeled fava beans (about 3 pounds unshelled beans)

2 cups quartered cherry tomatoes

1 cup very thinly vertically sliced red onion

1 (15½-ounce) can unsalted chickpeas (garbanzo beans), rinsed and drained

¼ cup canola mayonnaise

1 tablespoon minced fresh chives

❶ Combine oil, rind, 2 tablespoons lemon juice, thyme, ½ teaspoon pepper, and salt in a large bowl, stirring with a whisk.

❷ Bring 8 cups water to a boil in a large saucepan. Add wax beans; cook 2 minutes. Add fava beans to wax beans in pan; cook an additional 2 minutes or until beans are tender. Drain and rinse with cold water. Drain. Add bean mixture, cherry tomatoes, onion, and chickpeas to dressing; toss well.

❸ Combine 1½ tablespoons lemon juice, ¼ teaspoon pepper, mayonnaise, and chives in a small bowl, stirring with a whisk. Let stand 10 minutes. Drizzle mayonnaise mixture over bean mixture.

SERVES 8 (serving size: about 1 cup)

CALORIES 147; FAT 7.9g (sat 0.8g, mono 5g, poly 1.4g); PROTEIN 4g; CARB 15g; FIBER 4g; CHOL 0mg; IRON 1mg; SODIUM 160mg; CALC 43mg

Prep Pointer

If you purchase whole fava bean pods, you'll need to shell them, and then peel the beans: Blanch shelled beans in boiling water for a few seconds, remove to a bowl of ice water, drain, and slip off the opaque skins.

Simple Swap

You can also substitute shelled edamame.

Prep Pointer

This colorful Southwestern salad can be wrapped in tortillas and eaten like a burrito.

Pinto, Black, and Red Bean Salad with Grilled Corn and Avocado

HANDS-ON TIME: 42 MIN. | **TOTAL TIME:** 42 MIN.

1 cup halved heirloom grape or cherry tomatoes

1 teaspoon salt, divided

3 ears shucked corn

1 medium white onion, cut into ¼-inch-thick slices

1 jalapeño pepper

1 tablespoon olive oil

Cooking spray

⅓ cup chopped fresh cilantro

⅓ cup fresh lime juice

1 (15-ounce) can unsalted pinto beans, rinsed and drained

1 (15-ounce) can unsalted black beans, rinsed and drained

1 (15-ounce) can unsalted kidney beans, rinsed and drained

2 diced peeled avocados

❶ Preheat grill to medium-high heat.

❷ Place tomatoes in a large bowl, and sprinkle with ½ teaspoon salt. Let stand 10 minutes.

❸ Brush corn, onion, and jalapeño evenly with oil. Place vegetables on grill rack coated with cooking spray. Grill corn 12 minutes or until lightly charred, turning after 6 minutes. Grill onion slices and jalapeño 8 minutes or until lightly charred, turning after 4 minutes. Let vegetables stand 5 minutes.

❹ Cut kernels from cobs. Coarsely chop onion. Finely chop jalapeño; discard stem. Add corn, onion, and jalapeño to tomato mixture; toss well. Add ½ teaspoon salt, cilantro, and next 4 ingredients (through kidney beans) to corn mixture; toss well. Top with avocado.

SERVES 12 (serving size: ⅔ cup)

CALORIES 141; **FAT** 6.4g (sat 0.9g, mono 4.2g, poly 0.9g); **PROTEIN** 5g; **CARB** 18g; **FIBER** 7g; **CHOL** 0mg; **IRON** 1mg; **SODIUM** 211mg; **CALC** 38mg

Fresh Pea Salad with Radishes, Tomatoes, and Mint

HANDS-ON TIME: 15 MIN. | **TOTAL TIME:** 2 HR. 35 MIN.

1½ cups fresh pink-eyed peas
3 tablespoons fresh lemon juice
1 tablespoon rice wine vinegar
1 tablespoon olive oil
2 cups grape or cherry tomatoes, halved
1 cup thinly sliced radishes (about 8)
¼ cup chopped fresh mint
¼ teaspoon salt
¼ teaspoon freshly ground black pepper
Mint sprigs (optional)

❶ Sort and wash peas; place in a small saucepan. Cover with water to 2 inches above peas; bring to a boil. Cover, reduce heat, and simmer 20 minutes or until tender. Drain.

❷ Combine juice, vinegar, and oil in a small bowl; stir well with a whisk.

❸ Combine peas, tomatoes, and next 4 ingredients (through pepper) in a medium bowl. Drizzle juice mixture over salad, tossing to coat. Cover and chill 2 hours. Garnish with mint sprigs, if desired.

SERVES 6 (serving size: ⅔ cup)

CALORIES 217; FAT 5.4g (sat 0.7g, mono 2.4g, poly 1.6g); PROTEIN 10g; CARB 34g; FIBER 10g; CHOL 0mg; IRON 4mg; SODIUM 145mg; CALC 65mg

Simple Swap

Chickpeas, black-eyed peas, or lady peas could also be used in this salad.

Simple Swap

Sub whole-wheat spaghetti for the soba noodles. Just add 10 minutes longer to cook.

Soba Noodle Salad

HANDS-ON TIME: 10 MIN. | **TOTAL TIME:** 19 MIN.

4 ounces uncooked soba (buckwheat noodles)
1½ tablespoons lower-sodium soy sauce
1 tablespoon dark sesame oil
1 teaspoon brown sugar
1½ teaspoons fresh lemon juice
¼ teaspoon crushed red pepper
½ cup (2-inch-long) julienne-cut red bell pepper
½ cup julienne-cut snow peas
¼ cup thinly sliced green onions

❶ Cook soba according to package directions, omitting salt and fat; drain and rinse with cold water. Drain well.

❷ Combine soy sauce, dark sesame oil, brown sugar, lemon juice, and crushed red pepper in a medium bowl, stirring well with a whisk. Add noodles, red bell pepper, snow peas, and green onions; toss well.

SERVES 4 (serving size: ¾ cup)

CALORIES 151; **FAT** 4g (sat 0.5g, mono 1.6g, poly 1.7g); **PROTEIN** 4g; **CARB** 25g; **FIBER** 2g; **CHOL** 0mg; **IRON** 1mg; **SODIUM** 221mg; **CALC** 22mg

Quinoa with Broccoli and Bacon

HANDS-ON TIME: 25 MIN. | **TOTAL TIME:** 25 MIN.

3/4 cup uncooked quinoa, rinsed
1 cup water
3 teaspoons olive oil, divided
2 cups fresh broccoli florets
2 tablespoons water
1/8 teaspoon salt
2 bacon slices, cooked and crumbled

❶ Heat quinoa in a saucepan over medium-high heat; sauté 2 minutes. Add 1 cup water; bring to a boil. Cover, reduce heat, and simmer 13 minutes. Remove from heat; let stand 2 minutes. Heat 1 teaspoon olive oil in a saucepan over medium-high heat. Add broccoli florets; sauté 2 minutes. Add 2 tablespoons water; cover and reduce heat. Cook 2 minutes. Combine quinoa, broccoli, 2 teaspoons olive oil, salt, and bacon.

SERVES 4 (serving size: about 1 cup)

CALORIES 170; FAT 6.4g (sat 1.2g, mono 3g, poly 1.5g); PROTEIN 7g; CARB 22g; FIBER 3g; CHOL 4mg; IRON 2mg; SODIUM 139mg; CALC 32mg

Prep Pointer

Bacon adds a salty, full flavor to the other subtly flavored ingredients and gives the dish the right amount of crunch.

Quinoa Salad with Artichokes and Parsley

HANDS-ON TIME: 20 MIN. | **TOTAL TIME:** 38 MIN.

1 tablespoon olive oil
1 cup chopped spring or sweet onion
1/2 teaspoon chopped fresh thyme
1 (9-ounce) package frozen artichoke hearts, thawed
1 cup fat-free, lower-sodium chicken broth
1/2 cup uncooked quinoa
1 cup chopped fresh parsley
5 teaspoons grated lemon rind
1 1/2 tablespoons fresh lemon juice
1/4 teaspoon kosher salt

❶ Heat oil in a medium saucepan over medium-high heat. Add onion and thyme; sauté 5 minutes or until onion is tender. Add artichokes; sauté 2 minutes or until thoroughly heated. Add broth and quinoa; bring to a simmer. Cover and cook 18 minutes or until liquid is completely absorbed.
❷ Remove pan from heat. Stir in parsley, rind, juice, and salt. Serve warm or at room temperature.

SERVES 8 (serving size: about 1/3 cup)

CALORIES 83; FAT 2.8g (sat 0.3g, mono 1.4g, poly 0.6g); PROTEIN 3g; CARB 12g; FIBER 4g; CHOL 0mg; IRON 1mg; SODIUM 135mg; CALC 39mg

◄ *Bulgur Salad with Edamame*

HANDS-ON TIME: 10 MIN. | **TOTAL TIME:** 2 HR. 10 MIN.

1 cup uncooked bulgur
1 cup boiling water
1 cup frozen shelled edamame
  (green soybeans)
1 pound yellow and red cherry tomatoes,
  halved
1 cup finely chopped fresh flat-leaf
  parsley
⅓ cup finely chopped fresh mint
2 tablespoons chopped fresh dill
1 cup chopped green onions
¼ cup fresh lemon juice
¼ cup extra-virgin olive oil
¾ teaspoon kosher salt
½ teaspoon freshly ground black pepper

❶ Combine bulgur and 1 cup boiling water in a large bowl. Cover and let stand 1 hour or until bulgur is tender.
❷ Cook edamame in boiling water 3 minutes or until crisp-tender. Drain. Add edamame, tomatoes, and remaining ingredients to bulgur; toss well. Let stand at room temperature 1 hour before serving.

SERVES 6 (serving size: 1¼ cups)

CALORIES 208; FAT 10.5g (sat 1.3g, mono 6.7g, poly 1.2g); PROTEIN 6g; CARB 25g; FIBER 7g; CHOL 0mg; IRON 2mg; SODIUM 252mg; CALC 59mg

Prep Pointer

You can prepare the edamame mixture while the bulgur hydrates.

Tabbouleh Salad

HANDS-ON TIME: 15 MIN. | **TOTAL TIME:** 3 HR. 10 MIN.

2½ cups boiling water
1½ cups uncooked bulgur
  (about 8 ounces)
2 cups chopped fresh flat-leaf parsley
1 cup diced seeded tomato
¾ cup diagonally sliced green onions
¼ cup chopped fresh mint
6 tablespoons fresh lemon juice
3 tablespoons extra-virgin olive oil
1 teaspoon kosher salt
1 teaspoon freshly ground black pepper
½ teaspoon ground cumin

❶ Combine 2½ cups boiling water and bulgur in a large bowl; cover and let stand 1 hour. Add parsley and remaining ingredients to bulgur; toss well. Cover and chill at least 2 hours.

SERVES 8 (serving size: about ⅔ cup)

CALORIES 161; FAT 5.7g (sat 0.8g, mono 3.8g, poly 0.8g); PROTEIN 5g; CARB 26g; FIBER 7g; CHOL 0mg; IRON 3mg; SODIUM 259mg; CALC 54mg

Golden Beet Salad with Wheat Berries and Pumpkinseed Vinaigrette

HANDS-ON TIME: 20 MIN. | **TOTAL TIME:** 1 HR. 40 MIN.

4 medium golden beets

3 tablespoons extra-virgin olive oil, divided

1 cup uncooked wheat berries

2 cups water

½ cup unsalted pumpkinseed kernels, toasted and divided

1 tablespoon honey

1 tablespoon Dijon mustard

1 tablespoon sherry vinegar

¼ teaspoon kosher salt

¼ teaspoon freshly ground black pepper

⅓ cup diced celery

¼ cup thinly sliced shallots

2 tablespoons chopped fresh chives

¼ cup celery leaves

❶ Preheat oven to 400°.

❷ Leave root and 1 inch of stem on beets, and scrub with a brush. Place beets in center of a 16 x 12–inch sheet of foil; drizzle with 1 tablespoon oil. Fold foil over beets; tightly seal edges. Bake at 400° for 1 hour and 20 minutes or until tender. Unwrap beets; cool. Trim off beet roots; rub off skins. Cut beets into wedges.

❸ While beets cook, combine wheat berries and 2 cups water in a medium saucepan; bring to a boil. Cover, reduce heat, and simmer 1 hour or until tender, stirring occasionally. Drain; cool slightly.

❹ Place ¼ cup pumpkinseed kernels in a large bowl, and coarsely crush with back of a spoon. Add honey and next 4 ingredients (through pepper); stir well with a whisk. Gradually add 2 tablespoons olive oil, stirring constantly with a whisk. Add beets, wheat berries, celery, shallots, and chives; toss gently. Sprinkle with ¼ cup pumpkinseed kernels and celery leaves.

SERVES 8 (serving size: about ⅔ cup)

CALORIES 203; FAT 9g (sat 1.5g, mono 3.8g, poly 1g); PROTEIN 6g; CARB 27g; FIBER 5g; CHOL 0mg; IRON 1mg; SODIUM 174mg; CALC 16mg

Couscous and Dill Snap Peas

HANDS-ON TIME: 20 MIN. | **TOTAL TIME:** 20 MIN.

5 cups water, divided
6 ounces sugar snap peas, trimmed
5 teaspoons extra-virgin olive oil, divided
⅔ cup Israeli couscous
½ teaspoon grated lemon rind
2 tablespoons fresh lemon juice
1 teaspoon Dijon mustard
½ teaspoon minced fresh garlic
½ teaspoon sugar
¼ teaspoon kosher salt
¼ teaspoon freshly ground black pepper
1 tablespoon minced fresh dill
2 tablespoons shaved Parmesan cheese

❶ Bring 4 cups water to a boil in a large saucepan. Add peas; cook 30 seconds or until crisp-tender. Drain and plunge into ice water; drain. Slice half of peas diagonally.
❷ Heat 2 teaspoons olive oil in a saucepan over medium heat. Add couscous; sauté 3 minutes. Add 1 cup water; bring to a boil. Cover, reduce heat, and simmer 10 minutes. Drain and rinse; drain.
❸ Combine 1 tablespoon oil, lemon rind, and next 6 ingredients (through pepper) in a medium bowl; stir with a whisk. Add peas; toss to coat. Add couscous and dill; toss. Top with Parmesan cheese.

SERVES 4 (serving size: about 1 cup)

CALORIES 211; **FAT** 6.7g (sat 1.2g, mono 4.3g, poly 0.7g); **PROTEIN** 6.2g; **CARB** 31.5g; **FIBER** 2.5g; **CHOL** 2mg; **IRON** 1mg; **SODIUM** 195mg; **CALC** 52mg

Greek Orzo Salad

HANDS-ON TIME: 10 MIN. | **TOTAL TIME:** 20 MIN.

¾ cup orzo
1 tablespoon olive oil
1 tablespoon red wine vinegar
¼ teaspoon sugar
¼ teaspoon kosher salt
¼ teaspoon freshly ground black pepper
¾ cup diced seeded tomato
½ cup chopped green bell pepper
¼ cup chopped red onion
3 tablespoons chopped fresh parsley
4 Castelvetrano olives, sliced

❶ Cook orzo according to package directions, omitting salt and fat; drain.
❷ Combine oil, vinegar, sugar, salt, and black pepper in a large bowl, stirring with a whisk until sugar dissolves. Add orzo, tomato, bell pepper, onion, parsley, and olives; stir to combine.

SERVES 4 (serving size: about ¾ cup)

CALORIES 202; **FAT** 4.7g (sat 0.6g, mono 2.8g, poly 0.4g); **PROTEIN** 6g; **CARB** 35g; **FIBER** 3g; **CHOL** 0mg; **IRON** 2mg; **SODIUM** 157mg; **CALC** 16mg

Orzo, Corn, and Roasted Bell Pepper Salad

HANDS-ON TIME: 34 MIN. | **TOTAL TIME:** 34 MIN.

2 red bell peppers

1 cup uncooked orzo (rice-shaped pasta)

3 tablespoons extra-virgin olive oil, divided

3 ears shucked corn

1 medium red onion, peeled and cut into ½-inch-thick slices

Cooking spray

¼ cup thinly sliced green onions

¼ cup chopped fresh flat-leaf parsley

3 tablespoons white wine vinegar

1 teaspoon salt

½ teaspoon freshly ground black pepper

1 jalapeño pepper, minced

1 garlic clove, minced

❶ Preheat broiler.

❷ Cut bell peppers in half lengthwise; discard seeds and membranes. Place pepper halves, skin sides up, on a foil-lined baking sheet; flatten with hand. Broil 15 minutes or until blackened. Wrap in foil. Let stand 15 minutes. Peel and chop.

❸ Preheat grill to medium-high heat.

❹ Cook orzo according to package directions, omitting salt and fat. Drain. Place orzo in a large bowl; drizzle with 1 tablespoon oil. Cool slightly.

❺ Place corn and red onion on grill rack coated with cooking spray; grill 5 minutes or until lightly browned, turning occasionally. Cut kernels from ears of corn; chop red onion. Add bell pepper, corn, red onion, 2 tablespoons oil, green onions, and remaining ingredients to orzo. Toss gently to combine.

SERVES 8 (serving size: about ⅔ cup)

CALORIES 180; FAT 5.9g (sat 0.9g, mono 3.9g, poly 0.7g); PROTEIN 5g; CARB 29g; FIBER 3g; CHOL 0mg; IRON 1mg; SODIUM 302mg; CALC 15mg

Simple Swap

Use tricolored orzo to make the salad even more vibrant.

Prep Pointer

If you have a gas stove, you can also roast the peppers on the stovetop. Using metal tongs, hold pepper halves over a medium flame until charred all over.

Rotini Salad with Kalamata Olive Dressing

HANDS-ON TIME: 30 MIN. | **TOTAL TIME:** 30 MIN.

1 red bell pepper
½ yellow bell pepper
6 ounces uncooked rotini
   (corkscrew pasta)
¼ pound haricots verts
   (French green beans), trimmed
   and cut into 1-inch pieces
1½ cups quartered cherry tomatoes
½ cup sliced fresh basil
1½ ounces diced fresh mozzarella
4 pitted kalamata olives, sliced
1 ounce prosciutto, chopped
Cooking spray
3 garlic cloves, peeled and sliced
1 large shallot, peeled and cut into
   ½-inch pieces
2½ tablespoons white balsamic vinegar
1 tablespoon water
1 teaspoon Dijon mustard
¼ teaspoon kosher salt
¼ teaspoon freshly ground black pepper

❶ Preheat broiler.
❷ Cut red bell pepper in half lengthwise; discard seeds and membranes. Place red and yellow pepper halves, skin sides up, on a foil-lined baking sheet; flatten with hand. Broil 15 minutes or until blackened. Wrap peppers in foil. Let stand 10 minutes.
❸ Peel and dice peppers; place in a large bowl.
❹ Cook pasta according to package directions, omitting salt and fat. Add haricots verts to pasta during last 3 minutes of cooking time.
❺ Drain. Add pasta mixture, tomatoes, and next 4 ingredients (through prosciutto) to peppers; toss.
❻ Heat a small saucepan over medium-low heat. Coat pan with cooking spray.
❼ Add garlic and shallot to pan. Cook 15 minutes or until soft, stirring occasionally.
❽ Place garlic mixture, vinegar, and remaining ingredients in a blender; process until smooth. Pour dressing over pasta mixture; toss well.

SERVES 7 (serving size: about 1 cup)

CALORIES 147; FAT 3g (sat 1.3g, mono 1.1g, poly 0.3g); PROTEIN 7g; CARB 24g; FIBER 2g; CHOL 8mg; IRON 1mg; SODIUM 205mg; CALC 59mg

Black Pepper Pasta Salad with Prosciutto, Asparagus, and Romano

HANDS-ON TIME: 35 MIN. | **TOTAL TIME:** 35 MIN.

8 ounces uncooked cavatappi pasta or elbow macaroni

3 cups (1½-inch) slices asparagus (about 1 pound)

1 teaspoon olive oil

2 ounces prosciutto, chopped

½ cup thinly sliced shallots

6 tablespoons light mayonnaise

1 teaspoon grated lemon rind

1 tablespoon chopped fresh tarragon

2 tablespoons fresh lemon juice

1 teaspoon freshly ground black pepper

Dash of salt

1 cup diced tomato

1½ ounces pecorino Romano cheese, grated (about ⅓ cup packed)

❶ Cook pasta according to package directions, omitting salt and fat. Add asparagus during the last 2 minutes of cooking. Drain and rinse under cold water; drain.

❷ Heat a large nonstick skillet over medium-high heat. Add olive oil to pan, and swirl to coat. Add prosciutto, and cook 6 minutes or until crisp, stirring occasionally. Remove prosciutto from pan using a slotted spoon, leaving drippings in pan. Drain prosciutto on paper towels. Add shallots to drippings in pan; cook over medium heat 1 minute or until shallots are tender, stirring frequently.

❸ Combine mayonnaise, lemon rind, tarragon, juice, pepper, and salt in a large bowl; stir well. Add pasta, asparagus, three-fourths of prosciutto, shallots, tomato, and cheese; toss well to coat. Top servings evenly with remaining prosciutto.

SERVES 8 (serving size: about 1 cup)

CALORIES 208; **FAT** 7g (sat 1.9g, mono 1.8g, poly 2.3g); **PROTEIN** 9g; **CARB** 28g; **FIBER** 3g; **CHOL** 15mg; **IRON** 3mg; **SODIUM** 349mg; **CALC** 86mg

Prep Pointer

Look for prosciutto in the deli or prepared meats section of the supermarket.

Superfast

Ready in 15
minutes or less!

Macaroni Salad

HANDS-ON TIME: 8 MIN. | **TOTAL TIME:** 14 MIN.

4 ounces uncooked elbow macaroni
  (about 1 cup)
½ cup canola mayonnaise
1 tablespoon cider vinegar
1½ teaspoons sugar
¾ teaspoon dry mustard
½ teaspoon freshly ground black pepper
¼ teaspoon salt
⅓ cup thinly sliced celery
⅓ cup finely chopped red bell pepper
¼ cup finely chopped red onion
¼ cup grated carrot
1 tablespoon chopped fresh chives

❶ Cook pasta according to package directions, omitting salt and fat; drain.
❷ Combine mayonnaise and next 5 ingredients (through salt) in a large bowl, stirring with a whisk. Stir in cooked pasta, celery, and remaining ingredients. Cover and store in refrigerator up to 3 days.

SERVES 6 (serving size: ½ cup)

CALORIES 217; **FAT** 15.3g (sat 1.4g, mono 8.1g, poly 4.3g); **PROTEIN** 3g; **CARB** 17g; **FIBER** 1g; **CHOL** 7mg; **IRON** 1mg; **SODIUM** 242mg; **CALC** 13mg

Did You Know?

Farfalle, or bow-tie pasta, is named for its shape. In Italian, this word means "butterflies."

Spinach-Pasta Salad

HANDS-ON TIME: 18 MIN. | **TOTAL TIME:** 18 MIN.

½ cup mini farfalle
1½ tablespoons extra-virgin olive oil
1 tablespoon white wine vinegar
½ teaspoon Dijon mustard
¼ teaspoon freshly ground black pepper
⅛ teaspoon salt
2 garlic cloves, minced
3 cups baby spinach
¼ cup chopped red onion

❶ Cook mini farfalle according to package directions. Drain. Rinse with cold water; drain.
❷ Combine olive oil and next 5 ingredients (through garlic) in a large bowl, stirring well with a whisk. Add garlic vinaigrette, spinach, and onion to pasta.

SERVES 4 (serving size: about ⅔ cup)

CALORIES 106; **FAT** 5.4g (sat 0.8g, mono 3.7g, poly 0.7g); **PROTEIN** 3g; **CARB** 12g; **FIBER** 1g; **CHOL** 0mg; **IRON** 1mg; **SODIUM** 108mg; **CALC** 31mg

Macaroni Salad with Bacon, Peas, and Creamy Dijon Dressing

HANDS-ON TIME: 26 MIN. | **TOTAL TIME:** 26 MIN.

Prep Pointer

Tossing the salad with some, but not all, of the dressing before chilling allows the tangy Dijon dressing to flavor the pasta and veggies without making them soggy.

4 ounces ⅓-less-fat cream cheese (about ½ cup)

¼ cup chopped shallots

¼ cup canola mayonnaise (such as Hellmann's)

2 tablespoons fat-free sour cream

2 tablespoons Dijon mustard

2 tablespoons fresh lemon juice

1 tablespoon white wine vinegar

¾ teaspoon freshly ground black pepper

¼ teaspoon kosher salt

8 ounces uncooked large elbow macaroni

⅔ cup fresh green peas

⅔ cup finely diced red bell pepper

⅔ cup finely diced red onion

½ cup thinly sliced green onions

¼ cup chopped fresh flat-leaf parsley

½ teaspoon grated lemon rind

3 center-cut bacon slices, cooked and crumbled

❶ Place first 9 ingredients in a food processor; process until smooth. Cover and chill.

❷ Cook pasta according to package directions, omitting salt and fat; add peas during the last 3 minutes of cooking time. Drain; rinse with cold water. Drain. Combine pasta mixture, bell pepper, and next 4 ingredients (through rind) in a large bowl.

❸ Toss pasta mixture with half of dressing. Cover and chill until ready to serve.

❹ Toss salad with remaining dressing, and sprinkle with crumbled bacon; serve immediately.

SERVES 10 (serving size: about ¾ cup)

CALORIES 161; FAT 4.8g (sat 1.9g, mono 1g, poly 0.7g); PROTEIN 5g; CARB 23g; FIBER 2g; CHOL 10mg; IRON 1mg; SODIUM 242mg; CALC 32mg

BLT Panzanella Salad

HANDS-ON TIME: 25 MIN. | **TOTAL TIME:** 25 MIN.

1 tablespoon unsalted butter

3 ounces Italian bread, crusts trimmed, torn into ¼-inch pieces

¾ cup fresh corn kernels

4 large ripe heirloom tomatoes, cored and cut crosswise into ¼-inch-thick slices

1 cup small multicolored cherry tomatoes, halved

⅛ teaspoon plus dash of kosher salt, divided

¾ teaspoon freshly ground black pepper, divided

2 teaspoons balsamic vinegar

2 teaspoons extra-virgin olive oil

1 cup baby arugula

3 tablespoons canola mayonnaise (such as Hellmann's)

1 tablespoon fresh lemon juice

2 teaspoons minced fresh chives

¼ cup thinly sliced basil leaves

3 center-cut bacon slices, cooked and crumbled

❶ Melt butter in a large skillet over medium-high heat. Add bread; sauté 5 minutes or until bread is toasted, stirring occasionally. Remove from heat; stir in corn.

❷ Sprinkle tomatoes with dash of salt and ½ teaspoon pepper; let tomatoes stand 5 minutes.

❸ Combine ⅛ teaspoon salt, ¼ teaspoon pepper, vinegar, and oil in a large bowl. Add bread mixture and arugula; toss to coat. Combine mayonnaise, lemon juice, and chives in a small bowl.

❹ Arrange tomatoes and bread mixture on a large platter. Drizzle with mayonnaise mixture; sprinkle evenly with basil and bacon.

SERVES 6

CALORIES 132; FAT 6.9g (sat 1.9g, mono 3g, poly 1.3g); PROTEIN 4g; CARB 15g; FIBER 2g; CHOL 8mg; IRON 1mg; SODIUM 236mg; CALC 33mg

Did You Know?

Panzanella, essentially, is a salad made with bread and tomatoes.

Winter
Jeweled
Fruit Salad,
p. 225

Maduros,
p. 251

Spiced
Cranberry-
Mango
Chutney,
p. 235

fruit

Fruit is nature's candy: luscious, vibrant, and either sweet or tart. It's low in calories and high in all the good stuff—vitamins, minerals, phytonutrients, and fiber. Irresistible on its own, fruit is also the perfect complement to fish, pork, and poultry dishes. Use it raw, pickled, grilled, or roasted to make bright, simple, zero-effort salsas, chutneys, and salads.

Know Your Fruits

Even the smallest fruits can have big health benefits. Consuming the recommended daily amount of fruit can help you lose weight, improve heart health, and may reduce the risk of some chronic diseases. There's no match for just-picked fruity goodness: From the arrival of summer's peaches to the cranberries you'll find in winter, each season offers a variety of great flavors to keep your palate happy.

Berries

Berries are available year-round, but it is best to get them in peak season for the most concentrated flavor. Look for plump, colorful berries, and refrigerate them, unwashed, as soon as you get home. For longer storage, freeze them.

Citrus fruit

Oranges, tangerines, grapefruit, kumquats, and lemons are at their best midwinter, right when you need their bright flavors the most. For best quality, select blemish-free fruit that is firm to the touch and heavy for its size. To keep them fresh longer, refrigerate them. They'll last only a couple of days at room temperature but up to two weeks in the fridge.

Melons

Most melons hit their peak in summer months. Look for a symmetrical melon heavy for its size and free of cracks or soft spots. Melons store well at room temperature for a week or longer, depending on ripeness. Wash and dry the rind before cutting to prevent bacterial contamination.

Pome fruit

Pome fruits such as apples, pears, and quince signal the sweet passage of fall. They are excellent to pair with many sweet and savory ingredients, especially nuts, cheese, and warm spices.

Stone fruit

Choose nectarines, plums, and peaches that give slightly when pressed. Cherries should have a deep color and smooth skin. If not perfectly ripe, peaches and plums will continue to ripen on your counter; refrigerate once ripe. Eat cherries within two days of purchase or refrigerate, unwashed, in a plastic bag.

Tropical fruit

Tropical fruits include bananas, coconuts, dates, figs, papayas, mangos, persimmons, and pineapple. Make sure you buy ripe fruit. Look for papayas with yellowish skin and pineapples with a red-orange colored base. Judge mango ripeness by feel, not color: It's best when the flesh gives slightly.

How to Prepare

SECTION AND SLICE CITRUS

❶ Cut off top and bottom of fruit to create a level surface.

❷ Use a serrated knife to peel fruit, making short strokes from top to bottom of fruit, along where the rind meets the flesh.

❸ For rounds, lay the fruit parallel to the board, and slice.

❹ For sections, use a sharp paring knife to cut the sections between the membranes.

BROIL GRAPEFRUIT

Though this pink and red citrus is delicious enough on its own, if the tartness is too much try broiling— it makes the fruit even sweeter.

❶ Preheat broiler to high.

❷ Cut the grapefruit in half; place each half on a baking sheet with the cut side facing up.

❸ Sprinkle ½ teaspoon cinnamon and 2 teaspoons brown sugar on each side.

❹ Broil on high for 3 to 5 minutes or until bubbling.

CUT A MELON

❶ To trim, place washed melon on a cutting board, and use a sharp, heavy knife to slice about 1 inch from the stem end to make a stable cutting surface.

❷ Stand the melon up, cut side down, and vertically slice the melon in half. (At that point, remove and discard the seeds from cantaloupes and honeydew melons.)

❸ Lay halves cut side down, and make 1-inch cuts through the melon. Refrigerate cut melon in a covered container.

Winter Jeweled Fruit Salad

HANDS-ON TIME: 25 MIN. | **TOTAL TIME:** 25 MIN.

½ cup pomegranate arils
(about 1 pomegranate)
½ cup julienne-cut peeled jicama
⅓ cup sliced seeded kumquats
(about 6 medium)
2 medium ripe mangoes, peeled and cut
into thin slices
2 tangerines or clementines, peeled and
sectioned
2 blood oranges, peeled and sectioned
1 pear, thinly sliced
2 tablespoons fresh lime juice
2 tablespoons honey
¼ teaspoon ground red pepper
⅛ teaspoon coarse sea salt

❶ Combine first 7 ingredients in a large bowl;
toss gently. Combine lime juice, honey, pepper,
and salt in a small bowl, stirring well with a whisk.
Pour over fruit; toss gently to coat. Serve at room
temperature.

SERVES 8 (serving size: 1 cup)

CALORIES 118; **FAT** 0.4g (sat 0.1g, mono 0.1g, poly 0.1g);
PROTEIN 1g; **CARB** 30g; **FIBER** 4g; **CHOL** 0mg; **IRON** 0mg;
SODIUM 37mg; **CALC** 39mg

◄ Spiced Winter Fruit

HANDS-ON TIME: 30 MIN. | **TOTAL TIME:** 60 MIN.

1 large pink grapefruit
1 large red grapefruit
⅓ cup small pitted prunes
⅓ cup dried figs, cut into quarters
3 tablespoons light brown sugar
7 whole cloves
1 (3-inch) cinnamon stick
1 cup seedless red grapes, halved

❶ Peel and section grapefruit over a bowl;
squeeze membranes to extract juice. Set sections
aside; reserve juice and add water to equal 1¼ cups.
❷ Combine juice mixture, prunes, figs, sugar, cloves,
and cinnamon in a medium saucepan; bring to
a boil. Reduce heat; simmer 15 minutes, stirring
occasionally. Remove from heat; cool. Discard
cloves and cinnamon stick. Stir in grapefruit
sections and grapes.

SERVES 8 (serving size: ½ cup)

CALORIES 97; **FAT** 0.3g (sat 0g, mono 0.1g, poly 0.1g);
PROTEIN 1g; **CARB** 25g; **FIBER** 3g; **CHOL** 0mg; **IRON** 1mg;
SODIUM 3mg; **CALC** 32mg

Three-Fruit Salsa

HANDS-ON TIME: 17 MIN. | **TOTAL TIME:** 17 MIN.

1 cup finely chopped peeled cantaloupe
1 cup finely chopped peeled mango
1 cup sliced small strawberries
1/2 cup finely chopped seeded peeled cucumber
1/2 cup finely chopped green bell pepper
1/2 cup finely chopped red onion
1 1/2 tablespoons chopped fresh mint
1 tablespoon chopped fresh basil
2 tablespoons fresh lime juice
2 tablespoons finely chopped seeded jalapeño pepper
1 tablespoon honey
1/4 teaspoon salt

❶ Combine all ingredients in a bowl; toss to combine. Serve salsa with a slotted spoon.

SERVES 6 (serving size: about 3/4 cup)

CALORIES 59; **FAT** 0.4g (sat 0.1g, mono 0.1g, poly 0.1g); **PROTEIN** 1g; **CARB** 15g; **FIBER** 2g; **CHOL** 0mg; **IRON** 1mg; **SODIUM** 103mg; **CALC** 19mg

Fresh Fruit Salad

HANDS-ON TIME: 14 MIN. | **TOTAL TIME:** 14 MIN.

2 tablespoons sugar
1 teaspoon grated orange rind
2 tablespoons fresh orange juice
3 cups cubed honeydew melon
1 cup sliced strawberries
1 kiwifruit, peeled and sliced
1/4 cup raspberries (optional)
1/4 cup blueberries (optional)

❶ Place first 3 ingredients in a large bowl; stir until sugar dissolves. Add honeydew, strawberries, kiwifruit, and berries, if desired; toss gently to combine.

SERVES 4 (serving size: about 1 1/4 cups)

CALORIES 99; **FAT** 0.4g (sat 0.1g, mono 0g, poly 0.2g); **PROTEIN** 1g; **CARB** 25g; **FIBER** 3g; **CHOL** 0mg; **IRON** 1mg; **SODIUM** 24mg; **CALC** 22mg

Clementine Salad with Walnuts

HANDS-ON TIME: 48 MIN. | **TOTAL TIME:** 48 MIN.

½ cup water
½ cup red wine vinegar
¼ cup sugar
1 cup vertically sliced red onion
1 tablespoon fresh orange juice
2 teaspoons olive oil
1 teaspoon Dijon mustard
8 cups gourmet salad greens
2 cups clementine sections
　(about 6 clementines)
¾ cup Spiced Walnuts
6 tablespoons pomegranate arils

❶ Combine first 3 ingredients in a small saucepan. Bring to a boil; remove from heat. Reserve 2 tablespoons vinegar mixture. Combine remaining vinegar mixture and onion in a small bowl; cool to room temperature.
❷ Combine reserved 2 tablespoons vinegar mixture, orange juice, oil, and mustard; stir well.
❸ Combine dressing and salad greens in a large bowl; toss well. Divide salad greens mixture evenly among 6 salad plates. Top each with ⅓ cup clementines, about 2 tablespoons onions, 2 tablespoons Spiced Walnuts, and 1 tablespoon pomegranate seeds.

SERVES 6

CALORIES 175; FAT 5.3g (sat 0.6g, mono 2g, poly 2.5g); PROTEIN 3g; CARB 32g; FIBER 4g; CHOL 0mg; IRON 1mg; SODIUM 58mg; CALC 49mg

Spiced Walnuts

1 cup walnut halves
½ cup sugar
¼ cup water
½ teaspoon ground cinnamon
¼ teaspoon salt
Dash of ground red pepper
Cooking spray

❶ Preheat oven to 350°.
❷ Arrange walnuts in a single layer on a baking sheet. Bake at 350° for 10 minutes or until nuts are lightly browned.
❸ Combine sugar and next 4 ingredients (through red pepper) in a small saucepan. Cook, without stirring, until a candy thermometer registers 238° (about 8 minutes). Remove from heat; stir in walnuts. Pour walnut mixture onto baking sheet coated with cooking spray. Cool completely; break into small pieces.

SERVES 16 (serving size: 2 tablespoons)

CALORIES 60; FAT 3.4g (sat 0.3g, mono 0.8g, poly 2.2g); PROTEIN 0.8g; CARB 7g; FIBER 0g; CHOL 0mg; IRON 0mg; SODIUM 37mg; CALC 6mg

Prep Pointer

Good choices for gourmet salad greens are loose-leaf lettuce, arugula, romaine lettuce, radicchio, butterhead lettuce, cress, and escarole.

Prep Pointer

To make this ahead, refrigerate the orange mixture and juice mixture separately. Bring them to room temperature, and toss together before serving.

Orange and Olive Salad

HANDS-ON TIME: 16 MIN. | **TOTAL TIME:** 16 MIN.

4 oranges, peeled
1/2 cup green olives, pitted and halved
   (such as picholine or cerignola)
1/4 cup finely chopped fresh cilantro
1/4 teaspoon kosher salt
1/4 teaspoon freshly ground black pepper
2 1/2 tablespoons fresh lemon juice
1 1/2 tablespoons olive oil
1 teaspoon orange-flower water
Dash of sugar

❶ Cut each orange crosswise into 5 slices. Place orange slices in a bowl; toss with olives and cilantro. Sprinkle with salt and pepper.
❷ Combine juice, oil, orange-flower water, and sugar; stir with a whisk. Pour over salad; toss gently to combine.

SERVES 6 (serving size: about 2/3 cup)

CALORIES 77; **FAT** 5.1g (sat 0.5g, mono 3.7g, poly 0.8g); **PROTEIN** 1g; **CARB** 9g; **FIBER** 2g; **CHOL** 0mg; **IRON** 0mg; **SODIUM** 259mg; **CALC** 25mg

Pear Relish

HANDS-ON TIME: 7 MIN. | **TOTAL TIME:** 17 MIN.

2 cups chopped red Anjou pear
1/3 cup sliced kumquat
2 tablespoons fresh lemon juice
1 tablespoon honey
1/3 cup sliced green olives
3 tablespoons thinly sliced shallots
1 1/2 tablespoons extra-virgin olive oil
1 1/2 tablespoons chopped fresh chives
1 1/2 teaspoons chopped fresh flat-leaf
   parsley
1/4 teaspoon salt
1/8 teaspoon ground red pepper

❶ Combine pear, kumquat, lemon juice, and honey; let stand 10 minutes. Add olives, shallots, and remaining ingredients; toss.

SERVES 12 (serving size: 1/4 cup)

CALORIES 47; **FAT** 2.4g (sat 0.3g, mono 1.6g, poly 0.2g); **PROTEIN** 0g; **CARB** 7g; **FIBER** 1g; **CHOL** 0mg; **IRON** 0mg; **SODIUM** 105mg; **CALC** 22mg

Beet-Citrus Salad with Pistachios

HANDS-ON TIME: 5 MIN. | **TOTAL TIME:** 5 MIN.

½ teaspoon grated orange rind
2 tablespoons fresh orange juice
1 tablespoon extra-virgin olive oil
½ teaspoon ground cumin
¼ teaspoon kosher salt
¼ teaspoon freshly ground black pepper
1 (20-ounce) jar refrigerated citrus salad
   (such as Del Monte), drained
1 (8-ounce) package steamed,
   ready-to-eat beets, rinsed, drained,
   and cut into wedges
¼ cup shelled dry-roasted, unsalted
   pistachios

❶ Combine first 6 ingredients; stir with a whisk. Add citrus and beets; toss gently. Sprinkle with pistachios.

SERVES 4 (serving size: ¼ cup)

CALORIES 156; FAT 6.9g (sat 0.9g, mono 4.3g, poly 1.4g); PROTEIN 2g; CARB 20g; FIBER 3g; CHOL 0mg; IRON 1mg; SODIUM 141mg; CALC 40mg

Superfast

Ready in 15
minutes or less!

Lemon Balm Citrus Salad

HANDS-ON TIME: 15 MIN. | **TOTAL TIME:** 15 MIN.

2 navel oranges
1 red grapefruit
½ cup seedless red grapes, halved
2 tablespoons small fresh lemon balm
    or mint leaves
2 tablespoons honey

❶ Peel and section oranges and grapefruit over a bowl; squeeze membranes to extract juice. Add grapes, lemon balm, and honey; toss well. Chill.

SERVES 4 (serving size: about ½ cup)

CALORIES 110; FAT 0.1g (sat 0g, mono 0g, poly 0.1g); PROTEIN 1g; CARB 28g; FIBER 3g; CHOL 0mg; IRON 0mg; SODIUM 2mg; CALC 55mg

Grapefruit–Hearts of Palm Salad

HANDS-ON TIME: 22 MIN. | **TOTAL TIME:** 22 MIN.

2 tablespoons canola oil
½ teaspoon grated lime rind
1 tablespoon fresh lime juice
1 tablespoon canola mayonnaise
1 teaspoon honey
⅛ teaspoon freshly ground black pepper
4 cups baby kale
1½ cups ruby red grapefruit sections
    (about 2 large grapefruit)
½ cup thinly sliced red onion
2 (14-ounce) cans hearts of palm, rinsed,
    drained, and cut diagonally into
    ¼-inch slices
1 small red chile, seeded and thinly sliced
1 ripe peeled avocado, cut into thin wedges

❶ Combine first 6 ingredients in a small bowl; stir with a whisk until smooth.
❷ Place ⅔ cup kale on each of 6 plates. Arrange grapefruit sections, onion, hearts of palm, chile, and avocado evenly over kale. Drizzle with dressing.

SERVES 6 (serving size: about 1 cup salad and about 2 teaspoons dressing)

CALORIES 183; FAT 11.1g (sat 1.2g, mono 6.7g, poly 2.5g); PROTEIN 5g; CARB 20g; FIBER 6g; CHOL 0mg; IRON 4mg; SODIUM 240mg; CALC 122mg

Simple Swap

Use artichoke hearts in place of hearts of palm.

Grapefruit and Fennel Salad

HANDS-ON TIME: 26 MIN. | **TOTAL TIME:** 26 MIN.

4 pink grapefruit
12 cups gourmet salad greens
2 cups coarsely chopped fennel bulb
    (about 2 bulbs)
1 cup vertically sliced red onion
½ cup seasoned rice vinegar
2 tablespoons honey
1 tablespoon extra-virgin olive oil
1 teaspoon fennel seeds, crushed
¼ teaspoon salt

❶ Peel and section grapefruit over a bowl, and squeeze membranes to extract juice. Set 3 cups sections aside, and reserve ¼ cup juice for vinaigrette. Discard membranes.
❷ Combine grapefruit sections, salad greens, chopped fennel, and sliced onion in a large bowl. Combine vinegar, reserved ¼ cup juice, honey, oil, seeds, and salt. Drizzle salad with vinaigrette, and toss gently to coat. Serve immediately.

SERVES 8 (serving size: 1½ cups)

CALORIES 85; FAT 2.1g (sat 0.3g, mono 1.3g, poly 0.3g); PROTEIN 3g; CARB 15g; FIBER 2g; CHOL 0mg; IRON 2mg; SODIUM 84mg; CALC 68mg

Strawberry, Cucumber, and Basil Salad

HANDS-ON TIME: 14 MIN. | **TOTAL TIME:** 1 HR. 14 MIN.

4 cups hulled strawberries, quartered
  (1 pound)
2 tablespoons thinly sliced fresh basil
2 teaspoons balsamic vinegar
1 teaspoon sugar
2 medium cucumbers, peeled, halved
  lengthwise, seeded, and thinly sliced
  (about 2 cups)
1 teaspoon fresh lemon juice
1/4 teaspoon salt
1/4 teaspoon freshly ground black pepper

❶ Combine first 4 ingredients in a large bowl, and toss gently to coat. Cover and chill 1 hour.
❷ Combine cucumbers and juice; toss to coat. Add cucumber mixture, salt, and pepper to strawberry mixture; toss gently to combine. Serve immediately.

SERVES 4 (serving size: 1½ cups)

CALORIES 49; FAT 0.5g (sat 0.1g, mono 0.1g, poly 0.3g); PROTEIN 1g; CARB 12g; FIBER 3g; CHOL 0mg; IRON 1mg; SODIUM 150mg; CALC 26mg

Chunky Strawberry-Avocado Salsa

HANDS-ON TIME: 13 MIN. | **TOTAL TIME:** 13 MIN.

1½ cups quartered ripe strawberries
2/3 cup chopped radishes
1/2 cup chopped green onions
1 tablespoon white balsamic vinegar
1/4 teaspoon kosher salt
1 ripe avocado, peeled and diced

❶ Combine all ingredients in a medium bowl. Serve immediately.

SERVES 12 (serving size: 1/4 cup)

CALORIES 37; FAT 2.5g (sat 0.4g, mono 1.7g, poly 0.3g); PROTEIN 1g; CARB 4g; FIBER 2g; CHOL 0mg; IRON 0mg; SODIUM 44mg; CALC 9mg

Did You Know?

Strawberries and avocados make an amazing flavor combo. The rich and buttery flavor of avocado creates the perfect balance for the tangy sweetness of the strawberries.

Strawberries, Peaches, and Basil with Orange Vinaigrette

HANDS-ON TIME: 18 MIN. | **TOTAL TIME:** 18 MIN.

1 cup fresh orange juice
1½ tablespoons sugar
1½ tablespoons champagne vinegar or
    white wine vinegar
1 tablespoon extra-virgin olive oil
Dash of salt
1½ cups fresh blueberries
1 pound fresh strawberries, halved
1 large ripe peach or nectarine, cut into
    16 wedges
¼ cup small basil leaves

❶ Combine first 3 ingredients in a small sauce-pan; bring to a boil. Cook until reduced to ½ cup (about 15 minutes). Add oil and salt to pan, stirring with a whisk. Let stand 2 minutes.
❷ Combine berries and peach in a large bowl. Add juice mixture, stirring gently. Sprinkle with basil.

SERVES 4 (serving size: 1¼ cups)

CALORIES 163; FAT 4.2g (sat 0.5g, mono 2.6g, poly 0.7g); PROTEIN 2g; CARB 33g; FIBER 4g; CHOL 0mg; IRON 1mg; SODIUM 39mg; CALC 36mg

Prep Pointer

You'll need 2 to 4 medium-sized oranges to get 1 cup of juice.

Blueberry-Chipotle Chutney

HANDS-ON TIME: 38 MIN. | **TOTAL TIME:** 38 MIN.

4 cups fresh blueberries
1 cup finely chopped Granny Smith apple
½ cup white wine vinegar
⅓ cup sugar
⅓ cup honey
3 tablespoons grated orange rind
1 tablespoon mustard seeds
2 tablespoons chopped canned chipotle
   chiles in adobo sauce (about 2 chiles)
½ teaspoon salt
½ teaspoon ground ginger

❶ Combine all ingredients in a large saucepan; bring to a boil. Reduce heat, and simmer, uncovered, 25 minutes or until thick, stirring frequently. Cool; pour into airtight containers.

SERVES 32 (serving size: 2 tablespoons)

CALORIES 34; **FAT** 0.2g (sat 0g, mono 0.1g, poly 0.1g); **PROTEIN** 0g; **CARB** 9g; **FIBER** 1g; **CHOL** 0mg; **IRON** 0mg; **SODIUM** 48mg; **CALC** 4mg

Cranberry-Orange Relish

HANDS-ON TIME: 10 MIN. | **TOTAL TIME:** 10 MIN.

1 tablespoon grated orange rind
1 cup orange sections
⅓ cup sugar
2 teaspoons honey
½ teaspoon ground cinnamon
⅛ teaspoon salt
1 (12-ounce) bag fresh cranberries
Cinnamon stick (optional)

❶ Place all ingredients except cinnamon stick in a food processor; pulse to combine. Garnish with cinnamon stick, if desired.

SERVES 8 (serving size: ¼ cup)

CALORIES 68; **FAT** 0.1g (sat 0g, mono 0g, poly 0.1g); **PROTEIN** 0g; **CARB** 18g; **FIBER** 3g; **CHOL** 0mg; **IRON** 0mg; **SODIUM** 38mg; **CALC** 14mg

Grape and Hazelnut Salad

HANDS-ON TIME: 12 MIN. | **TOTAL TIME:** 12 MIN.

1 tablespoon extra-virgin olive oil
1 tablespoon white balsamic vinegar
1/2 teaspoon Dijon mustard
1 (5-ounce) package mixed salad greens
1/3 cup halved seedless red grapes
2 tablespoons coarsely chopped toasted
   hazelnuts

❶ Combine olive oil, vinegar, and Dijon mustard in a large bowl, stirring with a whisk. Add salad greens, grapes, and hazelnuts; toss to coat.

SERVES 4 (serving size: about 1 cup)

CALORIES 71; FAT 5.6g (sat 0.6g, mono 4.1g, poly 0.7g); PROTEIN 1g; CARB 5g; FIBER 1g; CHOL 0mg; IRON 1mg; SODIUM 29mg; CALC 6mg

Spiced Cranberry- Mango Chutney

HANDS-ON TIME: 23 MIN. | **TOTAL TIME:** 23 MIN.

1 1/2 tablespoons canola oil
1/2 cup finely chopped shallots
2 teaspoons mustard seeds
1 teaspoon minced peeled fresh ginger
1 teaspoon minced fresh garlic
1 teaspoon minced serrano chile
1/3 cup sugar
1/4 cup golden raisins
2 tablespoons red wine vinegar
1/4 teaspoon kosher salt
1 (12-ounce) package fresh cranberries
2 cups chopped peeled mango
   (about 2 large)
1/3 cup finely chopped toasted walnuts

❶ Heat a large skillet over medium heat. Add oil; swirl. Add shallots; sauté 2 minutes. Add mustard seeds, ginger, garlic, and serrano; sauté 2 minutes. Stir in sugar and next 4 ingredients (through cranberries); bring to a simmer. Reduce heat, and cook 4 minutes. Add mango; cook 1 minute. Stir in walnuts.

SERVES 12 (serving size: 1/4 cup)

CALORIES 105; FAT 4.2g (sat 0.4g, mono 1.4g, poly 2.1g); PROTEIN 1g; CARB 17g; FIBER 2g; CHOL 0mg; IRON 0mg; SODIUM 42mg; CALC 17mg

Spike your cranberry sauce by stirring in 1 to 2 tablespoons orange or black currant liqueur at the end. If you like it spiced, stir in ½ teaspoon ground cinnamon, ¼ teaspoon ground nutmeg, and ¼ teaspoon ground allspice.

Three-Ingredient Cranberry Sauce

HANDS-ON TIME: 12 MIN. | **TOTAL TIME:** 42 MIN.

1 navel orange
1 cup sugar
¼ cup water
1 (12-ounce) package fresh cranberries

❶ Grate orange to yield 2 teaspoons rind. Cut orange in half; squeeze to yield ½ cup juice. Combine rind, juice, and remaining ingredients in a small saucepan; bring to a boil. Reduce heat to low, and simmer 7 minutes or until cranberries begin to pop. Remove from heat; cover and refrigerate at least 30 minutes.

SERVES 12 (serving size: about ¼ cup)

CALORIES 83; FAT 0.1g (sat 0g, mono 0g, poly 0g); PROTEIN 0g; CARB 21g; FIBER 1g; CHOL 0mg; IRON 0mg; SODIUM 1mg; CALC 4mg

Cranberry Sauce with Cassis

HANDS-ON TIME: 18 MIN. | **TOTAL TIME:** 2 HR. 18 MIN.

1 tablespoon canola oil
½ cup finely chopped shallots
⅔ cup dried tart cherries
½ cup crème de cassis
   (black currant-flavored liqueur)
¾ cup sugar
1 (12-ounce) package fresh cranberries
1½ teaspoons grated lemon rind

❶ Heat a medium saucepan over medium heat. Add oil; swirl to coat. Add shallots; sauté 4 minutes or until tender, stirring occasionally. Increase heat to medium-high. Add cherries, crème de cassis, sugar, and cranberries; bring to a boil. Reduce heat, and simmer 8 minutes or until cranberries begin to pop, stirring occasionally. Remove from heat; stir in rind. Cool to room temperature.

SERVES 12 (serving size: ¼ cup)

CALORIES 143; FAT 1.2g (sat 0.1g, mono 0.7g, poly 0.4g); PROTEIN 1g; CARB 27g; FIBER 2g; CHOL 0mg; IRON 0mg; SODIUM 3mg; CALC 18mg

Simple Swap

If you can't find cassis, substitute orange liqueur.

Refrigerator Pickled Blackberries

HANDS-ON TIME: 35 MIN. | **TOTAL TIME:** 8 HR. 35 MIN.

3 cups white balsamic vinegar
2 whole cloves
2 (3-inch) cinnamon sticks
1 gallon fresh blackberries
2 cups honey

❶ Combine first 3 ingredients in a Dutch oven; bring to a boil. Cover; reduce heat, and simmer 10 minutes. Remove from heat; let stand 5 minutes. Add berries; cover and chill 8 hours.
❷ Drain berries in a colander over a bowl, reserving liquid. Discard spices. Divide berries among 12 (half-pint) jars.
❸ Bring vinegar mixture and honey to a boil in a saucepan. Divide hot vinegar mixture among jars, filling to ¼ inch from top. Cover with metal lids; screw on bands. Cool to room temperature. Refrigerate up to 2 weeks.

SERVES 32 (serving size: about ⅓ cup)

CALORIES 78; FAT 0.4g (sat 0g, mono 0.1g, poly 0.2g); PROTEIN 1g; CARB 19g; FIBER 4g; CHOL 0mg; IRON 0mg; SODIUM 1mg; CALC 22mg

Did You Know?

Refrigerator pickles are not shelf-stable like some other pickles, but they'll keep in the fridge for 2 weeks.

Simple Swap

Red beets and any garden tomatoes also work well.

Peach Salad with Tomatoes and Beets

HANDS-ON TIME: 25 MIN. | **TOTAL TIME:** 1 HR. 15 MIN.

2 medium-sized golden beets
2 medium-sized ripe tomatoes
½ teaspoon kosher salt, divided
½ teaspoon freshly ground black pepper
3 tablespoons extra-virgin olive oil
2 tablespoons fresh lemon juice, divided
1 tablespoon honey
1 medium shallot, thinly sliced
3 medium peaches, sliced
3 tablespoons small mint leaves
2 teaspoons thyme leaves
2 ounces goat cheese, crumbled
   (about ½ cup)

❶ Preheat oven to 425°.
❷ Scrub beets and trim tops to 1 inch. Place beets in a glass or ceramic baking dish; fill dish one-third full with water. Cover with foil; bake at 425° for 1 hour or until beets are tender. Cool. Peel beets, and cut into ¼-inch-thick slices. Core tomatoes; cut into ¼-inch-thick slices. Arrange the beet and tomato slices on a platter; sprinkle with ¼ teaspoon salt and pepper.
❸ Combine ¼ teaspoon salt, oil, 1 tablespoon juice, honey, and shallot in a medium bowl. Toss peach slices with remaining 1 tablespoon juice. Add peach mixture to honey mixture; toss. Mound peach mixture on top of beet and tomato slices; sprinkle salad with the mint, thyme, and goat cheese.

SERVES 8 (serving size: about 2 beet slices, 2 tomato slices, and ½ cup peach mixture)

CALORIES 167; **FAT** 9.9g (sat 4.3g, mono 4.1g, poly 0.6g); **PROTEIN** 5g; **CARB** 12g; **FIBER** 2g; **CHOL** 18mg; **IRON** 1mg; **SODIUM** 240mg; **CALC** 34mg

Grilled Peaches with Ginger Glaze

HANDS-ON TIME: 34 MIN. | **TOTAL TIME:** 34 MIN.

6 peaches
3 tablespoons brown sugar
2 tablespoons minced shallots
2 tablespoons lower-sodium soy sauce
1 tablespoon minced peeled fresh ginger
1 tablespoon hoisin sauce
1 teaspoon grated orange rind
2 tablespoons fresh orange juice
Cooking spray

❶ Cut an X on the bottoms of peaches, carefully cutting just through the skin. Fill a large Dutch oven with water; bring to a boil. Immerse peaches 20 seconds; remove with a slotted spoon, and plunge into ice water. Slip skins off peaches using a paring knife. Cut peaches in half; remove pits.
❷ Preheat grill to medium-high heat.
❸ Combine sugar and next 6 ingredients (through juice). Brush cut sides of peaches with marinade. Place peaches, cut sides down, on grill rack coated with cooking spray; grill 10 minutes or until tender, turning and basting once with marinade.

SERVES 6 (serving size: 2 peach halves)

CALORIES 80; **FAT** 0.3g (sat 0g, mono 0.1g, poly 0.1g); **PROTEIN** 1g; **CARB** 20g; **FIBER** 2g; **CHOL** 0mg; **IRON** 0mg; **SODIUM** 176mg; **CALC** 13mg

Simple Swap

Apricots are also great grilled. Brush with 1 tablespoon olive oil and 1 teaspoon honey, and grill. Serve alone or over a bed of greens.

◀ Triple-Plum Salsa

HANDS-ON TIME: 28 MIN. | **TOTAL TIME:** 58 MIN.

¼ cup finely chopped red onion
2 tablespoons chopped fresh cilantro
1 tablespoon minced jalapeño pepper
1 teaspoon grated lime rind
1 tablespoon fresh lime juice
2 teaspoons minced peeled fresh ginger
2 teaspoons canola oil
2 ripe red-skinned plums, pitted and sliced
2 ripe green-skinned plums, pitted and sliced
2 ripe purple or black-skinned plums, pitted and sliced

❶ Combine all ingredients in a bowl; toss well. Let stand 30 minutes.

SERVES 16 (serving size: ¼ cup)

CALORIES 20; **FAT** 0.7g (sat 0.1g, mono 0.3g, poly 0.3g); **PROTEIN** 0g; **CARB** 4g; **FIBER** 1g; **CHOL** 0mg; **IRON** 0mg; **SODIUM** 0mg; **CALC** 3mg

Marinated Grilled Apples with Mint

HANDS-ON TIME: 16 MIN. | **TOTAL TIME:** 1 HR. 16 MIN.

⅔ cup fresh orange juice
1 tablespoon chopped fresh mint
2 tablespoons honey
1 teaspoon vanilla extract
½ teaspoon ground ginger
¼ teaspoon black pepper
3 Granny Smith apples, cored and each cut crosswise into 4 (½-inch) slices
Cooking spray

❶ Combine first 6 ingredients in a large zip-top plastic bag. Add apple slices; seal and marinate in refrigerator 1 to 2 hours, turning bag occasionally.
❷ Preheat grill to medium-high heat.
❸ Remove apple from bag, reserving marinade. Place apple slices on grill rack coated with cooking spray; grill 3 minutes on each side, turning and basting frequently with reserved marinade. Arrange apple slices on a platter; drizzle with any remaining marinade.

SERVES 4 (serving size: 3 apple slices)

CALORIES 116; **FAT** 0.5g (sat 0.1g, mono 0g, poly 0.1g); **PROTEIN** 1g; **CARB** 29g; **FIBER** 3g; **CHOL** 0mg; **IRON** 0mg; **SODIUM** 1mg; **CALC** 14mg

Cinnamon Stewed Apples

HANDS-ON TIME: 58 MIN. | **TOTAL TIME:** 63 MIN.

6 cups chopped peeled Granny Smith apple (about 2 pounds)
½ cup packed brown sugar
¼ cup apple juice
1 teaspoon ground cinnamon
⅛ teaspoon ground nutmeg
⅛ teaspoon salt

❶ Combine all ingredients in a large, heavy saucepan. Cover and cook over medium-low heat 45 minutes or until apple is tender, stirring occasionally. Let stand 5 minutes.

SERVES 8 (serving size: ¼ cup)

CALORIES 121; **FAT** 0.4g (sat 0.1g, mono 0g, poly 0.1g); **PROTEIN** 0g; **CARB** 31g; **FIBER** 2g; **CHOL** 0mg; **IRON** 0mg; **SODIUM** 42mg; **CALC** 19mg

Sautéed Apples

HANDS-ON TIME: 22 MIN. | **TOTAL TIME:** 22 MIN.

3 tablespoons butter
6 cups sliced peeled Granny Smith
  apple (about 2 pounds)
½ cup packed brown sugar
⅛ teaspoon ground cinnamon

❶ Melt butter in a large skillet over medium-high heat. Add apple; sauté 6 minutes or until apple is just tender. Stir in sugar and cinnamon. Cook 1 minute or until sugar melts.

SERVES 8 (serving size: ½ cup)

CALORIES 137; FAT 4.6g (sat 2.7g, mono 1.3g, poly 0.2g);
PROTEIN 0g; CARB 26g; FIBER 2g; CHOL 12mg; IRON 0mg;
SODIUM 49mg; CALC 17mg

Did You Know?

The firmness and tart flavor of Granny Smith apples hold up well when heated, making them perfect for cooking and baking.

Easy "Baked" Apples

HANDS-ON TIME: 36 MIN. | **TOTAL TIME:** 36 MIN.

2 cups dried cranberries
1¼ cups coarsely chopped walnuts
1 cup packed brown sugar
1 cup water
2 teaspoons ground cinnamon
6 Gala Apples, cored and chopped (about 3 pounds)

❶ Combine all ingredients in a large microwave-safe dish. Microwave at HIGH 20 minutes or until apple is soft, stirring occasionally.

SERVES 24 (serving size: ¼ cup)

CALORIES 126; FAT 4.1g (sat 0.4g, mono 0.6g, poly 3g); PROTEIN 1g; CARB 24g; FIBER 2g; CHOL 0mg; IRON 1mg; SODIUM 4mg; CALC 16mg

Rustic Applesauce

HANDS-ON TIME: 48 MIN. | **TOTAL TIME:** 48 MIN.

4 cups cubed peeled Braeburn or Pink Lady apple
4 cups cubed peeled Granny Smith apple
½ cup packed brown sugar
2 teaspoons grated lemon rind
3 tablespoons fresh lemon juice
1 teaspoon ground cinnamon
1 teaspoon vanilla extract
Dash of salt
2 tablespoons crème fraîche

❶ Combine first 8 ingredients in a Dutch oven over medium heat. Cook 25 minutes or until apple is tender, stirring occasionally.
❷ Remove from heat; mash to desired consistency with a fork or potato masher. Stir in crème fraîche. Serve warm or chilled.

SERVES 7 (serving size: ½ cup)

CALORIES 140; FAT 1.8g (sat 1g, mono 0.5g, poly 0.2g); PROTEIN 0g; CARB 33g; FIBER 2g; CHOL 3mg; IRON 1mg; SODIUM 30mg; CALC 31mg

Chunky Spiced Applesauce

HANDS-ON TIME: 1 HR. 17 MIN. | **TOTAL TIME:** 3 HR. 17 MIN.

10 cups cubed peeled apple
   (about 3 pounds)
½ lemon
2 cups fresh cranberries
1 cup sugar
½ cup maple syrup
⅓ cup water
½ teaspoon ground cinnamon
Pinch of freshly grated nutmeg

❶ Place apple in a large bowl; cover with cold water. Squeeze juice from lemon half into bowl; place lemon half in bowl. Set aside.

❷ Combine cranberries and remaining ingredients in a Dutch oven; bring to a boil, stirring occasionally. Cook 3 minutes or until cranberries pop.

❸ Drain apple; discard lemon. Add apple to pan. Cover, reduce heat, and simmer 25 minutes or until apple is soft. Uncover, bring to a boil, and cook 15 minutes. Mash apple mixture with a potato masher. Pour into a serving dish; cover and chill at least 2 hours.

SERVES 14 (serving size: about ½ cup)

CALORIES 124; FAT 0.2g (sat 0g, mono 0g, poly 0.1g); PROTEIN 0g; CARB 33g; FIBER 3g; CHOL 0mg; IRON 0mg; SODIUM 2mg; CALC 14mg

Prep Pointer

Prepare this applesauce up to 1 day ahead.

Mango Salsa

HANDS-ON TIME: 13 MIN. | **TOTAL TIME:** 13 MIN.

2 cups diced peeled mango
  (about 2 mangoes)
2 cups diced seeded tomato
2 tablespoons chopped red onion
2 tablespoons chopped fresh cilantro
2 tablespoons diced jalapeño pepper
2 tablespoons fresh lime juice
1 teaspoon sugar
¼ teaspoon salt

❶ Combine all ingredients in a medium bowl; toss gently. Cover and chill.

SERVES 8 (serving size: ½ cup)

CALORIES 45; FAT 0.2g (sat 0g, mono 0.1g, poly 0.1g); PROTEIN 1g; CARB 12g; FIBER 2g; CHOL 0mg; IRON 0mg; SODIUM 77mg; CALC 11mg

Simple Swap

For a less spicy version, discard the seeds and ribs from the jalapeño before chopping.

◀ Green Papaya and Mango Salad

HANDS-ON TIME: 17 MIN. | **TOTAL TIME:** 47 MIN.

2 cups shredded green papaya
  (about ½ pound)
2 cups cherry tomatoes, halved
1½ cups (½-inch) cubed peeled ripe
  mango (about 1)
1 cup bean sprouts
2 tablespoons chopped green onions
3 tablespoons fresh lime juice
1 tablespoon fish sauce
2 teaspoons honey
1 small jalapeño pepper, chopped
Cilantro sprigs (optional)
Mint sprigs (optional)

❶ Combine first 5 ingredients in a large bowl. Combine juice, fish sauce, honey, and jalapeño in a small bowl; pour juice mixture over papaya mixture. Toss gently to combine. Cover and let stand 30 minutes. Garnish with cilantro and mint, if desired.

SERVES 6 (serving size: 1 cup)

CALORIES 64; FAT 0.4g (sat 0.1g, mono 0.1g, poly 0.1g); PROTEIN 2g; CARB 16g; FIBER 2g; CHOL 0mg; IRON 1mg; SODIUM 240mg; CALC 22mg

Spicy Grilled Mango with Chiles and Crema

HANDS-ON TIME: 15 MIN. | **TOTAL TIME:** 15 MIN.

3 tablespoons fresh lime juice, divided
1 thinly sliced green jalapeño pepper
1 thinly sliced red jalapeño pepper
2 ripe peeled mangoes, cut into
  ⅓-inch-thick slices
Cooking spray
¼ teaspoon kosher salt
¼ teaspoon freshly ground black pepper
⅛ teaspoon ground red pepper
3 tablespoons Mexican crema
¼ cup cilantro leaves

❶ Combine 2 tablespoons juice and jalapeños in a small bowl.
❷ Coat mango slices with cooking spray; sprinkle with salt, black pepper, and ground red pepper. Heat a grill pan over high heat until smoking hot. Coat pan with cooking spray. Add mango to pan. Cook, without moving, 4 minutes or until well marked. Turn and cook 2 minutes; place on a platter.
❸ Combine 1 tablespoon juice and crema in a small bowl, stirring until smooth. Spoon jalapeños over mango. Drizzle with crema mixture; sprinkle with cilantro leaves.

SERVES 4 (serving size: ½ mango and 1 tablespoon sauce)

CALORIES 128; FAT 2.6g (sat 1.8g, mono 0.2g, poly 0.1g); PROTEIN 2g; CARB 28g; FIBER 3g; CHOL 6mg; IRON 0mg; SODIUM 172mg; CALC 22mg

Asian Caramelized Pineapple ▶

HANDS-ON TIME: 21 MIN. | **TOTAL TIME:** 21 MIN.

1½ teaspoons canola oil
1½ tablespoons minced red onion
1 large garlic clove, minced
2 cups diced fresh pineapple
1 tablespoon lower-sodium soy sauce
1½ teaspoons chopped seeded red
   jalapeño pepper
1½ teaspoons fresh lime juice
1 teaspoon chopped peeled fresh ginger
1½ teaspoons chopped fresh cilantro

❶ Heat a large nonstick skillet over medium heat. Add oil to pan; swirl to coat. Add onion and garlic; cook 2 minutes. Add pineapple; cook 5 minutes or until lightly browned. Add soy sauce, pepper, juice, and ginger; cook 2 minutes. Remove from heat; stir in cilantro.

SERVES 4 (serving size: about ½ cup)

CALORIES 61; FAT 1.9g (sat 0.1g, mono 1.1g, poly 0.6g); PROTEIN 1g; CARB 12g; FIBER 1g; CHOL 0mg; IRON 0mg; SODIUM 135mg; CALC 15mg

Prep Pointer

Toasting coconut gives it a nutty flavor and a crunchy texture. To toast, spread the flakes in a single layer on a baking sheet, and bake at 325° for 5 to 10 minutes or until slightly brown, stirring occasionally.

Pineapple and Orange Salad with Toasted Coconut

HANDS-ON TIME: 23 MIN. | **TOTAL TIME:** 23 MIN.

2 cups orange sections (about 4 oranges)
½ cup pomegranate arils
4 sliced peeled kiwifruit
1 (4-pound) pineapple, peeled and cut into 1-inch cubes
1 teaspoon grated lime rind
1 tablespoon fresh lime juice
1 tablespoon fresh orange juice
⅛ teaspoon ground red pepper
½ cup flaked sweetened coconut, toasted and divided

❶ Combine first 4 ingredients in a medium bowl. Combine rind and next 3 ingredients (through pepper) in a small bowl. Gently stir lime mixture into fruit mixture; cover and chill.

❷ Just before serving, stir ¼ cup coconut into pineapple mixture. Sprinkle with ¼ cup coconut.

SERVES 8 (serving size: about ¾ cup)

CALORIES 140; FAT 1.9g (sat 1.4g, mono 0.1g, poly 0.2g); PROTEIN 2g; CARB 32g; FIBER 5g; CHOL 0mg; IRON 1mg; SODIUM 18mg; CALC 59mg

Maduros
(Sautéed Sweet Plantains)

HANDS-ON TIME: 16 MIN. | **TOTAL TIME:** 16 MIN.

4 cups (½-inch-thick) slices soft black
  plantains (about 6)
3 tablespoons sugar
¼ teaspoon salt
1½ tablespoons butter

❶ Combine first 3 ingredients in a large bowl; toss well.
❷ Melt butter in a large nonstick skillet over medium-high heat. Add plantains; sauté 5 minutes or until browned and tender.

SERVES 12 (serving size: about ⅓ cup)

**CALORIES 134; FAT 1.8g (sat 1g, mono 0.4g, poly 0.1g);
PROTEIN 1g; CARB 32g; FIBER 2g; CHOL 4mg; IRON 1mg;
SODIUM 62mg; CALC 3mg**

Machuquillo
(Plantain Mash)

HANDS-ON TIME: 7 MIN. | **TOTAL TIME:** 22 MIN.

2 medium plantains, peeled and thinly
  sliced
1 tablespoon olive oil
⅛ teaspoon salt
1 garlic clove, minced

❶ Cook plantain slices in boiling water 15 minutes or until tender; drain. Place plantains, oil, salt, and garlic in a bowl; mash with a potato masher until smooth. Serve immediately.

SERVES 4 (serving size: ½ cup)

**CALORIES 140; FAT 3.7g (sat 0.6g, mono 2.5g, poly 0.4g);
PROTEIN 1g; CARB 29g; FIBER 2g; CHOL 0mg; IRON 1mg;
SODIUM 224mg; CALC 4mg**

Prep Pointer

Use plantains with completely black skins, which indicate that they are fully ripe.

Jicama-Pomegranate Salad

HANDS-ON TIME: 21 MIN. | **TOTAL TIME:** 21 MIN.

3 cups julienne-cut peeled jicama
   (about 1 medium)
½ cup pomegranate arils
⅓ cup vertically sliced red onion
¼ cup chopped fresh cilantro
¼ cup fresh lime juice
2 tablespoons olive oil
1 tablespoon honey
¼ teaspoon salt
⅛ teaspoon ground red pepper

❶ Combine jicama, pomegranate arils, onion, and cilantro in a large bowl. Combine lime juice, olive oil, honey, salt, and ground red pepper in a bowl, stirring with a whisk. Add juice mixture to jicama mixture; toss gently to coat.

SERVES 6 (serving size: ⅔ cup)

CALORIES 144; FAT 4.7g (sat 0.7g, mono 3.3g, poly 0.6g); PROTEIN 2g; CARB 25g; FIBER 10g; CHOL 0mg; IRON 1mg; SODIUM 107mg; CALC 27mg

◀ Melon and Fig Salad with Prosciutto and Balsamic Drizzle

HANDS-ON TIME: 15 MIN. | **TOTAL TIME:** 30 MIN.

½ cup balsamic vinegar
2 teaspoons extra-virgin olive oil
1 teaspoon fresh lemon juice
¼ teaspoon freshly ground black pepper
4 cups gourmet salad greens
½ pound honeydew melon, peeled,
   seeded, and thinly sliced
½ pound cantaloupe, peeled, seeded,
   and thinly sliced
4 very thin slices prosciutto, torn
   (about 1 ounce)
4 fresh figs, quartered

❶ Bring vinegar to a simmer in a small saucepan over medium-low heat; cook until syrupy and reduced to 3 tablespoons (about 10 minutes), stirring occasionally. Remove from heat.
❷ Combine oil, juice, and pepper in a bowl, stirring with a whisk. Add salad greens; toss gently. Divide melon among 4 plates; top with salad greens. Arrange prosciutto and figs over salad greens; drizzle with balsamic syrup.

SERVES 4 (serving size: ¼ pound melon, about 1 cup salad greens, 1 slice prosciutto, 1 quartered fig, and about 2 teaspoons balsamic syrup)

CALORIES 153; FAT 3.2g (sat 0.6g, mono 1.7g, poly 0.3g); PROTEIN 4g; CARB 28g; FIBER 4g; CHOL 6mg; IRON 1mg; SODIUM 239mg; CALC 44mg

Did You Know?

Jicama is a root vegetable that looks like a potato yet tastes sweet. It easily absorbs the flavors of other foods, making it great to cook with.

Picante Three-Melon Salad

HANDS-ON TIME: 30 MIN. | **TOTAL TIME:** 45 MIN.

3 cups cubed seeded red watermelon
3 cups cubed seeded yellow watermelon
3 cups cubed honeydew melon
½ cup chopped white onion
2 tablespoons chopped fresh cilantro
2½ teaspoons finely chopped seeded
   serrano chile (about 1)
1 teaspoon grated lime rind
3 tablespoons fresh lime juice
½ teaspoon salt
¼ teaspoon chili powder
⅛ to ¼ teaspoon minced chipotle chile,
   canned in adobo sauce

❶ Combine first 6 ingredients in a large bowl. Combine rind and remaining ingredients in a small bowl. Pour juice mixture over melon mixture; toss well. Let stand 15 minutes before serving.

SERVES 8 (serving size: 1 cup)

CALORIES 63; FAT 0.3g (sat 0.1g, mono 0.1g, poly 0.1g); PROTEIN 1g; CARB 16g; FIBER 1g; CHOL 0mg; IRON 0mg; SODIUM 162mg; CALC 15mg

Shaved Melon Salad with Lemon-Sherry Dressing ▶

HANDS-ON TIME: 26 MIN. | **TOTAL TIME:** 26 MIN.

1 teaspoon grated lemon rind
2 tablespoons fresh lemon juice
1 tablespoon sherry
1 teaspoon honey
⅜ teaspoon kosher salt
¼ teaspoon freshly ground black pepper
2 tablespoons extra-virgin olive oil
½ medium cantaloupe
½ medium honeydew melon
3 tablespoons small mint leaves

❶ Combine first 6 ingredients in a large bowl. Gradually add oil, stirring constantly with a whisk. ❷ Remove and discard seeds from cantaloupe and honeydew melon. Cut melons into 2-inch-wide wedges; remove rinds. Cut melon wedges into long, thin ribbons using a mandoline. Add melon ribbons to dressing; toss gently to coat. Sprinkle with mint. Serve immediately.

SERVES 6 (serving size: about 1 cup)

CALORIES 94; FAT 4.7g (sat 0.7g, mono 3.3g, poly 0.6g); PROTEIN 1g; CARB 13g; FIBER 1g; CHOL 0mg; IRON 0mg; SODIUM 143mg; CALC 12mg

Did You Know?

The term "heirloom" is generally used to describe plants that have been grown from seed and naturally pollinated by wind or insects. Additionally, they are more than 50 years old and have been passed down through generations.

Heirloom Tomato, Watermelon, and Peach Salad

HANDS-ON TIME: 11 MIN. | **TOTAL TIME:** 2 HR. 11 MIN.

2 tablespoons fresh lime juice
1½ tablespoons extra-virgin olive oil
1 tablespoon honey
1 tablespoon white rum
¼ teaspoon salt
⅛ teaspoon ground red pepper
3 cups cubed seedless watermelon
1½ cups sliced peaches
½ cup vertically sliced red onion
¼ cup torn fresh mint leaves
2 tablespoons thinly sliced fresh basil
1 pound heirloom beefsteak tomatoes, cut into 1-inch chunks
1½ ounces crumbled goat cheese (about ⅓ cup)

❶ Combine first 6 ingredients in a large bowl, stirring with a whisk. Add watermelon and next 5 ingredients (through tomato); toss gently. Cover and refrigerate 2 hours or until thoroughly chilled. Sprinkle with goat cheese just before serving.

SERVES 8 (serving size: about ¾ cup)

CALORIES 90; **FAT** 3.8g (sat 1.1g, mono 2.3g, poly 0.4g); **PROTEIN** 2g; **CARB** 13g; **FIBER** 2g; **CHOL** 2mg; **IRON** 1mg; **SODIUM** 95mg; **CALC** 22mg

Watermelon and Fennel Salad with Honey-Lime Vinaigrette

HANDS-ON TIME: 10 MIN. | **TOTAL TIME:** 10 MIN.

3 tablespoons fresh lime juice
2 tablespoons olive oil
1 tablespoon honey
1/4 teaspoon kosher salt
1/4 teaspoon freshly ground black pepper
1 tablespoon finely minced shallots
3 1/4 cups thinly sliced fennel bulb
3 cups cubed watermelon
1/4 cup chopped fresh mint
2 ounces crumbled feta cheese
(about 1/2 cup)

❶ Combine first 5 ingredients, stirring with a whisk. Stir in shallots. Combine fennel and watermelon in a large bowl. Drizzle dressing over watermelon mixture; toss gently. Sprinkle with mint and cheese.

SERVES 8 (serving size: about 3/4 cup)

CALORIES 88; FAT 5g (sat 1.5g, mono 2.8g, poly 0.4g); PROTEIN 2g; CARB 10g; FIBER 1g; CHOL 6mg; IRON 1mg; SODIUM 159mg; CALC 60mg

Superfast

Ready in 15 minutes or less!

Watermelon-Cucumber Salad

HANDS-ON TIME: 20 MIN. | **TOTAL TIME:** 20 MIN.

6 cups watermelon, cut into 1-inch pieces
1 cup coarsely chopped watercress
3/4 cup thinly sliced Vidalia onion
1 medium English cucumber, sliced (about 3 cups)
2 tablespoons chopped fresh mint
2 tablespoons chopped fresh cilantro
2 tablespoons fresh lime juice
2 teaspoons extra-virgin olive oil
1/4 teaspoon kosher salt
2 ounces reduced-fat feta cheese, crumbled (about 1/2 cup)
Mint sprigs (optional)

❶ Combine first 4 ingredients in a large bowl. Combine mint and next 3 ingredients (through oil) in a small bowl, stirring with a whisk.
❷ Add juice mixture and salt to watermelon mixture; toss gently to coat. Sprinkle with feta; garnish with mint sprigs, if desired.

SERVES 6 (serving size: 1 1/2 cups)

CALORIES 93; FAT 3.1g (sat 1.1g, mono 1.2g, poly 0.2g); PROTEIN 4g; CARB 15g; FIBER 1g; CHOL 3mg; IRON 1mg; SODIUM 218mg; CALC 58mg

Prep Pointer

A 6-pound watermelon yields about 2 pounds of rind. Keep rind fully submerged in pickling liquid for best results, and leave the cheesecloth bag of spices in with the pickled rind so the flavor intensifies with time. Refrigerate for up to 2 weeks.

Pickled Watermelon Rind

HANDS-ON TIME: 35 MIN. | **TOTAL TIME:** 20 HR. 45 MIN.

1 (6-pound) watermelon
6 cups water
2 tablespoons salt, divided
1 teaspoon pickling spice
3 (¼-inch) slices fresh ginger
2 whole cloves
2 whole allspice
1 (3-inch) cinnamon stick
1¼ cups sugar
1 cup white vinegar

❶ Carefully remove outer green layer from watermelon rind using a vegetable peeler. Reserve remaining watermelon for another use.

❷ Cut rind into ½-inch pieces. Bring 6 cups water and 5 teaspoons salt to a boil in a large saucepan over medium-high heat. Add rind to pan. Reduce heat, and simmer 15 minutes or until crisp-tender. Drain rind. Place in a large bowl.

❸ Place pickling spice, ginger, cloves, allspice, and cinnamon on a double layer of cheesecloth. Gather edges of cheesecloth together; tie securely. Combine cheesecloth bag, 1 teaspoon salt, sugar, and vinegar in saucepan; bring to a boil, stirring until sugar dissolves. Pour hot vinegar mixture over rind. Cool to room temperature. Cover and chill 12 hours.

❹ Strain rind mixture through a sieve over a saucepan; return solids to bowl. Bring liquid to a boil; carefully pour over solids. Chill at least 8 hours before serving.

SERVES 10 (serving size: about ¼ cup)

CALORIES 35; FAT 0g (sat 0g, mono 0g, poly 0g); PROTEIN 1g; CARB 8g; FIBER 0g; CHOL 0mg; IRON 0mg; SODIUM 175mg; CALC 26mg

Sliced Avocado with Lime

HANDS-ON TIME: 6 MIN. | **TOTAL TIME:** 6 MIN.

1 medium ripe avocado, peeled and
  sliced
1 tablespoon fresh lime juice
1 teaspoon honey
¼ teaspoon salt
1 tablespoon chopped fresh cilantro

❶ Divide avocado among 4 plates. Combine juice, honey, and salt; drizzle over avocado. Sprinkle with cilantro.

SERVES 4 (serving size: one-fourth of avocado and about 1 teaspoon lime mixture)

CALORIES 87; FAT 7.4g (sat 1.1g, mono 4.9g, poly 0.9g); PROTEIN 1g; CARB 6g; FIBER 3g; CHOL 0mg; IRON 0mg; SODIUM 151mg; CALC 7mg

Superfast

Ready in 15 minutes or less!

Easy Guacamole

HANDS-ON TIME: 15 MIN. | **TOTAL TIME:** 15 MIN.

1½ tablespoons coarsely chopped red
  onion
1 tablespoon fresh lime juice
⅛ teaspoon salt
1 garlic clove
½ small jalapeño pepper
1 ripe peeled avocado
1 tablespoon cilantro leaves

❶ Place first 5 ingredients in a food processor; pulse 5 times or until finely chopped. Add avocado; process until smooth. Sprinkle with cilantro.

SERVES 4 (serving size: about ¼ cup)

CALORIES 85; FAT 7.7g (sat 1.2g, mono 4.8g, poly 1g); PROTEIN 1g; CARB 5g; FIBER 3g; CHOL 0mg; IRON 1mg; SODIUM 77mg; CALC 9mg

Avocado Salsa

HANDS-ON TIME: 10 MIN. | **TOTAL TIME:** 10 MIN.

½ cup finely chopped peeled avocado
⅓ cup chopped seeded tomato
2 tablespoons finely chopped onion
1 tablespoon finely chopped seeded
  jalapeño pepper
1 tablespoon chopped fresh cilantro
1 tablespoon fresh lime juice
⅛ teaspoon salt

❶ Combine all ingredients; toss mixture gently. Serve salsa immediately.

SERVES 6 (serving size: about 2½ tablespoons)

CALORIES 59; FAT 5.2g (sat 0.8g, mono 3.2g, poly 0.7g); PROTEIN 1g; CARB 4g; FIBER 2g; CHOL 0mg; IRON 1mg; SODIUM 54mg; CALC 6mg

Simple Swap

Try adding chopped orange and pink grapefruit.

Roasted Turnips,
Sweet Potatoes,
Apples, and
Cranberries,
p. 268

Spaghetti
Squash
Fritters,
p. 301

Balsamic
Collard
Greens,
p. 313

vegetables

Vegetables are the absolute foundation of a healthy diet. They are nutritional powerhouses— low in calories and brimming with a multitude of vitamins, minerals, antioxidants, and a host of other good-for-you compounds—plus they're full of flavor. Embracing the sheer variety of vegetables and the many ways to cook them ensures that you will never run out of exciting veggies to bring to the table.

Know Your Vegetables

Buying fresh seasonal produce ensures you don't have to do much to make them taste extraordinary. Choose vegetables of all colors to obtain the widest variety of nutrients.

Root vegetables

Root vegetables, including sweet potatoes, turnips, beets, parsnips, and carrots, create hearty meals. Root vegetables store well. Wrap them unwashed in a paper towel, place in a plastic bag, and store in the refrigerator for up to two weeks.

Corn

Look for green, moist husks that cling tightly to the corn. Pull back a portion to make sure the silk is slightly sticky and the kernels are plump. As soon as it's picked, the flavor of corn changes, so eat as soon as possible after purchasing, or store in the refrigerator with the husks intact. Don't shuck until ready to use.

Leafy greens

Leafy greens are available year-round and are also extremely versatile; in many instances, greens can be readily substituted for one another.

Winter squash

From green to yellow to orange, winter squash is a go-to vegetable in the fall. Winter squashes will keep in a cool, dark place for several months after being harvested. Look for squash that seems heavy for its size, since it contains more edible flesh.

Cruciferous

This category includes broccoli, cabbage, Brussels sprouts, bok choy, kohlrabi, and cauliflower. These hardy, cool-season veggies lend themselves to a wide variety of cooking methods. Store them in a produce bag in the coldest part of your refrigerator.

Tomatoes

Summer is the peak season for tomatoes. Look for ones with bright, shiny skin and firm flesh that yields slightly to pressure. Store them at room temperature but not in direct sunlight, and never store tomatoes in the refrigerator.

Snap beans

Snap beans, including green beans, haricots verts, pole beans, and wax beans, are all entirely edible, with tender, slightly sweet pods. Look for those with bright green pods and taut skin. Pick one up and break it in half; if you hear the signature snap, the bean is fresh. Cook snap beans as soon as possible. To preserve, wrap in a damp paper towel, place in a plastic bag, and refrigerate up to a week.

How to Prepare

It's easy to get into the routine of preparing the same vegetables and side dishes, but it's easy to break out of it: Combine two or three different vegetables to add appeal; use new flavors or spice things up with a sauce; or try different cooking techniques.

STEAMING VEGETABLES

❶ Fill a pan with a few inches of water, and bring to a boil.
❷ Place the vegetables in a metal steamer, and place steamer in the pan (the boiling water should not touch the vegetables).
❸ Cover the pan with a well-fitting lid, and steam until the vegetables are crisp-tender when pierced.

ROASTING VEGETABLES

❶ Cut the vegetables into equal-sized pieces to ensure they cook evenly.
❷ Place the cut vegetables on a baking sheet or roasting pan (for easy cleanup, line the pan with foil and coat with cooking spray). Toss with a little olive or canola oil, or coat with cooking spray. Spread the vegetables in a single layer, and sprinkle with kosher salt, freshly ground pepper, and any additional herbs you choose.

SAUTÉING VEGETABLES

❶ Cut vegetables to a uniform thickness and size to ensure they cook evenly. They shouldn't be larger than bite-sized.
❷ Heat the pan over medium-high heat for a few minutes.
❸ Once the pan is hot, add in the oil, such as olive oil (not extra-virgin) or canola oil. Heat the oil for 10 to 30 seconds; then add in the vegetables. Cook for about 3 minutes, stirring frequently.

Glazed Winter Vegetables ▶

HANDS-ON TIME: 20 MIN. | **TOTAL TIME:** 65 MIN.

8 cups water
1¾ cups (½-inch-thick) slices parsnip
   (about ½ pound)
1½ cups (½-inch) cubed peeled
   rutabaga (about ½ pound)
1½ cups pearl onions (about ½ pound)
1⅓ cups (½-inch-thick) slices carrot
   (about ½ pound)
2 cups trimmed Brussels sprouts, halved
   (about ½ pound)
Cooking spray
1 tablespoon butter
1 tablespoon extra-virgin olive oil
2 teaspoons chopped fresh thyme
½ teaspoon salt
¼ teaspoon freshly ground black pepper
⅛ teaspoon ground nutmeg
½ cup dry Marsala or Madeira

❶ Preheat oven to 450°.
❷ Bring 8 cups water to a boil in a Dutch oven. Add parsnip and next 3 ingredients (through carrot); cook 4 minutes. Add Brussels sprouts; cook 1 minute. Drain and place vegetables in a shallow roasting pan coated with cooking spray. Add butter and next 5 ingredients (through nutmeg), stirring gently until butter melts.
❸ Pour Marsala over vegetables; cover with foil. Bake at 450° for 30 minutes, stirring after 15 minutes. Uncover and stir vegetables (do not remove pan from oven). Bake an additional 15 minutes or until vegetables are tender, stirring after 8 minutes.

SERVES 6 (serving size: about 1 cup)

CALORIES 149; FAT 4.6g (sat 1.5g, mono 2.2g, poly 0.4g); PROTEIN 3g; CARB 24g; FIBER 4g; CHOL 5mg; IRON 1mg; SODIUM 256mg; CALC 71mg

Stir-Fried Vegetables

HANDS-ON TIME: 20 MIN. | **TOTAL TIME:** 20 MIN.

1 tablespoon dark sesame oil
1 tablespoon minced peeled fresh ginger
5 garlic cloves, minced
1 cup sliced red bell pepper
8 ounces sliced shiitake mushroom caps
2 baby bok choy, sliced vertically
¼ cup water
1 tablespoon lower-sodium soy sauce

❶ Place oil, ginger, and garlic in a large skillet over medium-high heat; cook 2 minutes or until garlic just begins to brown. Add pepper and mushrooms; stir-fry 4 minutes. Add bok choy and ¼ cup water; cook 2 minutes or until bok choy is crisp-tender and water evaporates. Remove from heat; stir in soy sauce.

SERVES 4 (serving size: about ½ cup)

CALORIES 67; FAT 3.8g (sat 0.5g, mono 1.4g, poly 1.5g); PROTEIN 2g; CARB 7g; FIBER 2g; CHOL 0mg; IRON 0mg; SODIUM 155mg; CALC 17mg

Prep Pointer

Use any combination of vegetables you like for this riotously colorful side dish. To ensure all the vegetables are done at the same time, place the second pan in the oven after the first pan has been in for 20 minutes.

Roasted Winter Vegetables

HANDS-ON TIME: 24 MIN. | **TOTAL TIME:** 69 MIN.

16 thyme sprigs, divided
4 medium beets, peeled and quartered
4 carrots, peeled and cut in half lengthwise
2 medium turnips, peeled and quartered
2 tablespoons extra-virgin olive oil, divided
½ teaspoon salt, divided
½ teaspoon freshly ground black pepper, divided
8 unpeeled garlic cloves
2 medium red onions, peeled and cut lengthwise into quarters
2 fennel bulbs, cored and cut lengthwise into quarters
1 teaspoon chopped fresh thyme

❶ Preheat oven to 425°.

❷ Place 8 thyme sprigs, beets, carrots, and turnips in a large bowl. Drizzle with 1 tablespoon oil; sprinkle with ¼ teaspoon salt and ¼ teaspoon pepper. Toss to coat. Arrange vegetables on a jelly-roll pan. Bake at 425° for 45 minutes or until vegetables are tender and begin to brown, stirring occasionally.

❸ Place 8 thyme sprigs, garlic, onions, and fennel in a bowl. Drizzle with remaining 1 tablespoon oil; sprinkle with ¼ teaspoon salt and ¼ teaspoon pepper. Arrange vegetables in a single layer on a jelly-roll pan. Bake at 425° for 25 minutes or until vegetables are tender and begin to brown, stirring occasionally. Combine beet mixture and onion mixture; sprinkle with chopped thyme.

SERVES 8 (serving size: 1 cup)

CALORIES 103; **FAT** 3.7g (sat 0.5g, mono 2.5g, poly 0.5g); **PROTEIN** 3g; **CARB** 17g; **FIBER** 5g; **CHOL** 0mg; **IRON** 1mg; **SODIUM** 253mg; **CALC** 67mg

Spring Vegetable Skillet

HANDS-ON TIME: 17 MIN. | **TOTAL TIME:** 17 MIN.

16 baby carrots with tops (about
   10 ounces)
¾ teaspoon kosher salt, divided
12 ounces sugar snap peas, trimmed
1½ tablespoons butter
1 tablespoon chopped fresh tarragon
¼ teaspoon freshly ground black pepper
1 teaspoon grated lemon rind
1 teaspoon fresh lemon juice

❶ Peel carrots and cut off tops to within 1 inch of carrot; cut in half lengthwise.
❷ Place ¼ teaspoon salt in a large saucepan of water; bring to a boil. Add carrots and peas; cook 3 minutes or until crisp-tender. Drain.
❸ Melt butter in a large nonstick skillet over medium-high heat. Add vegetables and cook 1 minute, stirring to coat. Stir in ½ teaspoon salt, tarragon, and pepper; cook 1 minute. Remove from heat; stir in rind and juice.

SERVES 6 (serving size: ⅔ cup)

CALORIES 69; FAT 2.9g (sat 1.8g, mono 0.7g, poly 0.1g); PROTEIN 2g; CARB 9g; FIBER 3g; CHOL 8mg; IRON 1mg; SODIUM 221mg; CALC 58mg

Did You Know?

Tarragon is one of the most unique herbs, with a strong flavor that has hints of licorice and an aroma of anise. It's considered one of the four *fines herbes*, the others being parsley, chives, and chervil.

Roasted Turnips, Sweet Potatoes, Apples, and Cranberries

HANDS-ON TIME: 12 MIN. | **TOTAL TIME:** 1 HR. 42 MIN.

3 cups (½-inch) cubed peeled turnips (about 1¼ pounds)
3 cups (½-inch) cubed peeled sweet potato (about 1¼ pounds)
2½ cups (¼-inch) cubed peeled Granny Smith apple (about 1½ pounds)
1 cup dried cranberries
½ cup packed dark brown sugar
1 tablespoon fresh lemon juice
Cooking spray
2 tablespoons butter, cut into small pieces

❶ Preheat oven to 350°.
❷ Combine first 6 ingredients in a shallow 2-quart glass or ceramic baking dish coated with cooking spray. Top with butter. Bake at 350° for 1½ hours or until tender, stirring after 45 minutes.

SERVES 7 (serving size: about ½ cup)

CALORIES 230; FAT 3.8g (sat 2.2g, mono 1g, poly 0.3g); PROTEIN 2g; CARB 50g; FIBER 5g; CHOL 9mg; IRON 1mg; SODIUM 85mg; CALC 52mg

Garlicky Turnip Fries

HANDS-ON TIME: 15 MIN. | **TOTAL TIME:** 38 MIN.

¾ cup pomegranate arils
¼ cup chopped shallots
2 tablespoons cider vinegar
3 tablespoons sugar
1 teaspoon tomato paste
⅛ teaspoon salt
4 turnips, peeled
2 tablespoons olive oil
2 tablespoons cornmeal
2 tablespoons grated Parmesan cheese
¼ teaspoon garlic salt

❶ Place 2 baking sheets in oven. Preheat oven to 450°.
❷ Place pomegranate arils, shallots, and vinegar in a mini food processor; process until blended. Strain through a sieve into a saucepan; discard solids. Stir in sugar, tomato paste, and salt. Simmer 10 minutes.
❸ Cut turnips into ½-inch matchsticks; toss with oil. Toss with cornmeal, Parmesan cheese, and garlic salt; divide between preheated pans. Bake at 450° for 15 minutes. Turn turnips over; rotate pans. Bake 8 minutes or until browned.

SERVES 4 (serving size: about ½ cup turnips and 1 tablespoon sauce)

CALORIES 137; FAT 5.3g (sat 1g, mono 3.5g, poly 0.6g); PROTEIN 2g; CARB 21g; FIBER 2g; CHOL 2mg; IRON 1mg; SODIUM 184mg; CALC 54mg

Spiced Oven Fries

HANDS-ON TIME: 10 MIN. | **TOTAL TIME:** 40 MIN.

3 (8-ounce) baking potatoes
1 tablespoon canola oil
½ teaspoon paprika
½ teaspoon dried oregano
¼ teaspoon kosher salt
¼ teaspoon ground cumin
Dash of ground red pepper

❶ Place a baking sheet in oven. Preheat oven to 450°.

❷ Cut each potato lengthwise into 8 wedges. Combine potatoes, canola oil, paprika, oregano, salt, cumin, and ground red pepper; toss to coat. Arrange potatoes on preheated pan in a single layer. Bake at 450° for 30 minutes or until browned, stirring after 15 minutes.

SERVES 4 (serving size: 6 wedges)

CALORIES 167; FAT 3.7g (sat 0.3g, mono 2.2g, poly 1.1g); PROTEIN 4g; CARB 31g; FIBER 2g; CHOL 0mg; IRON 2mg; SODIUM 129mg; CALC 26mg

Prep Pointer

Russet, Yukon gold, and even sweet potatoes are great for baking. Their starchy fibers readily absorb water, making them tender. Stay away from waxy or red-skinned potatoes when baking, as they do not soften as easily.

◀ *Truffled Roasted Potatoes*

HANDS-ON TIME: 5 MIN. | **TOTAL TIME:** 45 MIN.

2 (20-ounce) packages refrigerated
    red potato wedges (such as Simply
    Potatoes)
2 tablespoons olive oil
1 tablespoon minced fresh garlic
½ teaspoon kosher salt
½ teaspoon freshly ground black pepper
1 tablespoon white truffle oil
2 teaspoons thyme leaves

❶ Preheat oven to 450°.
❷ Place potatoes on a jelly-roll pan; drizzle with olive oil, and sprinkle with garlic, salt, and pepper. Toss well to combine. Bake at 450° for 35 minutes or until potatoes are browned and tender. Remove from the oven. Drizzle potatoes with truffle oil, and sprinkle with thyme. Toss gently to combine.

SERVES 8 (serving size: about ¾ cup)

CALORIES 134; FAT 5.1g (sat 0.7g, mono 3.7g, poly 0.5g); PROTEIN 4g; CARB 18g; FIBER 4g; CHOL 0mg; IRON 1mg; SODIUM 269mg; CALC 3mg

Roasted Rosemary Fingerling Potatoes

HANDS-ON TIME: 15 MIN. | **TOTAL TIME:** 42 MIN.

1 tablespoon chopped fresh rosemary
2 tablespoons olive oil
¾ teaspoon kosher salt
½ teaspoon freshly ground black pepper
3 shallots, thinly sliced
2 pounds fingerling potatoes, halved
    lengthwise (about 6 cups)
Cooking spray
2 teaspoons minced fresh chives

❶ Preheat oven to 425°.
❷ Combine first 6 ingredients in a large bowl, tossing to coat. Arrange potato mixture on a foil-lined jelly-roll pan coated with cooking spray. Bake at 425° for 27 minutes or until potatoes are tender, turning after 15 minutes. Sprinkle evenly with chives.

SERVES 10 (serving size: ⅔ cup)

CALORIES 94; FAT 2.8g (sat 0.4g, mono 2g, poly 0.3g); PROTEIN 2g; CARB 16g; FIBER 2g; CHOL 0mg; IRON 1mg; SODIUM 150mg; CALC 10mg

Prep Pointer

Using truffle oil is an easy way to get the delicious earthy flavor of truffles without the large expense. Find bottles of this pungent ingredient at your local specialty food store.

Simple Swap

American, Colby, or Cheshire cheese can be used instead of cheddar.

Spinach and Ham Stuffed Baked Potatoes

HANDS-ON TIME: 10 MIN. | **TOTAL TIME:** 28 MIN.

4 (8-ounce) baking potatoes
2 tablespoons water
1 (5-ounce) bag baby spinach
2 tablespoons plain fat-free Greek yogurt
¼ teaspoon freshly ground black pepper
2 ounces lower-sodium ham, diced (such as Boar's Head; about ½ cup)
2 ounces cheddar cheese, shredded (about ½ cup)
¼ cup chopped green onions

❶ Pierce potatoes liberally with a fork. Microwave at HIGH 14 minutes or until tender. Remove potatoes from microwave, and cool 10 minutes.

❷ While potatoes cook, bring 2 tablespoons water to a simmer in a large skillet over medium-high heat. Add spinach to pan; cook 2 minutes, stirring until spinach wilts. Cool 5 minutes. Place spinach in a paper towel, and squeeze out any excess liquid. Coarsely chop spinach.

❸ Cut one-third off each potato lengthwise. Remove pulp from potato, leaving a ⅛-inch-thick shell. Combine potato pulp, yogurt, pepper, ham, cheese, and spinach in a large bowl, stirring to combine. Evenly fill potato shells with spinach mixture; sprinkle with green onions.

SERVES 4 (serving size: 1 potato)

CALORIES 272; **FAT** 5.2g (sat 3.1g, mono 1.5g, poly 0.2g); **PROTEIN** 12g; **CARB** 46g; **FIBER** 5g; **CHOL** 21mg; **IRON** 3mg; **SODIUM** 309mg; **CALC** 166mg

Home Fries

HANDS-ON TIME: 46 MIN. | **TOTAL TIME:** 46 MIN.

2 pounds Yukon gold or red potato, cubed
2½ tablespoons canola oil, divided
3 cups chopped yellow onion
6 garlic cloves, minced
2 tablespoons butter
½ teaspoon kosher salt
½ teaspoon freshly ground black pepper
¼ cup coarsely chopped fresh flat-leaf parsley

❶ Place potato in a microwave-safe dish, and cover with plastic wrap. Microwave at HIGH 5 minutes. Uncover and cool slightly.

❷ Heat a large skillet over medium heat. Add 1½ tablespoons oil to pan; swirl to coat. Add onion; cook 20 minutes or until golden and tender, stirring occasionally. Add garlic; cook 1 minute, stirring constantly. Remove onion mixture from pan. Wipe pan clean with paper towels.

❸ Increase heat to medium-high. Add 1 tablespoon oil and butter to pan; swirl to coat. Add potato, and cook 4 minutes, without stirring. Turn potato over. Cook 6 minutes or until browned, without stirring. Reduce heat to medium-low; cook 10 minutes or until tender and golden brown, stirring occasionally. Remove from heat. Stir in onion mixture, salt, and black pepper; toss. Sprinkle with parsley.

SERVES 6 (serving size: about ¾ cup)

CALORIES 248; FAT 9.8g (sat 2.9g, mono 4.7g, poly 1.8g); PROTEIN 5g; CARB 35g; FIBER 3g; CHOL 10mg; IRON 2mg; SODIUM 201mg; CALC 29mg

Prep Pointer

Briefly microwaving the potatoes gives them a head start on cooking. Adding butter not only helps them brown better, but also lends rich flavor. Waxy potatoes won't break down in the pan when cubed and sautéed.

Prep Pointer

You'll need to cook latkes in batches. Place the cooked ones in a single layer on a baking sheet lined with paper towels, and keep them warm in a low oven as you fry the next batch.

Classic Potato Latkes

HANDS-ON TIME: 1 HR. 40 MIN. | **TOTAL TIME:** 1 HR. 40 MIN.

3½ cups shredded peeled baking potato (about 1½ pounds)
1¼ cups grated onion
6 tablespoons all-purpose flour
1 teaspoon chopped fresh thyme
½ teaspoon kosher salt
¼ teaspoon freshly ground black pepper
1 large egg
¼ cup olive oil, divided
¾ cup unsweetened applesauce
Dash of ground cinnamon

❶ Combine potato and onion in a colander. Drain 30 minutes, pressing with the back of a spoon until barely moist. Combine potato mixture, flour, and next 4 ingredients (through egg) in a large bowl; toss well.

❷ Heat a large skillet over medium-high heat. Add 2 tablespoons olive oil to pan, and swirl to coat. Spoon ¼ cup potato mixture loosely into a dry measuring cup. Pour mixture into pan, and flatten slightly. Repeat procedure 5 times to form 6 latkes. Sauté 3½ minutes on each side or until golden brown. Remove latkes from pan, and keep warm. Repeat procedure with 2 tablespoons olive oil and potato mixture to yield 12 latkes total. Combine applesauce and ground cinnamon in a bowl. Serve applesauce with latkes.

SERVES 6 (serving size: 2 latkes and 2 tablespoons applesauce)

CALORIES 215; FAT 8.7g (sat 1.3g, mono 6.1g, poly 1g); PROTEIN 4.4g; CARB 31.6g; FIBER 2.6g; CHOL 30mg; IRON 1.6mg; SODIUM 173mg; CALC 30mg

Did You Know?

The difference between mild, medium, sharp, and extra-sharp cheese is the aging time. Extra-sharp cheddar cheese has typically been aged for about 1½ to 2 years.

Bacon and Cheddar Mashed Potatoes

HANDS-ON TIME: 10 MIN. | **TOTAL TIME:** 40 MIN.

2½ pounds Yukon gold or baking potato, peeled and coarsely chopped
½ cup fat-free milk
2 ounces shredded extra-sharp cheddar cheese (about ½ cup)
½ cup fat-free sour cream
½ teaspoon freshly ground black pepper
¼ teaspoon kosher salt
⅓ cup sliced green onions
2 applewood-smoked bacon slices, cooked and finely chopped

❶ Place potato in a large saucepan; cover with cold water. Bring to a boil. Reduce heat; simmer 15 minutes or until tender. Drain well; return potato to pan over medium-low heat. Add milk; mash potato mixture with a potato masher to desired consistency. Cook 2 minutes or until thoroughly heated, stirring constantly. Remove from heat. Add cheese, and stir until cheese melts. Stir in sour cream, pepper, and salt. Top with green onions and bacon.

SERVES 6 (serving size: about 1 cup)

CALORIES 237; FAT 4.5g (sat 2.5g, mono 1.4g, poly 0.2g); PROTEIN 10g; CARB 38g; FIBER 3g; CHOL 15mg; IRON 2mg; SODIUM 238mg; CALC 129mg

Mashed Potato Casserole

HANDS-ON TIME: 25 MIN. | **TOTAL TIME:** 49 MIN.

1½ pounds Yukon gold potatoes, peeled
 and cut into ½-inch-thick slices
1½ pounds baking potatoes, peeled and
 cut into ½-inch-thick slices
5 garlic cloves, thinly sliced
1¼ teaspoons kosher salt, divided
6 ounces ⅓-less-fat cream cheese,
 softened (about ¾ cup)
Cooking spray
2 ounces Parmigiano-Reggiano cheese,
 grated (about ½ cup)
½ cup panko (Japanese breadcrumbs)
2 tablespoons thinly sliced fresh chives

❶ Preheat oven to 350°.
❷ Place potatoes, garlic, and ½ teaspoon salt in a
large saucepan, and cover with water. Bring to a boil.
Reduce heat; simmer 15 minutes or until tender.
Drain in a colander over a bowl, reserving ½ cup
cooking liquid.
❸ Press potato mixture in batches through a
ricer into a large bowl. Stir in reserved ½ cup
cooking liquid, ¾ teaspoon salt, and cream cheese.
❹ Spoon potato mixture into a broiler-safe
11 x 7–inch glass or ceramic baking dish coated
with cooking spray. Bake at 350° for 20 minutes
or until thoroughly heated.
❺ Preheat broiler.
❻ Combine Parmigiano-Reggiano and panko;
sprinkle evenly over top of potatoes. Broil
4 minutes or until golden brown. Sprinkle with
chives.

SERVES 8 (serving size: about ⅔ cup)

CALORIES 243; **FAT** 6.5g (sat 3.6g, mono 1.7g, poly 0.3g);
PROTEIN 8g; **CARB** 38g; **FIBER** 3g; **CHOL** 20mg; **IRON** 1mg;
SODIUM 361mg; **CALC** 93mg

Prep Pointer

Assemble this dish
a day ahead, and bake
shortly before serving.

Simple Swap

Make Parmesan-Sage Sweet Potatoes: Stir 1 tablespoon butter, 2 tablespoons fat-free milk, ½ teaspoon chopped fresh sage, 1 ounce freshly grated Parmesan cheese (about ¼ cup), and ⅛ teaspoon salt into the potatoes.

Prep Pointer

The key to perfect, fluffy spuds is not overworking them with an electric mixer; a ricer (or food mill, if you have one) or potato masher is the best tool for the job.

Butter-Pecan Mashed Sweet Potatoes ▶

HANDS-ON TIME: 15 MIN. | **TOTAL TIME:** 15 MIN.

4 sweet potatoes (about 2 pounds)
1½ tablespoons butter
2 tablespoons fat-free milk
¼ teaspoon salt
¼ cup chopped pecans, toasted

❶ Pierce each potato with a fork 3 to 4 times on each side. Wrap each potato in a damp paper towel. Microwave at HIGH 8 minutes, turning after 4 minutes. Cool slightly. Cut potatoes in half; scoop pulp into a bowl. Mash pulp.
❷ Heat butter in a small saucepan over medium heat; cook 3 minutes or until browned. Stir butter, milk, and salt into potato pulp. Top with pecans.

SERVES 4 (serving size: ½ cup)

CALORIES 262; FAT 9.2g (sat 3.2g, mono 3.9g, poly 1.6g); PROTEIN 4g; CARB 42g; FIBER 8g; CHOL 12mg; IRON 1mg; SODIUM 304mg; CALC 51mg

Golden Buttermilk-Chive Mashed Potatoes

HANDS-ON TIME: 15 MIN. | **TOTAL TIME:** 35 MIN.

3 pounds Yukon gold potatoes, peeled and cut into 1-inch pieces
⅔ cup warm low-fat buttermilk
¼ cup warm 1% low-fat milk
3 tablespoons butter, melted
1¼ teaspoons kosher salt
¼ teaspoon white pepper
8 teaspoons chopped fresh chives

❶ Place potatoes in a large saucepan; cover with water. Bring to a boil; reduce heat, and simmer 15 minutes or until tender. Drain. Press potatoes through a ricer back into pan, or mash with a potato masher to desired consistency.
❷ Add buttermilk, milk, melted butter, kosher salt, and white pepper to potato mixture; stir well. Top with chopped fresh chives.

SERVES 8 (serving size: about ⅔ cup)

CALORIES 190; FAT 4.6g (sat 2.9g, mono 1.2g, poly 0.2g); PROTEIN 5g; CARB 31g; FIBER 2g; CHOL 13mg; IRON 1mg; SODIUM 335mg; CALC 36mg

Prep Pointer

This delectable casserole is made even better by its layer of sweet topping. The crunch of the caramelized sugar is a nice balance to the creamy potatoes. You can use dark or light brown sugar in the topping.

Sweet Potato Casserole

HANDS-ON TIME: 10 MIN. | **TOTAL TIME:** 1 HR. 26 MIN.

2 pounds sweet potatoes, peeled and chopped
3/4 cup granulated sugar
1/4 cup evaporated low-fat milk
3 tablespoons butter, melted
1/2 teaspoon salt
1 teaspoon vanilla extract
2 large eggs
Cooking spray
1.5 ounces all-purpose flour (about 1/3 cup)
2/3 cup packed brown sugar
1/8 teaspoon salt
2 tablespoons melted butter
1/2 cup chopped pecans

❶ Preheat oven to 350°.

❷ Place potatoes in a Dutch oven; cover with water. Bring to a boil. Reduce heat, and simmer 20 minutes or until tender; drain. Cool 5 minutes.

❸ Place potatoes in a large bowl; add granulated sugar, evaporated milk, 3 tablespoons melted butter, 1/2 teaspoon salt, and vanilla. Beat with a mixer at medium speed until smooth. Add eggs; beat well. Pour potato mixture into a 13 x 9–inch baking dish coated with cooking spray.

❹ Weigh or lightly spoon flour into a dry measuring cup; level with a knife. Combine flour, brown sugar, and 1/8 teaspoon salt; stir with a whisk. Stir in 2 tablespoons melted butter. Sprinkle flour mixture evenly over potato mixture; arrange pecans evenly over top. Bake at 350° for 25 minutes or just until golden.

❺ Preheat broiler (remove casserole from oven).

❻ Broil casserole 45 seconds or until topping is bubbly. Let stand 10 minutes before serving.

SERVES 12 (serving size: about 2/3 cup)

CALORIES 258; **FAT** 9.2g (sat 3.6g, mono 3.6g, poly 1.5g); **PROTEIN** 3g; **CARB** 42g; **FIBER** 3g; **CHOL** 43mg; **IRON** 1mg; **SODIUM** 199mg; **CALC** 54mg

Maple-Glazed Sweet Potatoes

HANDS-ON TIME: 49 MIN. | **TOTAL TIME:** 49 MIN.

8 cups (1-inch) cubed peeled sweet
 potato (about 3 pounds)
4 cups water
¼ cup lemon sections (about 1 large
 lemon)
¼ cup packed dark brown sugar
3 tablespoons maple syrup
2 tablespoons butter
½ teaspoon ground cinnamon
⅛ teaspoon ground red pepper
Dash of salt

❶ Combine first 3 ingredients in a large saucepan; bring to boil. Cook 20 minutes or until tender, stirring occasionally. Remove sweet potatoes from pan with a slotted spoon, reserving cooking liquid. Bring cooking liquid to a boil; cook until reduced to ⅓ cup (about 12 minutes). Stir in sugar and remaining ingredients. Stir in sweet potatoes; cook 2 minutes or until thoroughly heated.

SERVES 12 (serving size: ½ cup)

CALORIES 142; FAT 2.2g (sat 1.3g, mono 0.6g, poly 0.2g); PROTEIN 2g; CARB 30g; FIBER 3g; CHOL 5mg; IRON 1mg; SODIUM 46mg; CALC 30mg

Gingered Sweet Potatoes

HANDS-ON TIME: 17 MIN. | **TOTAL TIME:** 17 MIN.

4 sweet potatoes
⅓ cup fresh orange juice
1½ tablespoons grated peeled fresh
 ginger
1 teaspoon grated orange rind
½ teaspoon kosher salt
½ teaspoon freshly ground black pepper

❶ Pierce sweet potatoes with a fork. Microwave at HIGH 10 to 12 minutes or until tender, turning over halfway through. Peel, cut into large chunks, and process in a food processor with orange juice, ginger, and orange rind until smooth. Stir in salt and pepper.

SERVES 4 (serving size: about ⅔ cup)

CALORIES 115; FAT 0.2g (sat 0.1g, mono 0g, poly 0.1g); PROTEIN 3g; CARB 26g; FIBER 4g; CHOL 0mg; IRON 1mg; SODIUM 282mg; CALC 48mg

Prep Pointer

When buying fresh ginger at the store, look for tubers that are smooth and firm. Store it wrapped in a dry paper towel in the refrigerator for up to 3 weeks.

Prep Pointer

The honey draws out the natural sweetness of the carrots. Use whatever variety you prefer.

Honey-Orange Carrots

HANDS-ON TIME: 10 MIN. | **TOTAL TIME:** 8 HR. 10 MIN.

3 pounds carrots, diagonally cut into 3-inch pieces
2 tablespoons water
½ cup honey
½ teaspoon salt
2 tablespoons butter, cut into pieces
½ teaspoon grated orange rind

❶ Place carrots, 2 tablespoons water, and ½ cup honey in a 4-quart electric slow cooker. Sprinkle salt over carrots. Sprinkle butter pieces over mixture. Cover and cook on LOW 8 hours or until carrots are very tender. Transfer carrots to a bowl; stir in orange rind.

SERVES 13 (serving size: ½ cup)

CALORIES 98; **FAT** 2g (sat 1.2g, mono 0.5g, poly 0.2g); **PROTEIN** 1g; **CARB** 21g; **FIBER** 3g; **CHOL** 5mg; **IRON** 0mg; **SODIUM** 176mg; **CALC** 36mg

Citrusy Carrots with Parsley

HANDS-ON TIME: 5 MIN. | **TOTAL TIME:** 13 MIN.

1 pound peeled carrots
¼ cup water
¼ cup fresh orange juice
1 tablespoon honey
1 tablespoon butter
¼ cup chopped fresh parsley
¼ teaspoon kosher salt
¼ teaspoon freshly ground black pepper

❶ Cut carrots into 1-inch pieces. Bring to a boil in a large skillet with ¼ cup water, orange juice, and honey; reduce heat to medium, cover, and cook 8 minutes or until crisp-tender. Drain and toss with butter, parsley, salt, and pepper.

SERVES 4 (serving size: about ½ cup)

CALORIES 97; FAT 3.2g (sat 1.9g, mono 0.8g, poly 0.3g); PROTEIN 1g; CARB 17g; FIBER 3g; CHOL 8mg; IRON 1mg; SODIUM 226mg; CALC 46mg

Superfast

Ready in 15 minutes or less!

Carrots Roasted with Smoked Paprika

HANDS-ON TIME: 7 MIN. | **TOTAL TIME:** 32 MIN.

2 tablespoons olive oil
1½ teaspoons Spanish smoked paprika
1 teaspoon kosher salt
½ teaspoon freshly ground black pepper
2½ pounds medium carrots, peeled and halved lengthwise
2 tablespoons finely chopped fresh cilantro

❶ Place a jelly-roll pan on bottom oven rack. Preheat oven to 450°.
❷ Combine first 5 ingredients in a large bowl; toss well. Arrange carrot mixture in a single layer on preheated pan. Bake at 450° for 25 minutes or until tender, stirring after 12 minutes. Sprinkle with cilantro.

SERVES 10 (serving size: about ⅓ cup)

CALORIES 72; FAT 3g (sat 0.4g, mono 2g, poly 0.4g); PROTEIN 1g; CARB 11g; FIBER 3g; CHOL 0mg; IRON 0mg; SODIUM 267mg; CALC 39mg

Prep Pointer

We like the smooth texture you get from pureeing in a food processor; if you prefer a chunkier texture, use a potato masher.

Carrot Mash with Crème Fraîche

HANDS-ON TIME: 15 MIN. | **TOTAL TIME:** 50 MIN.

⅓ cup crème fraîche
1½ tablespoons finely chopped green onions
¾ teaspoon grated orange rind
½ teaspoon freshly ground black pepper
2 pounds carrots, peeled and cut crosswise into ½-inch slices
2 tablespoons fresh orange juice
1 tablespoon butter
½ teaspoon kosher salt

❶ Combine first 4 ingredients; set aside.
❷ Place carrots in a saucepan; cover with water. Bring to a boil; cover, reduce heat, and simmer 35 minutes or until tender. Drain; place in a food processor. Add juice, butter, and salt; process until smooth. Add crème fraîche mixture; pulse to combine.

SERVES 8 (serving size: about ⅔ cup)

CALORIES 96; **FAT** 5.2g (sat 3.1g, mono 1.5g, poly 0.3g); **PROTEIN** 1g; **CARB** 12g; **FIBER** 3g; **CHOL** 13mg; **IRON** 0mg; **SODIUM** 215mg; **CALC** 40mg

Moroccan-Spiced Baby Carrots ▶

HANDS-ON TIME: 7 MIN. | **TOTAL TIME:** 22 MIN.

2 tablespoons extra-virgin olive oil
12 ounces peeled baby carrots
1 lemon, sliced
1 teaspoon ground cumin
½ teaspoon ground cinnamon
½ teaspoon kosher salt
¼ teaspoon ground red pepper
1 tablespoon chopped fresh cilantro

❶ Preheat oven to 450°.
❷ Combine first 3 ingredients in a medium bowl; sprinkle with cumin, cinnamon, salt, and pepper, tossing to coat carrots. Arrange carrot mixture in a single layer on a jelly-roll pan. Bake at 450° for 13 minutes, turning once. Sprinkle with cilantro.

SERVES 4 (serving size: about ⅔ cup)

CALORIES 96; **FAT** 7g (sat 1g, mono 4.9g, poly 0.8g); **PROTEIN** 1g; **CARB** 9g; **FIBER** 3g; **CHOL** 0mg; **IRON** 1mg; **SODIUM** 187mg; **CALC** 39mg

Roasted Beets with Jalapeño Cream

HANDS-ON TIME: 9 MIN. | **TOTAL TIME:** 60 MIN.

1 pound medium-sized red beets
1 pound medium-sized golden beets
1/3 cup reduced-fat sour cream
1/4 cup finely chopped green onions
1/4 teaspoon salt
1 jalapeño pepper, finely chopped
16 Bibb or Boston lettuce leaves

1 Preheat oven to 450°.

2 Remove stems and roots from beets; wrap beets in foil. Bake at 450° for 45 minutes or until tender. Cool beets slightly; peel and cut into 1-inch wedges.

3 Combine sour cream, onions, salt, and jalapeño in a small bowl. Divide lettuce leaves among 8 plates; top evenly with beets and jalapeño mixture.

SERVES 8 (serving size: 2 lettuce leaves, 1/2 cup beets, and about 1 tablespoon jalapeño cream)

CALORIES 68; FAT 1.5g (sat 0.8g, mono 0g, poly 0.1g); PROTEIN 3g; CARB 12g; FIBER 4g; CHOL 5mg; IRON 1mg; SODIUM 170mg; CALC 43mg

Artichoke and Pea Sauté

HANDS-ON TIME: 12 MIN. | **TOTAL TIME:** 12 MIN.

2 teaspoons canola oil

3 cups frozen, quartered artichoke hearts, thawed (about 12 ounces)

1½ tablespoons butter

¼ cup chopped shallots

1 cup frozen green peas, thawed

¼ teaspoon kosher salt

⅛ teaspoon freshly ground black pepper

2 tablespoons flat-leaf parsley leaves

1 tablespoon torn fresh mint

6 lemon wedges

❶ Heat a large skillet over medium-high heat. Add oil to pan; swirl to coat. Add artichokes; sauté 4 minutes, stirring occasionally. Remove artichokes from pan.

❷ Melt butter in pan. Add shallot, and sauté 3 minutes or until shallots are tender and butter just begins to brown, stirring occasionally. Stir in artichokes, peas, salt, and pepper; sauté 30 seconds or until thoroughly heated. Remove from heat, and sprinkle with herbs. Serve with lemon wedges.

SERVES 6 (serving size: about ½ cup)

CALORIES 90; **FAT** 5.2g (sat 2g, mono 1.7g, poly 0.6g); **PROTEIN** 3g; **CARB** 9g; **FIBER** 5g; **CHOL** 8mg; **IRON** 1mg; **SODIUM** 168mg; **CALC** 38mg

Superfast

Ready in 15 minutes or less!

Broiled Artichoke Hearts with Lemon Crumbs

HANDS-ON TIME: 10 MIN. | **TOTAL TIME:** 10 MIN.

½ cup panko (Japanese breadcrumbs)

1 tablespoon grated fresh Parmesan cheese

2 teaspoons butter, melted

1 teaspoon grated lemon rind

½ teaspoon freshly ground black pepper

2 (9-ounce) packages thawed frozen artichoke hearts

1½ teaspoons olive oil

⅛ teaspoon kosher salt

❶ Preheat broiler.

❷ Combine panko, Parmesan cheese, melted butter, lemon rind, and pepper. Toss thawed artichoke hearts with olive oil and salt on a baking sheet. Top with crumbs. Broil 6 inches from heat 5 to 6 minutes, until slightly browned.

SERVES 4 (serving size: about ⅔ cup)

CALORIES 127; **FAT** 5.8g (sat 1.7g, mono 1.8g, poly 0.3g); **PROTEIN** 5g; **CARB** 16g; **FIBER** 8g; **CHOL** 6mg; **IRON** 1mg; **SODIUM** 201mg; **CALC** 78mg

Radishes in Browned Butter

HANDS-ON TIME: 19 MIN. | **TOTAL TIME:** 19 MIN.

3 cups radishes, halved lengthwise, with
   root and 1-inch stem left on
1 tablespoon butter
½ teaspoon grated lemon rind
2 teaspoons fresh lemon juice
¼ teaspoon salt
1 cup torn radish leaves
¼ teaspoon freshly ground black pepper

❶ Bring a medium pot of water to a boil. Add radishes to pan; cook 4 minutes or until crisp-tender. Drain.
❷ Melt butter in a medium skillet over medium-high heat. Add radishes to pan; sauté 3 minutes or until butter is browned and fragrant. Add rind, juice, and salt; cook 1 minute, stirring occasionally. Remove pan from heat; stir in radish leaves and pepper.

SERVES 4 (serving size: ³⁄₄ cup)

CALORIES 42; FAT 3g (sat 1.9g, mono 0.8g, poly 0.2g); PROTEIN 1g; CARB 4g; FIBER 2g; CHOL 8mg; IRON 0mg; SODIUM 208mg; CALC 32mg

Prep Pointer

Browning the butter gives it a nutty flavor, which adds complexity to the flavor profile of the dish.

Sweet Onion Casserole

HANDS-ON TIME: 20 MIN. | **TOTAL TIME:** 65 MIN.

1 tablespoon canola oil
4 cups chopped sweet onion (about
   1¾ pounds)
½ cup uncooked long-grain rice
²⁄₃ cup 2% reduced-fat milk
2 ounces shredded Gruyère cheese
   (about ½ cup)
¼ teaspoon salt
¼ teaspoon freshly ground black pepper
⅛ teaspoon ground allspice
Cooking spray
1⅓ ounces grated fresh Parmesan
   cheese (about ⅓ cup)
2 tablespoons chopped fresh parsley
   (optional)

❶ Preheat oven to 325°.
❷ Heat a large skillet over medium-high heat. Add oil to pan; swirl. Add onion; sauté 5 minutes or until tender. Place onion in a large bowl.
❸ Cook rice in a large pot of boiling water 5 minutes. Drain.
❹ Stir rice and next 5 ingredients (through allspice) into onions. Spoon onion mixture into an 8-inch square glass or ceramic baking dish coated with cooking spray. Sprinkle evenly with Parmesan cheese. Cover and bake at 325° for 40 minutes. Uncover and bake an additional 5 minutes. Top with parsley, if desired.

SERVES 6 (serving size: about ²⁄₃ cup)

CALORIES 192; FAT 7.4g (sat 3.1g, mono 3g, poly 0.9g); PROTEIN 8g; CARB 24g; FIBER 2g; CHOL 16mg; IRON 1mg; SODIUM 213mg; CALC 203mg

Diner-Style Onion Rings

HANDS-ON TIME: 20 MIN. | **TOTAL TIME:** 20 MIN.

4 cups canola oil

4.4 ounces gluten-free all-purpose flour (about 1 cup; such as Bob's Red Mill)

5 ounces white rice flour (about 1 cup; such as Bob's Red Mill)

1 tablespoon chili powder

1 teaspoon baking soda

1¼ cups club soda, chilled

1 medium onion, cut into ½-inch-thick slices and separated into rings (8 ounces)

¼ teaspoon salt

¼ teaspoon garlic powder

¼ teaspoon freshly ground black pepper

½ cup ketchup (optional)

❶ Preheat oven to 200°.

❷ Clip a candy thermometer onto the side of a 4-quart Dutch oven; add oil to pan. Heat oil to 385°.

❸ While oil heats, weigh or lightly spoon flours into dry measuring cups; level with a knife. Combine flours, chili powder, and baking soda in a medium bowl. Gradually add club soda, stirring with a whisk until smooth.

❹ Dip onion rings, 1 at a time, in batter, coating completely. Add to hot oil. (Do not crowd pan.) Fry 1 minute on each side or until golden, maintaining temperature of oil at 375°. Drain onion rings on a paper towel–lined jelly-roll pan. Place pan in oven, and keep warm at 200° until ready to serve.

❺ Combine salt, garlic powder, and black pepper. Sprinkle onion rings evenly with salt mixture just before serving. Serve with ketchup, if desired.

SERVES 6 (serving size: about 5 onion rings)

CALORIES 234; **FAT** 19g (sat 1.4g, mono 11.9g, poly 5.3g); **PROTEIN** 2g; **CARB** 15g; **FIBER** 2g; **CHOL** 0mg; **IRON** 0mg; **SODIUM** 177mg; **CALC** 17mg

Sweet and Sour Cipollini

HANDS-ON TIME: 22 MIN. | **TOTAL TIME:** 22 MIN.

20 ounces cipollini onions
4 teaspoons extra-virgin olive oil, divided
3 tablespoons red wine vinegar
1½ tablespoons light brown sugar
½ teaspoon kosher salt
¼ teaspoon freshly ground black pepper

1 Soak cipollini in a bowl of boiling water 1 minute. Drain. Trim top and root ends from onions; peel. Cut each onion in half crosswise.
2 Heat a large nonstick skillet over medium-high heat. Add 2 teaspoons olive oil; swirl to coat. Place half of onions, cut sides down, in pan, and cook 2 minutes on each side or until browned. Remove from pan. Repeat procedure with 2 teaspoons oil and remaining onions.
3 Return onions to pan, and sprinkle with vinegar and brown sugar. Swirl to melt sugar and coat onions with syrupy mixture. Stir in salt and pepper. Serve cipollini hot or at room temperature.

SERVES 6 (serving size: about 3 cipollini halves)

CALORIES 114; FAT 3.1g (sat 0.5g, mono 2.2g, poly 0.3g); PROTEIN 1g; CARB 21g; FIBER 2g; CHOL 0mg; IRON 0mg; SODIUM 168mg; CALC 33mg

Simple Swap

To add a floral note, replace the brown sugar with clover honey.

Did You Know?

Delicata squash are yellow or cream-colored with green stripes. They are creamier than other varieties of winter squash and taste best when eaten in early fall.

Roasted Red Onions and Delicata Squash

HANDS-ON TIME: 5 MIN. | **TOTAL TIME:** 30 MIN.

1 tablespoon unsalted butter, melted
1 tablespoon chopped fresh thyme
1 tablespoon honey
2 teaspoons olive oil
3 garlic cloves, sliced
2 (12-ounce) delicata squash, halved lengthwise, seeded, and cut into ½-inch slices
1 (1-pound) red onion, cut into 12 wedges
½ teaspoon salt, divided
½ teaspoon freshly ground black pepper, divided
Cooking spray
3 tablespoons chopped fresh flat-leaf parsley

❶ Place a baking sheet in oven. Preheat oven to 475° (leave pan in oven).

❷ Combine first 5 ingredients in a large bowl, stirring with a whisk. Add squash and onion; toss gently to coat. Sprinkle vegetable mixture with ¼ teaspoon salt and ¼ teaspoon pepper. Carefully remove preheated pan from oven; coat pan with cooking spray. Arrange vegetable mixture in a single layer on pan. Bake at 475° for 20 minutes or until tender, turning once. Sprinkle with ¼ teaspoon salt, ¼ teaspoon pepper, and chopped parsley.

SERVES 6 (serving size: about 1 cup)

CALORIES 120; FAT 3.6g (sat 1.5g, mono 1.6g, poly 0.3g); PROTEIN 2g; CARB 23g; FIBER 3g; CHOL 5mg; IRON 1mg; SODIUM 205mg; CALC 63mg

Roasted Delicata with Cranberries and Pumpkinseeds

HANDS-ON TIME: 10 MIN. | **TOTAL TIME:** 45 MIN.

2 (12-ounce) delicata squash
4 teaspoons canola oil, divided
½ teaspoon kosher salt, divided
¼ teaspoon freshly ground black
    pepper, divided
Cooking spray
4 thyme sprigs
3 tablespoons dried sweetened
    cranberries
2 teaspoons butter
1 teaspoon fresh lemon juice
2 tablespoons pumpkinseed kernels,
    toasted

❶ Preheat oven to 425°.

❷ Cut each squash in half lengthwise; scoop out and discard seeds and membranes. Brush flesh with 2 teaspoons oil; sprinkle evenly with ¼ teaspoon salt and ⅛ teaspoon pepper. Place squash halves, cut sides down, in a 13 x 9–inch glass or ceramic baking dish coated with cooking spray. Bake at 425° for 15 minutes. Turn over (cut sides up); place 1 thyme sprig in each. Bake an additional 17 minutes or until tender. Sprinkle with ¼ teaspoon salt and ⅛ teaspoon pepper.

❸ Preheat broiler to high.

❹ Broil squash 2 minutes or until lightly browned.

❺ Place cranberries in a small bowl; cover with water. Microwave at HIGH 45 seconds; drain.

❻ Melt butter in a small skillet over medium heat; cook 3 minutes or until browned. Stir in 2 teaspoons oil and lemon juice. Drizzle butter mixture over squash. Divide cranberries and pumpkinseeds among squash halves.

SERVES 4 (serving size: 1 squash half)

CALORIES 160; FAT 8.6g (sat 1.9g, mono 4.1g, poly 2.2g); PROTEIN 3g; CARB 19g; FIBER 2g; CHOL 5mg; IRON 1mg; SODIUM 257mg; CALC 44mg

Prep Pointer

Cranberries add tanginess to this rich and creamy dish. Microwaving them with water helps rehydrate them and plump them up.

Simple Swap

If you can't find kabocha, use two medium delicata or acorn squash.

Kabocha Squash Puree

HANDS-ON TIME: 12 MIN. | **TOTAL TIME:** 1 HR. 27 MIN.

1 (3-pound) kabocha squash
½ cup water
½ cup packed brown sugar
3 tablespoons butter, melted
½ teaspoon salt
¼ teaspoon freshly ground black pepper

❶ Preheat oven to 450°.
❷ Cut squash in half, and discard seeds. Place squash halves, cut sides down, in a 13 x 9–inch glass or ceramic baking dish, and add ½ cup water to dish. Cover and bake at 450° for 40 minutes or until squash is tender. Remove squash from pan, and let stand 10 minutes. Remove pulp from skin, and discard skin. Place squash pulp, ½ cup brown sugar, and remaining ingredients in a food processor; process until smooth.

SERVES 6 (serving size: ½ cup)

CALORIES 201; FAT 5.8g (sat 3.7g, mono 1.5g, poly 0.2g); PROTEIN 3g; CARB 37g; FIBER 3g; CHOL 15mg; IRON 1mg; SODIUM 244mg; CALC 71mg

Sugar-Roasted Pumpkin

HANDS-ON TIME: 8 MIN. | **TOTAL TIME:** 43 MIN.

1 small pumpkin (about 2½ pounds)
Cooking spray
2 teaspoons butter, divided
2 tablespoons dark brown sugar, divided

❶ Preheat oven to 425°.
❷ Cut pumpkin into 4 wedges, discarding seeds and membrane. Place pumpkin wedges, cut sides up, in an 11 x 7–inch glass or ceramic baking dish coated with cooking spray. Place ½ teaspoon butter on each wedge, and sprinkle each wedge with 1½ teaspoons sugar.
❸ Bake at 425° for 35 minutes or until tender.

SERVES 4 (serving size: 1 wedge)

CALORIES 94; FAT 2.1g (sat 1.3g, mono 0.6g, poly 0.1g); PROTEIN 2g; CARB 20g; FIBER 1g; CHOL 5mg; IRON 2mg; SODIUM 24mg; CALC 48mg

294
vegetables

Acorn Squash Wedges with Maple-Harissa Glaze

HANDS-ON TIME: 5 MIN. | **TOTAL TIME:** 55 MIN.

4 small acorn squash (about 10 ounces
   each), cut into wedges
Cooking spray
½ teaspoon kosher salt
4½ tablespoons maple syrup
1½ tablespoons unsalted butter, melted
1½ tablespoons water
2¼ teaspoons harissa paste
4 teaspoons sesame seeds

❶ Preheat oven to 400°.
❷ Arrange squash wedges, cut sides up, on a baking sheet lined with parchment paper. Coat squash wedges lightly with cooking spray; sprinkle with salt. Combine syrup and next 3 ingredients (through harissa paste) in a small bowl; drizzle into cavity of each squash wedge.
❸ Bake at 400° for 30 minutes. Sprinkle squash wedges with sesame seeds; bake an additional 20 minutes or until seeds are toasted and squash is tender.

SERVES 8

CALORIES 135; FAT 4.1g (sat 2g, mono 1.1g, poly 0.6g);
PROTEIN 2g; CARB 26g; FIBER 2g; CHOL 8mg; IRON 1mg;
SODIUM 168mg; CALC 84mg

Prep Pointer

Different brands of harissa, also known as Moroccan chile paste, can have varying intensities. Be sure to taste it before to decide how much your taste buds can handle.

Simple Swap

Replace the harissa with a couple of teaspoons minced canned chipotle chiles in adobo sauce and about 1 teaspoon of the adobo sauce from the can.

Prep Pointer

Though it tastes delicious when prepared with its skin on, the butternut squash can also be peeled with a vegetable peeler before baking, if you prefer.

Honey-Roasted Butternut Squash

HANDS-ON TIME: 12 MIN. | **TOTAL TIME:** 1 HR. 12 MIN.

2 large butternut squash, halved lengthwise and seeded (about 4 pounds)
2 tablespoons honey
1½ tablespoons butter
½ teaspoon kosher salt
¼ teaspoon freshly ground black pepper
2 tablespoons finely chopped toasted pecans
1 tablespoon minced fresh flat-leaf parsley

❶ Preheat oven to 400°.
❷ Place squash halves, cut sides up, on a foil-lined baking sheet. Place honey and butter in a microwave-safe bowl. Microwave at HIGH 30 seconds or until butter melts; stir to combine. Brush half of honey mixture over cut sides of squash; reserve remaining honey mixture. Sprinkle squash with salt and pepper. Bake at 400° for 1 hour or until tender.
❸ Carefully place squash, cut sides up, on a cutting board. Halve squash lengthwise; cut each half crosswise into thirds. Place squash on a platter. Heat reserved honey mixture in microwave at HIGH 20 seconds. Drizzle remaining honey mixture over squash; sprinkle evenly with pecans and parsley.

SERVES 8 (serving size: 3 pieces)

CALORIES 133; FAT 3.6g (sat 1.5g, mono 1.3g, poly 0.5g); PROTEIN 2g; CARB 27g; FIBER 4g; CHOL 6mg; IRON 1mg; SODIUM 147mg; CALC 95mg

Simple Swap

Each of the three types of mushrooms adds its own pungent twist. You can substitute other varieties, if you like.

Butternut Squash au Gratin

HANDS-ON TIME: 50 MIN. | **TOTAL TIME:** 1 HR. 50 MIN.

1 tablespoon extra-virgin olive oil
2 thinly sliced green onions
8 cups finely diced peeled butternut squash, divided (about 4 pounds)
½ teaspoon kosher salt, divided
2 center-cut bacon slices
4 ounces sliced chanterelle mushrooms
4 ounces sliced shiitake mushroom caps
1½ tablespoons chopped fresh sage
¼ cup unsalted beef stock (such as Swanson)
2 ounces Parmigiano-Reggiano cheese, grated and divided (about ½ cup)
2 tablespoons part-skim ricotta cheese
¼ teaspoon freshly ground black pepper
Cooking spray
6 ounces oyster mushrooms, sliced

❶ Preheat oven to 350°.

❷ Heat a large skillet over medium-high heat. Add oil; swirl to coat. Add green onions; sauté 30 seconds. Add 6 cups squash; sauté 2 minutes. Reduce heat to medium-low, and stir in ¼ teaspoon salt. Cook, covered, 15 minutes or until tender. Increase heat to medium-high. Cook, uncovered, 2 minutes or until liquid evaporates, stirring frequently. Place squash mixture in a large bowl; mash with a potato masher or fork until smooth.

❸ Cook bacon in a large nonstick skillet over medium-high heat until crisp. Remove bacon from pan, reserving drippings in pan; crumble bacon. Add chanterelles, shiitakes, and sage to drippings; sauté 8 minutes or until browned. Add stock; cook 3 minutes or until liquid almost evaporates. Add mushroom mixture, 2 cups diced squash, ¼ teaspoon salt, 1 ounce Parmigiano-Reggiano cheese, ricotta cheese, and black pepper to mashed squash mixture, stirring to combine.

❹ Spoon squash mixture into a broiler-safe 11 x 7–inch glass or ceramic baking dish coated with cooking spray. Cover with foil; bake at 350° for 1 hour. Remove pan from oven; discard foil.

❺ Preheat broiler to high.

❻ Combine bacon, 1 ounce Parmigiano-Reggiano, and oyster mushrooms in a bowl; sprinkle over gratin. Broil 6 minutes or until lightly browned. Let stand 5 minutes before serving.

SERVES 8 (serving size: about 1 cup)

CALORIES 163; **FAT** 5g (sat 1.9g, mono 1.9g, poly 0.4g); **PROTEIN** 7g; **CARB** 26g; **FIBER** 5g; **CHOL** 9mg; **IRON** 2mg; **SODIUM** 286mg; **CALC** 188mg

Baked Spaghetti Squash with Tomato Sauce and Olives

HANDS-ON TIME: 8 MIN. | **TOTAL TIME:** 1 HR. 39 MIN.

1 spaghetti squash (about 3¼ pounds)
1½ tablespoons olive oil
1 cup minced fresh onion
1 teaspoon dried oregano
½ teaspoon dried thyme
2 bay leaves
Dash of crushed red pepper
3 garlic cloves, minced and divided
1 cup dry red wine
½ cup water
⅓ cup coarsely chopped pitted
   kalamata olives
1 tablespoon capers
¼ teaspoon freshly ground black pepper
1 (28-ounce) can crushed tomatoes,
   undrained
1 ounce grated fresh Parmesan cheese
   (about ¼ cup)
¼ cup chopped fresh parsley

❶ Preheat oven to 375°.
❷ Pierce squash with a fork. Place squash on a baking sheet; bake at 375° for 1½ hours or until tender. Cool. Cut squash in half lengthwise; discard seeds. Scrape inside of squash with a fork to remove spaghetti-like strands to measure 6 cups. Keep warm.
❸ While squash is baking, heat a large nonstick skillet over medium heat. Add oil to pan; swirl to coat. Add onion, oregano, thyme, bay leaves, and red pepper; sauté 5 minutes. Add 2 minced garlic cloves, wine, and next 5 ingredients (through tomatoes); bring to a boil. Reduce heat, and simmer until thick (about 30 minutes). Discard bay leaves.
❹ Combine 1 minced garlic clove, Parmesan cheese, and parsley. Place ½ cup squash on each of 12 plates. Top each serving with about ⅓ cup sauce and 1½ teaspoons topping.

SERVES 12

**CALORIES 95; FAT 3.7g (sat 0.8g, mono 2.2g, poly 0.5g);
PROTEIN 3g; CARB 13g; FIBER 3g; CHOL 2mg; IRON 1mg;
SODIUM 242mg; CALC 81mg**

Did You Know?

There are only
42 calories in 1 cup
of cooked spaghetti
squash, making it
a healthy substitute
for pasta.

Spaghetti Squash Fritters

HANDS-ON TIME: 35 MIN. | **TOTAL TIME:** 55 MIN.

1 (2-pound) spaghetti squash
1 (8-ounce) package baby spinach
½ cup panko (Japanese breadcrumbs)
2 tablespoons grated fresh Parmesan cheese
1 tablespoon minced fresh garlic
½ teaspoon freshly ground black pepper
¼ teaspoon baking powder
2 large egg whites
1 tablespoon olive oil, divided
5 teaspoons canola mayonnaise
2 teaspoons 2% reduced-fat milk
1 teaspoon Sriracha (hot chile sauce, such as Huy Fong)
1 teaspoon cider vinegar

❶ Cut squash in half lengthwise. Scoop out seeds; discard. Place squash halves, cut sides up, in a microwave-safe bowl. Cover with a damp paper towel. Microwave at HIGH 20 minutes or until tender. Let stand 10 minutes. Scrape inside of squash with a fork to remove spaghetti-like strands to measure 4 cups.

❷ Heat a large skillet over medium-high heat. Add spinach to pan; cook 2 minutes or until spinach wilts. Place squash and spinach on a clean dish towel; squeeze until barely moist. Coarsely chop squash mixture, and place in a large bowl. Add panko and next 4 ingredients (through baking powder), and toss well to combine. Place egg whites in a medium bowl; beat with a mixer at high speed until soft peaks form. Gently fold egg whites into squash mixture.

❸ Fill a ¼-cup dry measuring cup with squash mixture. Invert onto work surface; gently pat into a ¾-inch-thick patty. Repeat procedure with remaining squash mixture, forming 10 patties total. Heat a large nonstick skillet over medium heat. Add 1½ teaspoons oil to pan, and swirl to coat. Add 5 patties to pan; cook 3 minutes on each side or until browned. Remove patties from pan; keep warm. Repeat procedure with 1½ teaspoons oil and squash patties.

❹ Combine mayonnaise and remaining ingredients in a small bowl. Serve with fritters.

SERVES 5 (serving size: 2 patties and about 2 teaspoons sauce)

CALORIES 172; FAT 8.8g (sat 1.5g, mono 4.3g, poly 1.8g); PROTEIN 6g; CARB 20g; FIBER 4g; CHOL 4mg; IRON 2mg; SODIUM 228mg; CALC 139mg

Prep Pointer

Sriracha packs a punch of heat that is tempered by the mayonnaise. You can adjust the amount depending on your heat tolerance.

Prep Pointer

This dish can be made ahead. Once all the ingredients are assembled in the gratin dish, cover and refrigerate for up to 3 days or freeze up to 3 weeks, until you are ready to bake it.

Zucchini and Onion Gratin

HANDS-ON TIME: 21 MIN. | **TOTAL TIME:** 45 MIN.

2 tablespoons olive oil, divided
1 large onion, quartered lengthwise and thinly sliced
1 tablespoon tomato paste
2 teaspoons grated lemon rind
1 teaspoon thyme leaves
$\frac{3}{8}$ teaspoon kosher salt, divided
$\frac{1}{4}$ teaspoon freshly ground black pepper
$1\frac{1}{2}$ pounds zucchini, diagonally sliced into $\frac{1}{4}$-inch-thick pieces
1 ounce Parmesan cheese, grated (about $\frac{1}{4}$ cup)

1 Heat a large skillet over medium heat. Add 1 tablespoon oil to pan; swirl to coat. Add onion; cook 6 minutes, stirring occasionally. Stir in tomato paste; cook 2 minutes. Stir in rind, thyme, $\frac{1}{8}$ teaspoon salt, and pepper; cook 2 minutes, stirring occasionally.

2 Preheat broiler to high.

3 Arrange zucchini on a jelly-roll pan. Drizzle with 1 tablespoon oil; toss. Broil 7 minutes or until lightly charred. Sprinkle with $\frac{1}{4}$ teaspoon salt.

4 Preheat oven to 375°.

5 Spread onion mixture in a 2-quart gratin dish. Arrange zucchini mixture over onion mixture. Sprinkle with cheese. Cover and bake at 375° for 25 minutes. Remove from oven.

6 Preheat broiler to high.

7 Uncover zucchini mixture; broil $1\frac{1}{2}$ minutes or until lightly browned.

SERVES 6 (serving size: about 1 cup)

CALORIES 92; FAT 6.3g (sat 1.6g, mono 3.7g, poly 0.6g); PROTEIN 4g; CARB 7g; FIBER 2g; CHOL 4mg; IRON 1mg; SODIUM 224mg; CALC 79mg

Caprese Zucchini

HANDS-ON TIME: 14 MIN. | **TOTAL TIME:** 14 MIN.

2 medium zucchini, sliced
½ cup diced seeded tomato
2 tablespoons chopped fresh basil
2 teaspoons olive oil
1 teaspoon red wine vinegar
¼ teaspoon kosher salt
¼ teaspoon freshly ground black pepper
1 ounce shredded part-skim mozzarella
  cheese (about ¼ cup)

❶ Preheat grill to medium-high heat.
❷ Place zucchini on grill rack. Grill zucchini 2 minutes on each side.
❸ Preheat broiler. Combine tomato, basil, olive oil, vinegar, salt, and pepper in a bowl. Arrange grilled zucchini on a foil-lined baking sheet; top evenly with tomato mixture and mozzarella cheese. Broil 2 minutes or until cheese melts.

SERVES 4 (serving size: 4 zucchini slices, 2 tablespoons tomato mixture, and 1 tablespoon cheese)

CALORIES 64; **FAT** 4.2g (sat 1.2g, mono 2g, poly 0.4g); **PROTEIN** 3g; **CARB** 4g; **FIBER** 1g; **CHOL** 4mg; **IRON** 1mg; **SODIUM** 175mg; **CALC** 73mg

Seared Cabbage Steaks

HANDS-ON TIME: 15 MIN. | **TOTAL TIME:** 30 MIN.

1 head cabbage
8 teaspoons canola oil, divided
2 teaspoons butter, divided
Cooking spray

❶ Preheat oven to 425°.
❷ Cut 4 (1-inch) vertical slices from head of cabbage. Heat 2 teaspoons canola oil and ½ teaspoon butter in a cast-iron skillet over medium-high heat. Add 1 cabbage steak; cook 4 minutes. Place, seared side up, on a baking sheet coated with cooking spray. Repeat with remaining oil, butter, and cabbage. Bake cabbage steaks at 425° for 15 to 20 minutes.

SERVES 4 (serving size: 1 steak)

CALORIES 157; **FAT** 11.5g (sat 2g, mono 6.4g, poly 2.7g); **PROTEIN** 3g; **CARB** 13g; **FIBER** 6g; **CHOL** 5mg; **IRON** 1mg; **SODIUM** 238mg; **CALC** 92mg

Sautéed Cabbage and Apples

HANDS-ON TIME: 19 MIN. | **TOTAL TIME:** 19 MIN.

1 tablespoon unsalted butter
2 teaspoons canola oil
8 cups sliced green cabbage
2 cups thinly sliced apple
1 teaspoon caraway seeds
½ teaspoon salt

❶ Heat a large skillet over medium-high heat. Add butter and oil to pan; swirl until butter melts. Add cabbage, apple, caraway seeds, and salt; cover and cook 5 minutes. Uncover and cook 5 minutes or until cabbage and apples are tender, stirring occasionally.

SERVES 6 (serving size: 1 cup)

CALORIES 73; FAT 3.7g (sat 1.4g, mono 1.5g, poly 0.6g); PROTEIN 1g; CARB 10g; FIBER 3g; CHOL 5mg; IRON 1mg; SODIUM 214mg; CALC 42mg

Prep Pointer

Use the slicing blade of your food processor to shorten the cabbage prep time.

Did You Know?

Cooking Brussels sprouts too long causes them to take on a strong sulphuric odor. As the sprouts become too soft, they release a glucosinolate compound which contributes to the bitterness that most people dislike.

Brussels Sprouts with Bacon, Garlic, and Shallots

HANDS-ON TIME: 27 MIN. | **TOTAL TIME:** 27 MIN.

6 slices center-cut bacon, chopped
½ cup sliced shallot (about 1 large)
1½ pounds Brussels sprouts, trimmed and halved
6 garlic cloves, thinly sliced
¾ cup fat-free, lower-sodium chicken broth
⅛ teaspoon salt
⅛ teaspoon freshly ground black pepper

❶ Heat a large nonstick skillet over medium-high heat. Add bacon, and sauté 5 minutes or until bacon begins to brown. Remove pan from heat. Remove bacon from pan with a slotted spoon, reserving 1 tablespoon drippings in pan (discard remaining drippings).
❷ Return pan to medium-high heat, and stir in bacon, shallot, and Brussels sprouts; sauté 4 minutes. Add garlic, and sauté 4 minutes or until garlic begins to brown, stirring frequently. Add chicken broth, and bring to a boil. Cook 2 minutes or until broth mostly evaporates and sprouts are crisp-tender, stirring occasionally. Remove from heat; stir in salt and pepper.

SERVES 6 (serving size: about ⅔ cup)

CALORIES 90; FAT 2.4g (sat 1.1g, mono 0.6g, poly 0.3g); PROTEIN 7g; CARB 14g; FIBER 5g; CHOL 8mg; IRON 2mg; SODIUM 263mg; CALC 60mg

Brussels Sprouts Gratin

HANDS-ON TIME: 34 MIN. | **TOTAL TIME:** 34 MIN.

2 hickory-smoked bacon slices
4 large shallots, thinly sliced
2 pounds Brussels sprouts, trimmed and halved
1 cup water
$3/8$ teaspoon kosher salt, divided
$1/4$ teaspoon freshly ground black pepper
Cooking spray
1 (2-ounce) slice French bread baguette
3 tablespoons butter

1 Preheat broiler.

2 Cook bacon in a large skillet over medium heat until crisp. Remove bacon from pan, reserving drippings; crumble. Increase heat to medium-high. Add shallots to drippings in pan; sauté 2 minutes or until tender, stirring occasionally. Add Brussels sprouts and 1 cup water; bring to a boil. Cover pan loosely with aluminum foil; cook 6 minutes or until Brussels sprouts are almost tender.

3 Uncover and remove from heat. Sprinkle with $1/4$ teaspoon salt and pepper; toss to combine. Spoon Brussels sprouts mixture into a 2-quart broiler-safe glass or ceramic baking dish coated with cooking spray.

4 Place bread in a food processor, and process until finely ground. Melt butter in skillet over medium-high heat. Add breadcrumbs and $1/8$ teaspoon salt to pan; sauté 2 minutes or until toasted, stirring frequently. Sprinkle breadcrumb mixture over Brussels sprouts mixture. Broil 3 minutes or until golden and thoroughly heated.

SERVES 6 (serving size: about $3/4$ cup)

CALORIES 133; **FAT** 5.8g (sat 3.2g, mono 1.1g, poly 0.3g); **PROTEIN** 6g; **CARB** 18g; **FIBER** 5g; **CHOL** 14mg; **IRON** 2mg; **SODIUM** 240mg; **CALC** 57mg

Prep Pointer

Braise the Brussels sprouts and toast the breadcrumbs up to a day ahead; then assemble and reheat before serving.

Superfast

Ready in 15 minutes or less!

Simple Swap

If you don't have dry white wine, use white wine vinegar instead.

Lemony Broccolini

HANDS-ON TIME: 15 MIN. | **TOTAL TIME:** 15 MIN.

2 teaspoons butter
1 pound trimmed Broccolini
¼ cup dry white wine
2 teaspoons grated lemon rind
1 tablespoon fresh lemon juice
¼ teaspoon salt
¼ teaspoon freshly ground black pepper

❶ Melt butter in a large skillet over medium-high heat; swirl to coat. Add Broccolini to pan; cook 4 minutes, stirring occasionally. Add wine to pan. Cover, reduce heat to medium-low, and cook 6 minutes or until Broccolini is tender. Add lemon rind, lemon juice, salt, and pepper to Broccolini; toss.

SERVES 4 (serving size: about 5 stalks)

CALORIES 73; FAT 1.9g (sat 1.2g, mono 0.5g, poly 0.1g); PROTEIN 4g; CARB 9g; FIBER 1g; CHOL 5mg; IRON 1mg; SODIUM 196mg; CALC 84mg

Roasted Chile-Garlic Broccoli

HANDS-ON TIME: 8 MIN. | **TOTAL TIME:** 18 MIN.

6 cups broccoli florets
2 tablespoons dark sesame oil
2 teaspoons sambal oelek (ground fresh
  chile paste)
$3/8$ teaspoon salt
$1/8$ teaspoon sugar
6 large garlic cloves, coarsely chopped

❶ Place a small roasting pan in oven. Preheat oven to 450°.
❷ Place broccoli in a large bowl; drizzle with oil. Toss to coat. Add sambal oelek, salt, and sugar to broccoli mixture; toss. Add broccoli mixture to preheated pan; toss. Bake at 450° for 5 minutes; remove from oven. Add garlic to pan; stir. Bake an additional 5 minutes or until broccoli is lightly browned.

SERVES 5 (serving size: 1 cup)

CALORIES 79; FAT 5.8g (sat 0.8g, mono 2.2g, poly 2.4g); PROTEIN 3g; CARB 6g; FIBER 2g; CHOL 0mg; IRON 1mg; SODIUM 260mg; CALC 47mg

Prep Pointer

Don't let the name sambal oelek scare you away from this recipe. You can actually find this chile paste at most supermarkets.

Charred Broccoli with Orange Browned Butter

HANDS-ON TIME: 10 MIN. | **TOTAL TIME:** 25 MIN.

10 ounces broccoli florets ($2^{1}/_{2}$ cups)
Cooking spray
1 tablespoon butter
1 teaspoon grated orange rind
2 tablespoons fresh orange juice
$1/4$ teaspoon salt
$1/4$ teaspoon freshly ground black pepper

❶ Preheat oven to 450°.
❷ Arrange broccoli on a foil-lined baking sheet; coat with cooking spray. Bake at 450° for 12 minutes or until crisp-tender and lightly browned, stirring once. Heat broiler to high, leaving pan in oven; broil 2 minutes or until lightly charred.
❸ Melt butter in a skillet over medium heat; cook 3 minutes or until browned. Remove from heat. Stir in rind and juice. Combine broccoli and butter mixture in a bowl. Sprinkle with salt and pepper; toss to coat.

SERVES 4 (serving size: about $2/_3$ cup)

CALORIES 50; FAT 3.2g (sat 1.9g, mono 0.8g, poly 0.2g); PROTEIN 2g; CARB 5g; FIBER 2g; CHOL 8mg; IRON 1mg; SODIUM 192mg; CALC 37mg

Cauliflower with Anchovy Breadcrumbs

HANDS-ON TIME: 24 MIN. | **TOTAL TIME:** 24 MIN.

6 cups cauliflower florets
1½ ounces torn French bread
2 teaspoons chopped fresh sage
¼ teaspoon freshly ground black pepper
¼ teaspoon salt
3 anchovy fillets, rinsed and drained
3 garlic cloves
1½ tablespoons butter

❶ Bring a large saucepan of water to a boil; add cauliflower. Boil 6 minutes; drain.
❷ Place bread and next 5 ingredients (through garlic) in a mini food processor; process until finely chopped. Melt butter in a medium skillet over medium heat. Add crumb mixture; cook 4 minutes. Toss crumbs with cauliflower.

SERVES 6 (serving size: 1 cup)

CALORIES 76; FAT 3.5g (sat 1.9g, mono 0.8g, poly 0.1g); PROTEIN 3g; CARB 9g; FIBER 2g; CHOL 9mg; IRON 1mg; SODIUM 223mg; CALC 33mg

Roasted Cauliflower, Chickpeas, and Olives

HANDS-ON TIME: 16 MIN. | **TOTAL TIME:** 38 MIN.

5½ cups cauliflower florets
   (about 1 pound)
12 green Spanish olives, pitted and
   halved
8 garlic cloves, coarsely chopped
1 (15-ounce) can unsalted chickpeas
   (garbanzo beans), rinsed and drained
3 tablespoons olive oil
½ teaspoon crushed red pepper
3 tablespoons fresh flat-leaf parsley
   leaves

❶ Preheat oven to 450°.
❷ Combine first 4 ingredients in a small roasting pan. Drizzle with oil; sprinkle with pepper. Toss well to coat. Bake at 450° for 22 minutes or until cauliflower is browned and crisp-tender, stirring after 10 minutes. Sprinkle with parsley.

SERVES 6 (serving size: about ⅔ cup)

CALORIES 185; **FAT** 10.4g (sat 1.3g, mono 6.5g, poly 0.8g); **PROTEIN** 6g; **CARB** 18g; **FIBER** 5g; **CHOL** 0mg; **IRON** 1mg; **SODIUM** 249mg; **CALC** 69mg

Wilted Kale with Toasted Shallots

HANDS-ON TIME: 15 MIN. | **TOTAL TIME:** 15 MIN.

1 tablespoon olive oil
2 shallots, very thinly sliced
1 pound stemmed chopped Lacinato kale
¼ teaspoon kosher salt
¼ teaspoon freshly ground black pepper

❶ Heat a large skillet over medium-high heat. Add oil to pan; swirl to coat. Add shallots; sauté 2 minutes or until golden brown. Add kale; cook 3 minutes or until kale wilts. Stir in salt and pepper.

SERVES 4 (serving size: about 1 cup)

CALORIES 92; **FAT** 4.2g (sat 0.6g, mono 2.5g, poly 0.7g); **PROTEIN** 4g; **CARB** 13g; **FIBER** 2g; **CHOL** 0mg; **IRON** 2mg; **SODIUM** 169mg; **CALC** 154mg

Did You Know?

Because chickpeas have a high protein and fiber content and have a low glycemic index, they satisfy hunger cravings, helping you eat less.

Superfast

Ready in 15 minutes or less!

Balsamic Collard Greens

HANDS-ON TIME: 15 MIN. | **TOTAL TIME:** 3 HR. 45 MIN.

3 bacon slices
1 cup chopped onion
1 (16-ounce) package chopped fresh
    collard greens
¼ teaspoon salt
2 garlic cloves, minced
1 bay leaf
1 (14.5-ounce) can fat-free,
    lower-sodium chicken broth
3 tablespoons balsamic vinegar
1 tablespoon honey

❶ Cook bacon in a large Dutch oven over medium heat until crisp. Remove bacon from pan; crumble. Add onion to drippings in pan; sauté 5 minutes or until tender. Add collard greens, and cook 2 to 3 minutes or until greens begin to wilt, stirring occasionally.

❷ Place collard green mixture, salt, and next 3 ingredients (through broth) in a 3-quart electric slow cooker. Cover and cook on LOW for 3½ to 4 hours. Remove bay leaf; discard.

❸ Combine balsamic vinegar and honey in a small bowl. Stir vinegar mixture into collard greens just before serving. Sprinkle with bacon.

SERVES 5 (serving size: ½ cup collard greens and 2½ teaspoons bacon)

CALORIES 82; **FAT** 1.8g (sat 0.8g, mono 0.8g, poly 0.4g); **PROTEIN** 5g; **CARB** 14g; **FIBER** 4g; **CHOL** 6mg; **IRON** 0mg; **SODIUM** 260mg; **CALC** 144mg

Prep Pointer

A "bunch" of collard greens at the store is typically 12 to 16 ounces. If you prefer unpackaged greens, you'll need one to two bunches.

Did You Know?

Agrodolce means "sweet and sour" in Italian and is a sauce typically made by reducing a mixture of sugar and vinegar. This preparation further tenderizes the chewy chard.

Sautéed Chard Agrodolce ▶

HANDS-ON TIME: 17 MIN. | **TOTAL TIME:** 17 MIN.

2 teaspoons olive oil
½ cup thinly sliced shallots
4 garlic cloves, minced
6 cups chopped Swiss chard
½ cup dried sweet cherries
1 tablespoon water
½ teaspoon freshly ground black pepper
¼ teaspoon kosher salt
2 teaspoons balsamic vinegar

❶ Heat a large skillet over medium-high heat. Add oil to pan; swirl to coat. Add shallots; sauté 2 minutes. Add garlic; sauté 1 minute. Add chard, cherries, 1 tablespoon water, pepper, and salt; toss to coat. Sauté 2 minutes or until chard begins to wilt. Stir in vinegar.

SERVES 4 (serving size: ½ cup)

CALORIES 122; FAT 2.4g (sat 0.3g, mono 1.7g, poly 0.3g); PROTEIN 2g; CARB 23g; FIBER 4g; CHOL 0mg; IRON 2mg; SODIUM 241mg; CALC 62mg

Wilted Swiss Chard and Mushrooms

HANDS-ON TIME: 18 MIN. | **TOTAL TIME:** 18 MIN.

10 ounces Swiss chard
1 tablespoon olive oil
1 thinly sliced shallot
6 ounces sliced cremini mushrooms
¼ teaspoon freshly ground black pepper
2 teaspoons lower-sodium soy sauce
1 tablespoon water

❶ Remove stems from Swiss chard. Thinly slice stems to measure 1 cup; coarsely chop leaves to measure 3 cups.
❷ Heat a large skillet over medium heat. Add olive oil to pan; swirl to coat. Add shallot; cook 1 minute. Add mushrooms, chard stems, and black pepper to pan; cook 5 minutes, stirring occasionally. Add chard leaves, soy sauce, and 1 tablespoon water to pan. Cover and cook 2 minutes or until chard wilts.

SERVES 4 (serving size: ½ cup)

CALORIES 55; FAT 3.5g (sat 0.5g, mono 2.5g, poly 0.4g); PROTEIN 2g; CARB 5g; FIBER 1g; CHOL 0mg; IRON 1mg; SODIUM 176mg; CALC 27mg

Simple Swap

If you can't find mirin, substitute an equal amount of white wine plus 2 teaspoons sugar.

Mirin-Braised Bok Choy with Shiitake Mushrooms

HANDS-ON TIME: 20 MIN. | **TOTAL TIME:** 32 MIN.

2 tablespoons peanut oil, divided
1 cup thinly sliced shiitake mushrooms
½ cup thinly sliced shallots
6 baby bok choy, halved lengthwise
½ cup unsalted chicken stock
   (such as Swanson)
¼ cup mirin (sweet rice wine)
1 tablespoon lower-sodium soy sauce
2 slices peeled fresh ginger

❶ Heat a large skillet over medium-high heat. Add 2 teaspoons oil to pan; swirl to coat. Add mushrooms and shallots to pan; cook 5 minutes or until mushrooms begin to brown, stirring occasionally. Remove mushroom mixture from pan.

❷ Add 2 teaspoons oil to pan. Add half of bok choy, cut sides down, to pan; cook 3 minutes. Remove bok choy from pan. Repeat procedure with remaining 2 teaspoons oil and remaining bok choy. Return mushroom mixture and bok choy to pan.

❸ Stir in stock, mirin, soy sauce, and ginger; bring to a boil. Reduce heat to medium-low; partially cover, and cook 10 minutes or until bok choy is crisp-tender. Uncover and remove bok choy from pan. Bring liquid to a boil; cook 6 minutes or until reduced to about ¼ cup. Drizzle liquid over bok choy.

SERVES 4 (serving size: 3 bok choy halves and about 1 tablespoon sauce)

CALORIES 118; **FAT** 7g (sat 1.2g, mono 3.1g, poly 2.2g); **PROTEIN** 2g; **CARB** 9g; **FIBER** 1g; **CHOL** 0mg; **IRON** 1mg; **SODIUM** 199mg; **CALC** 66mg

Cider Vinegar–Spiked Steamed Baby Spinach

HANDS-ON TIME: 2 MIN. | **TOTAL TIME:** 5 MIN.

Superfast

Ready in 15
minutes or less!

1 (16-ounce) container baby spinach
1 tablespoon water
2 tablespoons cider vinegar
¼ teaspoon crushed red pepper
⅛ teaspoon kosher salt

❶ Place spinach and 1 tablespoon water in a large bowl covered with plastic wrap. Microwave at HIGH 3 minutes or until spinach wilts. Drain well. Toss with vinegar, crushed red pepper, and salt.

SERVES 4 (serving size: ³/₄ cup)

CALORIES 49; FAT 0g; PROTEIN 3g; CARB 12g; FIBER 5g; CHOL 0mg; IRON 4mg; SODIUM 241mg; CALC 81mg

Steamed Spinach with Curry Butter

HANDS-ON TIME: 10 MIN. | **TOTAL TIME:** 10 MIN.

1 tablespoon unsalted butter
1 tablespoon mild curry powder
2 (16-ounce) containers fresh spinach
1 tablespoon fresh orange juice
⅛ teaspoon kosher salt
½ teaspoon ground red pepper

❶ Heat butter and curry powder in a large Dutch oven; cook 2 minutes. Add spinach in batches; cook 3 to 5 minutes or just until wilted. Remove from heat; stir in orange juice, salt, and ground red pepper.

SERVES 4 (serving size: about 1½ cups)

CALORIES 85; FAT 4g (sat 2g, mono 0.9g, poly 0.5g); PROTEIN 7g; CARB 10g; FIBER 6g; CHOL 8mg; IRON 7mg; SODIUM 240mg; CALC 233mg

◀ *Asparagus with Balsamic Tomatoes*

HANDS-ON TIME: 19 MIN. | **TOTAL TIME:** 19 MIN.

1 pound asparagus, trimmed
2 teaspoons extra-virgin olive oil
1½ cups halved grape tomatoes
½ teaspoon minced fresh garlic
2 tablespoons balsamic vinegar
¼ teaspoon salt
3 tablespoons crumbled goat cheese
½ teaspoon freshly ground black pepper

❶ Cook asparagus in boiling water 2 minutes or until crisp-tender. Drain.
❷ Heat olive oil in a large skillet over medium-high heat. Add tomatoes and garlic; cook 5 minutes. Stir in vinegar; cook 3 minutes. Stir in salt. Arrange asparagus on a platter; top with tomato mixture. Sprinkle with cheese and pepper.

SERVES 4

CALORIES 69; FAT 3.9g (sat 1.4g, mono 2g, poly 0.3g); PROTEIN 3g; CARB 7g; FIBER 2g; CHOL 4mg; IRON 2mg; SODIUM 181mg; CALC 45mg

Simple Swap

Crumbled feta cheese can be substituted for goat cheese.

Asparagus with Caper Vinaigrette

HANDS-ON TIME: 12 MIN. | **TOTAL TIME:** 12 MIN.

1½ pounds asparagus, trimmed
3 tablespoons extra-virgin olive oil, divided
½ teaspoon kosher salt, divided
Cooking spray
1 tablespoon red wine vinegar
½ teaspoon Dijon mustard
¼ teaspoon freshly ground black pepper
1 garlic clove, minced
2 teaspoons capers, coarsely chopped
¼ cup small basil leaves

❶ Preheat grill to medium-high heat.
❷ Place asparagus in a dish. Add 1 tablespoon oil and ¼ teaspoon salt, tossing well. Place asparagus on grill rack coated with cooking spray; grill 4 minutes or until crisp-tender, turning after 2 minutes.
❸ Combine ¼ teaspoon salt, vinegar, and next 3 ingredients (through garlic); stir with a whisk. Slowly pour 2 tablespoons oil into vinegar mixture, stirring constantly with a whisk. Stir in capers. Arrange asparagus on a serving platter; drizzle with vinaigrette, and sprinkle with basil.

SERVES 6 (serving size: about 4 asparagus spears and about 2 teaspoons vinaigrette)

CALORIES 91; FAT 7.2g (sat 1.1g, mono 5g, poly 1.1g); PROTEIN 3g; CARB 5g; FIBER 3g; CHOL 0mg; IRON 3mg; SODIUM 198mg; CALC 32mg

Superfast

Ready in 15 minutes or less!

Prep Pointer

Make individual servings of this soufflé by using ramekins rather than a 2-quart soufflé dish. You'll need to decrease your bake time, though. Check them through the oven door at 15 minutes. Avoid opening the oven door since fluctuations in temperature can cause the soufflé to deflate.

Asparagus and Gruyère Soufflé

HANDS-ON TIME: 30 MIN. | **TOTAL TIME:** 1 HR. 15 MIN.

Cooking spray
½ cup dry breadcrumbs
¾ pound asparagus, trimmed
1.5 ounces all-purpose flour
　(about ⅓ cup)
½ teaspoon salt
⅛ teaspoon ground nutmeg
1 teaspoon dry mustard
⅛ teaspoon freshly ground black
　pepper
1¼ cups 1% low-fat milk
1 large egg yolk, lightly beaten
2 ounces shredded Gruyère cheese
　(about ½ cup)
6 large egg whites
Dash of cream of tartar

❶ Preheat oven to 350°.

❷ Coat a 2-quart soufflé dish with cooking spray; sprinkle breadcrumbs over bottom and sides of dish.

❸ Cook asparagus in boiling water 4 minutes; drain and rinse with cold water. Cut a 1-inch tip from each asparagus spear; finely chop stalks.

❹ Weigh or lightly spoon flour into a dry measuring cup; level with a knife. Place flour, salt, ground nutmeg, dry mustard, and black pepper in a medium saucepan. Gradually add milk, stirring with a whisk until blended. Bring to a boil over medium heat, stirring constantly. Cook 1 minute or until thick.

❺ Gradually stir about one-fourth of hot milk mixture into egg yolk, stirring constantly with a whisk, and add to remaining hot milk mixture, stirring constantly. Cook 30 seconds, and remove from heat. Stir in asparagus tips, chopped asparagus, and cheese. Cool slightly.

❻ Place egg whites and cream of tartar in a large bowl, and beat with a mixer at high speed until stiff peaks form. Gently stir one-fourth of egg white mixture into asparagus mixture; gently fold in remaining egg white mixture. Spoon into prepared soufflé dish. Bake at 350° for 45 minutes or until puffed, golden, and set. Serve immediately.

SERVES 8

CALORIES 119; **FAT** 4g (sat 2g, mono 1.1g, poly 0.3g); **PROTEIN** 9g; **CARB** 12g; **FIBER** 1g; **CHOL** 33mg; **IRON** 1mg; **SODIUM** 279mg; **CALC** 131mg

Braising the fennel makes it so tender that you don't have to remove the tough core beforehand.

Braised Fennel with Parmesan Breadcrumbs

HANDS-ON TIME: 15 MIN. | **TOTAL TIME:** 35 MIN.

3 medium fennel bulbs, trimmed and halved lengthwise
4 teaspoons butter, divided
½ cup dry white wine
½ cup unsalted chicken stock (such as Swanson)
¼ teaspoon kosher salt
¼ teaspoon freshly ground black pepper
4 thyme sprigs
½ cup fresh breadcrumbs
1 tablespoon chopped fresh flat-leaf parsley
1 ounce Parmigiano-Reggiano cheese, grated (about ¼ cup)

❶ Cut each fennel half into 3 wedges. Melt 2 teaspoons butter in a large nonstick skillet over medium-high heat. Add fennel; cook 7 minutes or until browned, stirring occasionally. Add wine, stock, salt, pepper, and thyme sprigs; bring to a simmer. Cover, reduce heat, and simmer 20 minutes or until tender. Increase heat to medium-high; cook, uncovered, 1 minute or until liquid is slightly thickened. Remove thyme sprigs from pan; discard.

❷ Melt 2 teaspoons butter in a small skillet over medium heat. Add breadcrumbs; cook 3 minutes or until browned, stirring frequently. Remove pan from heat; stir in parsley and cheese. Arrange fennel wedges on a platter. Sprinkle breadcrumb mixture evenly over fennel.

SERVES 6 (serving size: 3 fennel wedges and about 2 tablespoons breadcrumb mixture)

CALORIES 117; **FAT** 4.3g (sat 2.5g, mono 1.1g, poly 0.2g); **PROTEIN** 5g; **CARB** 13g; **FIBER** 4g; **CHOL** 11mg; **IRON** 1mg; **SODIUM** 282mg; **CALC** 117mg

Warm-Spiced Okra

HANDS-ON TIME: 12 MIN. | **TOTAL TIME:** 12 MIN.

½ teaspoon curry powder
⅛ teaspoon crushed red pepper
1 shallot, minced
2 teaspoons olive oil
2 cups okra, halved lengthwise
¼ teaspoon salt

❶ Toast curry powder, crushed red pepper, and minced shallot in olive oil in a skillet over medium-low heat 2 minutes or until fragrant. Increase heat to high. Add okra; cook 3 minutes or just until tender. Sprinkle with salt.

SERVES 4 (serving size: ½ cup)

CALORIES 41; FAT 2.4g (sat 0.3g, mono 1.7g, poly 0.3g); PROTEIN 1g; CARB 5g; FIBER 2g; CHOL 0mg; IRON 1mg; SODIUM 153mg; CALC 44mg

Stewed Okra and Tomatoes

HANDS-ON TIME: 12 MIN. | **TOTAL TIME:** 32 MIN.

1 teaspoon canola oil
½ cup chopped onion
4 cups okra pods, trimmed (about 1 pound)
½ cup water
½ teaspoon sugar
¼ teaspoon salt
¼ teaspoon freshly ground black pepper
1 (14.5-ounce) can unsalted diced tomatoes, undrained

❶ Heat oil in a medium saucepan over medium heat. Add onion; sauté 2 minutes. Add okra and remaining ingredients; bring to a boil. Cover, reduce heat, and simmer 20 minutes.

SERVES 4 (serving size: 1 cup)

CALORIES 72; FAT 1.4g (sat 0.2g, mono 0.3g, poly 0.8g); PROTEIN 3g; CARB 14g; FIBER 5g; CHOL 0mg; IRON 2mg; SODIUM 198mg; CALC 114mg

Superfast

Ready in 15 minutes or less!

Prep Pointer

Just as toasting transforms a slice of bread, toasting spices adds another dimension to the flavor and brings out aromas that will enhance the dish.

◄ *Sautéed Snap Peas with Ricotta Salata and Mint*

HANDS-ON TIME: 5 MIN. | **TOTAL TIME:** 5 MIN.

1 tablespoon olive oil
2 (8-ounce) packages trimmed sugar snap peas
3 tablespoons chopped fresh mint
1½ teaspoons grated lemon rind
³⁄₈ teaspoon freshly ground black pepper
¼ teaspoon kosher salt
1.5 ounces ricotta salata or goat cheese, crumbled (about ⅓ cup)

❶ Heat a large skillet over medium-high heat. Add oil to pan; swirl to coat. Add peas; sauté 3 minutes or until crisp-tender. Stir in mint, rind, pepper, and salt. Sprinkle with cheese.

SERVES 6 (serving size: about 1 cup)

CALORIES 75; FAT 4.3g (sat 1.5g, mono 1.6g, poly 0.2g); PROTEIN 3g; CARB 6g; FIBER 2g; CHOL 8mg; IRON 2mg; SODIUM 197mg; CALC 39mg

Prep Pointer

To speed preparation, chop the mint, grate the lemon rind, and crumble the cheese while the peas cook.

Steamed Sugar Snap Peas

HANDS-ON TIME: 4 MIN. | **TOTAL TIME:** 12 MIN.

3 cups fresh sugar snap peas
1 tablespoon chopped fresh mint or tarragon
1 tablespoon butter
⅛ teaspoon salt
⅛ teaspoon freshly ground black pepper

❶ Steam peas 5 minutes or until crisp-tender; drain. Combine peas, mint or tarragon, butter, salt, and pepper; toss well.

SERVES 4 (serving size: ³⁄₄ cup)

CALORIES 46; FAT 3g (sat 1.8g, mono 0.8g, poly 0.2g); PROTEIN 1g; CARB 4g; FIBER 1g; CHOL 8mg; IRON 1mg; SODIUM 96mg; CALC 22mg

Simple Swap

Instead of mint, butter, salt, and pepper, give this an Asian spin by adding 1½ tablespoons soy sauce, 2 teaspoons rice vinegar, ½ teaspoon grated ginger, and 1½ tablespoons olive oil.

Simple Swap

White pearl onions
can be used if red
are unavailable.

Balsamic-Glazed Green Beans and Pearl Onions

HANDS-ON TIME: 30 MIN. | **TOTAL TIME:** 40 MIN.

1¼ pounds green beans, trimmed
1 tablespoon butter, divided
6 ounces red pearl onions, halved
    lengthwise and peeled
¼ cup fat-free, lower-sodium chicken
    broth
3 tablespoons balsamic vinegar
1 tablespoon sugar
½ teaspoon kosher salt
½ teaspoon freshly ground black
    pepper

❶ Place beans in a large saucepan of boiling water; cook 3 minutes. Drain and rinse with cold water; drain well. Place beans in a large bowl; set aside.

❷ Heat 1½ teaspoons butter in a large nonstick skillet over medium-high heat. Add onions; sauté 3 minutes or until lightly browned, stirring frequently. Add broth, vinegar, and sugar; bring to a boil. Simmer 3 minutes or until syrupy. Add beans, 1½ teaspoons butter, salt, and pepper; toss to coat. Cook 2 minutes or until thoroughly heated.

SERVES 8 (serving size: about ⅔ cup)

CALORIES 56; FAT 1.6g (sat 0.9g, mono 0.4g, poly 0.1g); PROTEIN 2g; CARB 10g; FIBER 3g; CHOL 4mg; IRON 1mg; SODIUM 149mg; CALC 34mg

Green Bean Casserole with Madeira Mushrooms

HANDS-ON TIME: 40 MIN. | **TOTAL TIME:** 60 MIN.

1½ pounds green beans, trimmed and halved crosswise

2 tablespoons olive oil

3 cups chopped sweet onion

1 teaspoon chopped fresh thyme

8 ounces shiitake mushrooms, stemmed and sliced

1 (8-ounce) package presliced button mushrooms

⅓ cup Madeira wine or dry sherry

¼ teaspoon salt

¼ teaspoon freshly ground black pepper

3 tablespoons all-purpose flour

1 cup fat-free, lower-sodium chicken broth

1 cup canned fried onions (about 2 ounces; such as French's)

2 ounces grated fresh Parmigiano-Reggiano cheese (about ½ cup)

❶ Preheat oven to 425°.

❷ Place beans in a large saucepan of boiling water; cook 4 minutes. Drain and rinse with cold water; drain well. Place beans in a large bowl; set aside.

❸ Heat a large skillet over medium-high heat. Add oil to pan; swirl to coat. Add onion and thyme to pan; sauté 4 minutes or until onion is tender, stirring occasionally. Add mushrooms; sauté 10 minutes or until liquid almost evaporates, stirring frequently. Stir in wine, salt, and pepper; cook 2 minutes or until liquid almost evaporates. Stir in flour; cook 1 minute, stirring constantly. Gradually stir in chicken broth; bring to a boil. Cook 1 minute or until thick, stirring constantly. Add mushroom mixture to green beans; toss well.

❹ Place green bean mixture in a 2-quart glass or ceramic baking dish. Combine fried onions and grated cheese in a small bowl. Top green bean mixture evenly with fried onion mixture. Bake at 425° for 17 minutes or until top is lightly browned.

SERVES 8 (serving size: ¾ cup)

CALORIES 173; **FAT** 8.5g (sat 2.3g, mono 4.9g, poly 0.6g); **PROTEIN** 7g; **CARB** 19g; **FIBER** 5g; **CHOL** 4mg; **IRON** 1mg; **SODIUM** 249mg; **CALC** 119mg

Prep Pointer

Cleaning mushrooms with a damp paper towel is better than soaking them in water because mushrooms quickly get water logged.

Prep Pointer

Stripping leaves from fresh herbs, especially thyme and rosemary, is easy if you pull from top to bottom. Hold a stem with one hand and gently pinch with the thumb and index finger of your other hand. Slide your fingers down the length of the stem to release the leaves.

Sherried Green Beans ▶

HANDS-ON TIME: 30 MIN. | **TOTAL TIME:** 30 MIN.

1½ pounds haricots verts (French green beans), trimmed
3 tablespoons butter, divided
⅓ cup thinly sliced shallots
¾ pound exotic mushroom blend, coarsely chopped
¼ cup dry sherry
3 tablespoons chopped fresh flat-leaf parsley
2 teaspoons chopped fresh thyme
¾ teaspoon kosher salt
½ teaspoon freshly ground black pepper

❶ Steam haricots verts 5 minutes or until crisp-tender; remove from heat.
❷ Melt 2 tablespoons butter in a large skillet over medium-high heat. Add shallots to pan; sauté 3 minutes, stirring occasionally. Add mushrooms; sauté 5 minutes or until liquid evaporates. Stir in sherry; bring to a boil. Cook until liquid almost evaporates (about 2 minutes). Add 1 tablespoon butter and haricots verts; cook 30 seconds or until thoroughly heated, tossing to coat. Remove from heat. Add parsley, thyme, salt, and pepper; toss to combine.

SERVES 8 (serving size: about 1 cup)

CALORIES 80; **FAT** 4.3g (sat 2.7g, mono 1.1g, poly 0.2g); **PROTEIN** 2g; **CARB** 8g; **FIBER** 4g; **CHOL** 11mg; **IRON** 1mg; **SODIUM** 256mg; **CALC** 56mg

Green Beans Provençale

HANDS-ON TIME: 21 MIN. | **TOTAL TIME:** 21 MIN.

4 cups (2-inch) cut green beans (about ¾ pound)
1 teaspoon olive oil
½ cup sliced green onions
4 garlic cloves, crushed
2 cups plum tomato, seeded and thinly sliced (about ¾ pound)
2 tablespoons chopped fresh or 2 teaspoons dried basil
¼ teaspoon salt
⅛ teaspoon freshly ground black pepper

❶ Steam green beans, covered, 5 minutes or until tender. Drain well, and set aside. Heat oil in a large nonstick skillet over medium-high heat. Add onions and garlic; sauté 1 minute. Add green beans; sauté 3 minutes. Add tomato and remaining ingredients; sauté 2 minutes.

SERVES 4 (serving size: 1 cup)

CALORIES 72; **FAT** 1.6g (sat 0.2g, mono 0.9g, poly 0.3g); **PROTEIN** 3g; **CARB** 14g; **FIBER** 4g; **CHOL** 0mg; **IRON** 2mg; **SODIUM** 164mg; **CALC** 62mg

Poblano-Corn Pudding

HANDS-ON TIME: 20 MIN. | **TOTAL TIME:** 3 HR. 20 MIN.

4 large poblano chiles (10 ounces)
Cooking spray
½ cup 1% low-fat milk
¼ cup yellow cornmeal
1.1 ounces all-purpose flour (about ¼ cup)
2 tablespoons sugar
2 tablespoons butter, melted
1 teaspoon baking powder
¼ teaspoon salt
2 large eggs, lightly beaten
1 (8¼-ounce) can cream-style corn
2 cups frozen whole-kernel corn
4 ounces reduced-fat cheddar cheese, shredded (about 1 cup)

❶ Preheat broiler.
❷ Place poblano chiles on a foil-lined baking sheet. Broil 8 minutes or until blackened and charred, turning after 6 minutes. Wrap chiles in foil. Let stand 15 minutes. Peel and discard skins. Discard seeds and stems. Chop chiles.
❸ Coat an oval 3-quart electric slow cooker with cooking spray. Place milk and next 7 ingredients (through eggs) in slow cooker; stir with a whisk until blended. Stir in chiles, cream-style corn, whole-kernel corn, and cheese. Cover and cook on LOW 2½ hours or until set. Remove lid. Cook on LOW 15 minutes.

SERVES 8 (serving size: ½ cup)

CALORIES 183; FAT 5.8g (sat 2.9g, mono 1.6g, poly 0.5g); PROTEIN 9g; CARB 27g; FIBER 2g; CHOL 65mg; IRON 1mg; SODIUM 353mg; CALC 185mg

Prep Pointer

Wrapping the chiles in foil after broiling them allows them to steam and makes it easier to peel their skins.

◄ Corn with Feta-Mint Butter

HANDS-ON TIME: 17 MIN. | **TOTAL TIME:** 17 MIN.

4 ears shucked corn
Cooking spray
2 tablespoons crumbled feta cheese
1 tablespoon unsalted butter, softened
1 tablespoon minced fresh mint
1½ teaspoons fresh lime juice

❶ Preheat grill to high heat.
❷ Place corn on grill rack coated with cooking spray; grill 8 minutes or until lightly charred, turning occasionally.
❸ Place feta, butter, mint, and lime juice in a small bowl. Mash with a fork to combine. Press mixture onto cobs using hands.

SERVES 4 (serving size: 1 corn cob)

CALORIES 128; FAT 5.4g (sat 2.9g, mono 1.4g, poly 0.6g); PROTEIN 4g; CARB 19g; FIBER 2g; CHOL 12mg; IRON 1mg; SODIUM 68mg; CALC 27mg

Prep Pointer

For a browner top, broil the eggplant for about 1 minute before serving.

Mediterranean Stuffed Eggplant

HANDS-ON TIME: 40 MIN. | **TOTAL TIME:** 1 HR. 33 MIN.

3 medium eggplant (about 3½ pounds)
Cooking spray
3 tablespoons plus 1 teaspoon canola oil, divided
1½ cups chopped onion
3 cups chopped plum tomato (about 1 pound)
1½ cups chopped summer squash
1 cup chopped zucchini
1 cup chopped red bell pepper
1 cup chopped green bell pepper
¼ cup dry white wine
1 tablespoon chopped fresh oregano
1 tablespoon chopped fresh basil
3 garlic cloves, minced
½ teaspoon salt
¼ teaspoon freshly ground black pepper
3 ounces crumbled feta cheese (about ¾ cup)
1¼ cups panko (Japanese breadcrumbs), divided
Chopped fresh parsley (optional)

1 Preheat oven to 350°.

2 Cut each eggplant in half lengthwise. Carefully scoop out pulp, leaving a ¼-inch-thick shell; reserve pulp. Place eggplant shells, skin sides down, on a baking sheet coated with cooking spray; brush eggplant halves with 2 tablespoons oil. Bake at 350° for 45 minutes or until tender.

3 While eggplant shells bake, chop reserved eggplant pulp to measure 6 cups. Heat 1 tablespoon oil in a Dutch oven over medium-high heat. Add chopped eggplant to pan; sauté 6 minutes or until eggplant is lightly browned and soft. Place eggplant in a bowl.

4 Coat pan with cooking spray. Add onion; sauté 5 minutes or until tender. Stir in tomato and next 8 ingredients (through garlic); sauté 6 minutes. Return chopped eggplant to pan. Stir in salt and black pepper; sauté 8 minutes or until vegetables begin to fall apart. Remove from heat; stir in cheese and ¼ cup panko. Cool slightly. Spoon about 1 cup eggplant mixture into each eggplant shell.

5 Combine 1 cup panko and 1 teaspoon oil in a small bowl. Sprinkle panko mixture evenly over stuffed eggplant; lightly coat with cooking spray. Bake at 350° for 25 minutes or until tops begin to brown. Sprinkle with parsley before serving, if desired.

SERVES 12 (serving size: ½ stuffed eggplant half)

CALORIES 119; FAT 4.1g (sat 1.7g, mono 1.6g, poly 0.4g); PROTEIN 5g; CARB 18g; FIBER 6g; CHOL 8mg; IRON 1mg; SODIUM 226mg; CALC 75mg

Roasted Eggplant with Pomegranate, Pickled Chiles, and Pecans

HANDS-ON TIME: 20 MIN. | **TOTAL TIME:** 50 MIN.

¼ cup white wine vinegar
¼ cup water
2 teaspoons sugar
20 thin jalapeño pepper slices
2 medium globe eggplant (about 2 pounds)
¼ cup plain whole-milk yogurt
2 teaspoons tahini (roasted sesame seed paste)
½ teaspoon kosher salt, divided
2 garlic cloves, minced
2 tablespoons extra-virgin olive oil, divided
2 teaspoons fresh lemon juice
2 cups arugula or watercress
¼ cup pomegranate arils
¼ cup pecans, toasted and crushed

❶ Combine first 3 ingredients in a small saucepan; bring to a boil. Remove from heat, and add jalapeño; let stand 15 minutes. Drain.
❷ Preheat grill to medium-high heat.
❸ Place whole eggplant on grill rack; grill 15 minutes or until charred on all sides and tender when pierced with a thin knife, turning frequently. Remove from heat; gently scrape off charred skin, if desired. Cool eggplant slightly; halve lengthwise. Lightly score flesh.
❹ Combine yogurt, tahini, ¼ teaspoon salt, and garlic, stirring well. Drizzle 4 teaspoons oil and lemon juice over eggplant flesh; top with yogurt mixture.
❺ Combine arugula, 2 teaspoons olive oil, and ¼ teaspoon salt in a medium bowl; toss gently. Top each eggplant half with about ½ cup arugula, 5 jalapeño slices, 1 tablespoon pomegranate arils, and 1 tablespoon pecans.

SERVES 4 (serving size: 1 topped eggplant half)

CALORIES 205; FAT 14.2g (sat 2g, mono 8.4g, poly 3g); PROTEIN 5g; CARB 20g; FIBER 9g; CHOL 2mg; IRON 1mg; SODIUM 256mg; CALC 69mg

Prep Pointer

Cook the eggplant whole over a gas stovetop burner or on a hot grill. The outside gets all charred as the inside steams, gathering a nice smoky overtone and becoming perfectly cooked.

Did You Know?

A terrine classically involves chopped meats formed into a loaf and served cold. The vibrant reds, yellows, and oranges of the heirloom tomatoes are showcased using this technique.

Tomato and Eggplant Terrine

HANDS-ON TIME: 33 MIN. | **TOTAL TIME:** 10 HR.

4 medium heirloom tomatoes, cut into ¼-inch-thick slices

1 cup water

2 garlic cloves, crushed

1 medium leek, chopped

1 medium tomato, quartered

¾ teaspoon salt, divided

½ teaspoon freshly ground black pepper, divided

1 tablespoon unflavored gelatin

6 (¼-inch-thick) slices medium eggplant

1½ tablespoons extra-virgin olive oil

Cooking spray

4 ounces fresh mozzarella cheese, cut into ⅛-inch-thick slices

1 tablespoon chopped thyme leaves, divided

1 tablespoon finely chopped fresh chives, divided

Thyme leaves (optional)

1 Preheat oven to 450°.

2 Place heirloom tomato slices on several layers of paper towels. Top with a single layer of paper towels. Let stand 15 minutes.

3 Combine 1 cup water, garlic, leek, and quartered tomato in a medium saucepan; bring to a boil. Reduce heat; simmer 10 minutes. Strain through a sieve over a bowl, pressing to extract liquid; discard solids. Pour liquid into pan; stir in ½ teaspoon salt and ¼ teaspoon pepper. Cool to room temperature. Sprinkle with gelatin; let stand 5 minutes. Bring gelatin mixture to a boil; boil 3 minutes. Remove from heat.

4 Lightly brush eggplant slices with oil; arrange in a single layer on a baking sheet lined with parchment paper. Bake at 450° for 10 minutes; turn and bake an additional 5 minutes or until tender.

5 Lightly coat a 9 x 5–inch loaf pan with cooking spray. Line pan with plastic wrap. Arrange tomato slices in a double layer on bottom of pan; sprinkle with ¼ teaspoon salt and ¼ teaspoon pepper. Top tomatoes with a thin layer of cheese; sprinkle with 1½ teaspoons thyme and 1½ teaspoons chives. Arrange 3 eggplant slices over cheese. Repeat layers, ending with tomatoes. Pour gelatin mixture over terrine. Cover with plastic wrap. Chill 8 hours or overnight.

6 Turn terrine out onto a platter. Let stand 1 hour (or until room temperature). Garnish with thyme leaves, if desired.

SERVES 12 (serving size: 1 slice)

CALORIES 78; FAT 4.7g (sat 2g, mono 1.3g, poly 0.3g); PROTEIN 3g; CARB 7g; FIBER 3g; CHOL 7mg; IRON 1mg; SODIUM 182mg; CALC 19mg

Toasty Tomatoes

HANDS-ON TIME: 5 MIN. | **TOTAL TIME:** 5 MIN.

1 teaspoon grated lemon rind
1/8 teaspoon freshly ground black
   pepper
1 small garlic clove, minced
1 1/2 tablespoons olive oil
1/2 cup panko (Japanese breadcrumbs)
4 Roma tomatoes, halved
Cooking spray
2 teaspoons grated fresh Parmesan
   cheese
1/4 teaspoon salt

❶ Preheat broiler.
❷ Combine lemon rind, pepper, and minced garlic. Mix in olive oil; toss in panko. Arrange Roma tomato halves, cut sides up, on a baking sheet; coat lightly with cooking spray. Top each with 1 teaspoon panko mixture; sprinkle Parmesan and salt evenly over tomatoes; broil 3 minutes or until cheese is bubbly.

SERVES 4 (serving size: 2 tomato halves)

CALORIES 97; **FAT** 5.6g (sat 0.8g, mono 3.8g, poly 0.6g); **PROTEIN** 2g; **CARB** 10g; **FIBER** 2g; **CHOL** 0mg; **IRON** 0mg; **SODIUM** 178mg; **CALC** 17mg

Breaded Broiled Tomatoes

HANDS-ON TIME: 10 MIN. | **TOTAL TIME:** 25 MIN.

1 (1-ounce) slice white bread
4 large plum tomatoes
2 ounces grated fresh Parmesan cheese
   (about 1/2 cup)
1 teaspoon freshly ground black pepper
1 large egg white, lightly beaten
1/2 cup low-fat buttermilk
Cooking spray
8 teaspoons chopped fresh cilantro

❶ Preheat oven to 400°.
❷ Place bread in a food processor; pulse 10 times or until coarse crumbs measure 3/4 cup.
❸ Core tomatoes; cut each tomato in half lengthwise, discarding seeds. Combine breadcrumbs, cheese, pepper, and egg white in a small bowl. Spoon 1 tablespoon buttermilk into each tomato half. Divide breadcrumb mixture among tomato halves. Place tomato halves on a baking sheet coated with cooking spray. Bake at 400° for 15 minutes or until tomatoes are tender.
❹ Increase oven temperature to broil.
❺ Broil tomato halves 1 minute or until lightly browned. Sprinkle each half with 1 teaspoon cilantro.

SERVES 8 (serving size: 1 tomato half)

CALORIES 57; **FAT** 2.5g (sat 1.4g, mono 0.6g, poly 0.2g); **PROTEIN** 4g; **CARB** 4g; **FIBER** 1g; **CHOL** 7mg; **IRON** 0mg; **SODIUM** 151mg; **CALC** 108mg

Pickled "Fried" Green Tomatoes with Buttermilk-Herb Sauce

HANDS-ON TIME: 37 MIN. | **TOTAL TIME:** 40 MIN.

Prep Pointer

Coating the tomatoes with cooking spray helps the breading mixture adhere and allows you to use less oil in the pan for crisping.

1 cup water
1 cup cider vinegar
2 tablespoons sugar
¾ teaspoon kosher salt, divided
16 (¼-inch-thick) slices green tomato (about 4 tomatoes)
7 tablespoons nonfat buttermilk, divided
2 tablespoons finely chopped fresh basil
3 tablespoons canola mayonnaise
1 teaspoon finely chopped fresh thyme
2 teaspoons cider vinegar
1 garlic clove, minced
½ teaspoon freshly ground black pepper, divided
¾ cup panko (Japanese breadcrumbs)
⅓ cup masa harina
1 large egg
1 large egg white
1 ounce all-purpose flour (about ¼ cup)
3 tablespoons extra-virgin olive oil, divided
Cooking spray

❶ Combine 1 cup water, 1 cup vinegar, sugar, and ½ teaspoon salt in a medium saucepan; bring to a boil. Add tomatoes; cook 2 minutes. Remove from heat; let stand 15 minutes, stirring occasionally. Drain tomatoes; pat dry.

❷ Combine 5 tablespoons buttermilk and next 5 ingredients (through garlic), stirring with a whisk. Stir in ¼ teaspoon pepper.

❸ Heat a large skillet over medium heat. Add panko to pan; cook 2 minutes or until toasted, stirring frequently. Remove from heat; stir in masa harina, ¼ teaspoon salt, and ¼ teaspoon pepper. Place panko mixture in a shallow dish. Combine 2 tablespoons buttermilk, egg, and egg white, stirring with a whisk. Place flour in another shallow dish. Dredge tomato slices in flour; dip in egg mixture, and dredge in panko mixture, turning to coat.

❹ Heat a large nonstick skillet over medium-high heat. Add 1 tablespoon oil to pan; swirl to coat. Add half of tomatoes; cook 4 minutes. Coat tops of tomatoes with cooking spray. Turn; add 1½ teaspoons oil to pan. Cook 4 minutes or until golden. Repeat procedure with 1½ tablespoons oil, tomatoes, and cooking spray. Serve with sauce.

SERVES 8 (serving size: 2 tomato slices and about 1 tablespoon sauce)

CALORIES 154; FAT 7.7g (sat 0.9g, mono 4.8g, poly 1.2g); PROTEIN 4g; CARB 16g; FIBER 1g; CHOL 23mg; IRON 1mg; SODIUM 215mg; CALC 41mg

Prep Pointer

Use a variety of hot and sweet peppers in red, orange, and yellow for superior flavor and color in this dish.

Sweet and Spicy Pepperonata

HANDS-ON TIME: 20 MIN. | **TOTAL TIME:** 55 MIN.

2 tablespoons olive oil
½ teaspoon kosher salt
2 pounds assorted peppers, such as mini sweet, bell, and hot long peppers, seeded and cut into strips
6 shallots, peeled and halved (about ½ pound)
3 tablespoons red wine vinegar
2 teaspoons sugar
1 teaspoon chopped fresh thyme

❶ Heat a Dutch oven over medium-high heat. Add oil to pan; swirl to coat. Add salt, peppers, and shallots; cook 3 minutes or until shallots begin to brown. Reduce heat to medium-low; cook, covered, 20 minutes or until peppers are tender.
❷ Increase heat to medium-high. Add vinegar, sugar, and thyme; cook 15 minutes or until peppers are tender and shallots are golden brown, stirring occasionally. Serve warm or at room temperature.

SERVES 6 (serving size: about ½ cup)

CALORIES 119; **FAT** 5g (sat 0.7g, mono 3.3g, poly 0.6g); **PROTEIN** 3g; **CARB** 17g; **FIBER** 3g; **CHOL** 0mg; **IRON** 1mg; **SODIUM** 167mg; **CALC** 12mg

Prep Pointer

A serrated knife slices easily through a tomato's skin without squashing it.

Roasted Peppers and Tomatoes with Herbs and Capers

HANDS-ON TIME: 35 MIN. | **TOTAL TIME:** 2 HR.

2 red bell peppers
2 yellow bell peppers
1½ pounds Campari tomatoes, halved
3/8 teaspoon kosher salt, divided
¼ teaspoon freshly ground black pepper
⅓ cup flat-leaf parsley leaves
3 tablespoons extra-virgin olive oil
1 tablespoon chopped fresh oregano
1 tablespoon capers, rinsed and drained
2 teaspoons minced fresh garlic
12 niçoise olives, pitted and halved

❶ Preheat broiler to high.
❷ Cut bell peppers in half lengthwise; discard seeds and membranes. Place halves, skin sides up, on a foil-lined baking sheet; flatten with hand. Broil 10 minutes or until blackened. Wrap peppers in foil; let stand 10 minutes. Peel; cut into ½-inch strips.
❸ Preheat oven to 400°.
❹ Combine tomatoes, ¼ teaspoon salt, and black pepper in a medium bowl.
❺ Combine ⅛ teaspoon salt, parsley, and remaining ingredients in a small bowl. Place one-third of tomatoes in bottom of a 1½-quart gratin dish. Top with one-third of peppers and one-third of parsley mixture. Repeat layers twice, ending with parsley mixture. Cover and bake at 400° for 30 minutes or until vegetables are thoroughly heated. Cool to room temperature; cover and chill.

SERVES 8 (serving size: ¾ cup)

CALORIES 97; FAT 6.9g (sat 0.9g, mono 4.9g, poly 0.8g); PROTEIN 2g; CARB 8g; FIBER 2g; CHOL 0mg; IRON 1mg; SODIUM 222mg; CALC 23mg

Summery Stuffed Poblanos

HANDS-ON TIME: 30 MIN. | **TOTAL TIME:** 60 MIN.

6 poblano chiles

2 ears shucked corn

Cooking spray

2 cups chopped seeded tomato, divided

1 cup hot cooked brown rice

¼ cup chopped fresh cilantro, divided

2 tablespoons pine nuts, toasted

2 tablespoons ⅓-less-fat cream cheese

2 teaspoons fresh lime juice

¼ teaspoon kosher salt

3 garlic cloves, minced

3 ounces Monterey Jack cheese, shredded (about ¾ cup)

2 ounces queso fresco, crumbled (about ½ cup)

Jalapeño pepper sauce (optional)

❶ Preheat grill to high heat.

❷ Lightly coat poblanos and corn with cooking spray. Place poblanos and corn on grill rack. Grill poblanos 12 minutes or until charred, turning occasionally. Grill corn 10 minutes or until lightly charred, turning occasionally. Wrap poblanos in foil; let stand 15 minutes. Peel and discard skins. Cut a lengthwise slit in each chile; discard seeds and membranes. Set aside.

❸ Preheat oven to 400°.

❹ Cut kernels from ears of corn. Combine kernels, 1 cup tomato, rice, 2 tablespoons cilantro, pine nuts, and next 5 ingredients (through Monterey Jack); toss well to combine. Open each poblano; divide rice mixture evenly among chiles (chiles will be very full). Place on a baking sheet. Bake at 400° for 7 minutes or until hot. Turn broiler to high. Sprinkle chiles with queso fresco. Broil 3 minutes or until cheese is lightly browned. Place chiles on a platter. Sprinkle with 1 cup tomato and 2 tablespoons cilantro. Serve with hot sauce, if desired.

SERVES 6 (serving size: 1 stuffed chile)

CALORIES 210; **FAT** 9.6g (sat 4.2g, mono 2.2g, poly 1.4g); **PROTEIN** 10g; **CARB** 25g; **FIBER** 5g; **CHOL** 19mg; **IRON** 1mg; **SODIUM** 197mg; **CALC** 165mg

Prep Pointer

Use a bristle brush or a damp paper towel to help remove silks from the ears of corn.

◀ *Sautéed Black Trumpets with Asparagus and Lemon*

HANDS-ON TIME: 12 MIN. | **TOTAL TIME:** 12 MIN.

8 cups water
2¼ teaspoons kosher salt, divided
1 pound asparagus, trimmed and cut diagonally into 1½-inch pieces
1 tablespoon extra-virgin olive oil
8 ounces black trumpet mushrooms
2 teaspoons butter
1½ teaspoons grated lemon rind
⅛ teaspoon freshly ground black pepper

❶ Combine 8 cups water and 2 teaspoons salt in a Dutch oven; bring to a boil. Add asparagus; cook 2 minutes or until crisp-tender. Drain; plunge asparagus into ice water. Drain well.
❷ Heat a large skillet over medium-high heat. Add oil; swirl to coat. Add mushrooms; sauté 4 minutes or until mushrooms release most of their liquid. Add asparagus; cook 1 minute or until thoroughly heated. Remove from heat; stir in ¼ teaspoon salt, butter, lemon rind, and pepper. Serve immediately.

SERVES 4 (serving size: about ¾ cup)

CALORIES 72; **FAT** 5.6g (sat 1.7g, mono 3g, poly 0.6g); **PROTEIN** 3g; **CARB** 4g; **FIBER** 2g; **CHOL** 5mg; **IRON** 2mg; **SODIUM** 237mg; **CALC** 18mg

Simple Swap

You can also use chanterelle, morel, or reconstituted dried wood ear mushrooms.

Buttery Mirin Mushrooms

HANDS-ON TIME: 12 MIN. | **TOTAL TIME:** 12 MIN.

1 tablespoon butter
8 ounces button mushrooms, halved
1 garlic clove, minced
¼ cup unsalted chicken stock (such as Swanson)
1 tablespoon mirin
⅜ teaspoon kosher salt
¼ teaspoon freshly ground black pepper

❶ Melt butter in a large skillet over medium heat. Add halved button mushrooms and minced garlic; cook 3 minutes or until mushrooms release their liquid. Add chicken stock and mirin; cook 2 minutes or until liquid is syrupy. Sprinkle with salt and pepper.

SERVES 4 (serving size: about ½ cup)

CALORIES 49; **FAT** 3.1g (sat 1.9g, mono 0.8g, poly 0.2g); **PROTEIN** 2g; **CARB** 3g; **FIBER** 1g; **CHOL** 8mg; **IRON** 0mg; **SODIUM** 240mg; **CALC** 5mg

Superfast

Ready in 15 minutes or less!

Pairs With Guide

Trying to find the right protein to pair with a side can sometimes be confusing. These easy-to-use charts give you some guidance when you're planning a meal, and take the guesswork out of finding complementary flavors.

pastas, rices, and grains

	Pork	Chicken/Poultry	Beef	Lamb	Fish	Seafood	Vegetarian
Lemon-Orange Orzo					■		
Orzo with Garlicky Spinach	■						
Broccoli and Penne with Asiago						■	
Lemon-Parsley Pasta							■
Mushroom-Ginger Noodles			■		■		
Couscous Pilaf	■	■	■		■	■	
Curried Currant–Couscous Pilaf		■					
Couscous with Winter Vegetables							■
Red Pepper Couscous		■			■		
Double Sesame Rice		■			■		
Golden Saffron Rice		■					
Thai Cilantro and Serrano Rice	■						
Yogurt Rice with Cumin and Chile		■		■	■		
Curried Sweet Potato–Apple Pilaf	■	■					
Nutty Rice					■		
Red Coconut Rice	■	■	■				
Cashew Rice					■		■
Coconut-Ginger Rice			■				

	Pork	Chicken/Poultry	Beef	Lamb	Fish	Seafood	Vegetarian
Wild Rice and Carrots		■					
Wild Rice Dressing with Roasted Chestnuts and Cranberries		■				■	
Black Bean–Cilantro Rice					■		
Spicy Brown Rice						■	
Toasted Millet with Cilantro Vinaigrette					■		
Mint and Pistachio Tabbouleh				■			
Balsamic and Grape Quinoa		■			■		
Nutty Almond-Sesame Red Quinoa	■						
Kale, Brown Rice, and Quinoa Pilaf		■					
Two-Corn Polenta with Tomato, Basil, and Cheese	■						
Goat Cheese and Basil Polenta			■				
Polenta-Sausage Triangles		■					
Awendaw	■	■	■			■	
Creamy Grits	■						
Mushroom and Leek Stuffing		■					
Ham, Gruyère, and Onion Stuffing		■					
Greek-Style Stuffing		■					
Simply Herby Stuffing		■					

beans, lentils, and peas

	Pork	Chicken/Poultry	Beef	Lamb	Fish	Seafood	Vegetarian
The Ultimate Baked Beans	■	■					
Spicy Black Beans		■	■				

	Pork	Chicken/Poultry	Beef	Lamb	Fish	Seafood	Vegetarian
Quick Classic Baked Beans	▬		▬				
Simmered Pinto Beans with Chipotle Sour Cream	▬		▬				
Cranberry Beans with Parsley Pesto	▬			▬			
Spicy Black-Eyed Peas	▬						
Black-Eyed Peas with Swiss Chard		▬					
Fava Beans with Tomato and Onion					▬		
Buttery Lentils with Shallots					▬		
Warm Spiced Lentils							▬
Tomato-Chickpea Curry	▬	▬					

salads and slaws

	Pork	Chicken/Poultry	Beef	Lamb	Fish	Seafood	Vegetarian
Simple Salad with Lemon Dressing	▬						
Grilled Caesar Salad		▬	▬		▬		
Lemony Kale Salad							▬
Spinach with Garlic Vinaigrette	▬						
Arugula Salad with Parmesan Vinaigrette							▬
Bitter Greens Salad with Spiced Mirin Dressing		▬			▬		
Jalapeño-Lime Slaw	▬	▬					
Sesame-Miso Cucumber Salad		▬				▬	
Summer Peach and Tomato Salad	▬						
Tomato and Grilled Bread Salad		▬				▬	
Grapefruit, Walnut, and Feta Salad		▬					▬

	Pork	Chicken/Poultry	Beef	Lamb	Fish	Seafood	Vegetarian
Fennel Salad with Lemon		■					
Zucchini Ribbons with Pecorino							■
Grilled Corn, Poblano and Black Bean Salad	■	■	■		■		
Roasted Potato Salad with Creamy Dijon Vinaigrette			■				
Zesty Three Bean and Sautéed Corn Salad							■
Fresh Pea Salad with Radishes, Tomato, and Mint	■						
Soba Noodle Salad	■		■		■		
Tabbouleh Salad	■	■		■		■	
Spinach–Pasta Salad		■					

fruit

	Pork	Chicken/Poultry	Beef	Lamb	Fish	Seafood	Vegetarian
Winter Jeweled Fruit Salad		■					■
Fresh Fruit Salad	■						■
Orange and Olive Salad		■					■
Pear Relish	■	■			■		■
Beet-Citrus Salad with Pistachios	■	■			■		
Grapefruit and Fennel Salad						■	
Chunky Strawberry-Avocado Salsa		■			■		■
Blueberry-Chipotle Chutney	■						
Cranberry-Orange Relish		■					
Grape and Hazelnut Salad							■
Spiced Cranberry-Mango Chutney		■					

	Pork	Chicken/Poultry	Beef	Lamb	Fish	Seafood	Vegetarian
Refrigerator Pickled Blackberries		■					■
Grilled Peaches with Ginger Glaze		■					
Triple-Plum Salsa	■	■			■		
Marinated Grilled Apples with Mint	■	■					
Cinnamon Stewed Apples	■						
Sautéed Apples	■						
Easy "Baked" Apples							■
Chunky Spiced Applesauce	■						
Green Papaya and Mango Salad	■	■					
Spicy Grilled Mango with Chiles and Crema	■	■	■				
Asian Caramelized Pineapple	■				■		
Pineapple and Orange Salad with Toasted Coconut	■						■
Watermelon-Cucumber Salad	■	■			■	■	
Pickled Watermelon Rind	■	■				■	

vegetables

	Pork	Chicken/Poultry	Beef	Lamb	Fish	Seafood	Vegetarian
Stir-Fried Vegetables	■		■				
Roasted Winter Vegetables		■					
Spiced Oven Fries			■				
Truffled Roasted Potatoes	■	■	■				
Roasted Rosemary Fingerling Potatoes		■	■	■	■		
Maple-Glazed Sweet Potatoes	■	■	■				

	Pork	Chicken/Poultry	Beef	Lamb	Fish	Seafood	Vegetarian
Honey-Orange Carrots	■	■	■	■	■		
Carrot Mash with Crème Fraîche			■				
Moroccan-Spiced Baby Carrots			■				
Radishes in Browned Butter		■					■
Sweet and Sour Cipollini	■	■					
Spaghetti Squash Fritters							■
Sautéed Cabbage and Apples	■	■					
Brussels Sprouts with Bacon, Garlic, and Shallots	■	■					
Lemony Broccolini		■					■
Roasted Chile-Garlic Broccoli			■		■		
Roasted Cauliflower, Chickpeas, and Olives		■			■		
Wilted Kale with Toasted Shallots		■					
Balsamic Collard Greens	■						
Wilted Swiss Chard and Mushrooms						■	
Asparagus with Balsamic Tomatoes	■				■		
Braised Fennel with Parmesan Breadcrumbs	■	■					
Warm-Spiced Okra				■			■
Steamed Sugar Snap Peas	■	■			■		
Toasty Tomatoes		■					
Sweet and Spicy Pepperonata	■		■		■		

Seasonal Produce Guide

When you use fresh fruits, vegetables, and herbs, you don't have to do much to make them taste great. Although many fruits, vegetables, and herbs are available year-round, you'll get better flavor and prices when you buy what's in season. This guide helps you choose the best produce so you can create tasty meals all year long.

Fall

Fruits
- Apples
- Cranberries
- Figs
- Grapes
- Pears
- Persimmons
- Pomegranates
- Quinces

Vegetables
- Belgian endive
- Bell peppers
- Broccoli
- Brussels sprouts
- Cabbage
- Cauliflower
- Eggplant
- Escarole
- Fennel
- Frisée
- Leeks
- Mushrooms
- Parsnips
- Pumpkins
- Red potatoes
- Rutabagas
- Shallots
- Sweet potatoes
- Winter squash
- Yukon gold potatoes

Herbs
- Basil
- Bay leaves
- Parsley
- Rosemary
- Sage
- Tarragon
- Thyme

Winter

Fruits
- Apples
- Blood oranges
- Cranberries
- Grapefruit
- Kiwifruit
- Kumquats
- Lemons
- Limes
- Mandarin oranges
- Navel oranges
- Pears
- Persimmons
- Pomegranates
- Pomelos
- Tangelos
- Tangerines
- Quinces

Vegetables
- Baby turnips
- Beets
- Belgian endive
- Brussels sprouts
- Celery root
- Escarole
- Fennel
- Frisée
- Jerusalem artichokes
- Kale
- Leeks
- Mushrooms
- Parsnips
- Potatoes
- Rutabagas
- Sweet potatoes
- Turnips
- Watercress
- Winter squash

Spring

Fruits
Bananas
Blood oranges
Coconuts
Grapefruit
Kiwifruit
Lemons
Limes
Mangoes
Navel oranges
Papayas
Passion fruit
Pineapples
Strawberries
Tangerines
Valencia oranges

Vegetables
Artichokes
Arugula
Asparagus
Avocados
Baby leeks
Beets
Belgian endive
Broccoli
Cauliflower
Dandelion greens
Fava beans
Green onions
Green peas
Kale
Lettuce
Mushrooms
Radishes
Red potatoes
Rhubarb
Snap beans
Snow peas
Spinach
Sugar snap peas
Sweet onions
Swiss chard

Herbs
Chives
Dill
Garlic chives
Lemongrass
Mint
Parsley
Thyme

Summer

Fruits
Apricots
Blackberries
Blueberries
Boysenberries
Cantaloupes
Casaba melons
Cherries
Crenshaw melons
Figs
Grapes
Guava
Honeydew melons
Mangoes
Nectarines
Papayas
Peaches
Plums
Raspberries
Strawberries
Watermelons

Vegetables
Avocados
Beans: snap, pole, and shell
Beets
Bell peppers
Cabbage
Carrots
Celery
Chile peppers
Collards
Corn
Cucumbers
Eggplant
Green beans
Jicama
Lima beans
Okra
Pattypan squash
Peas
Radicchio
Radishes
Summer squash
Tomatoes

Herbs
Basil
Bay leaves
Borage
Chives
Cilantro
Dill
Lavender
Lemon balm
Marjoram
Mint
Oregano
Rosemary
Sage
Summer savory
Tarragon
Thyme

Nutritional Information

How to Use It and Why

To interpret the nutritional analysis in *The Healthy Sides Cookbook*, use the figures below as a daily reference guide. One size doesn't fit all, so take lifestyle, age, and circumstances into consideration. For example, pregnant or breast-feeding women need more protein, calories, and calcium. Go to choosemyplate.gov for your own individualized plan.

~~~~~~

In Our Nutritional Analysis, We Use These Abbreviations

sat	saturated fat	**carb**	carbohydrates	**g**	gram
mono	monounsaturated fat	**chol**	cholesterol	**mg**	milligram
poly	polyunsaturated fat	**calc**	calcium		

Daily Nutrition Guide

	Women ages 25 to 50	Women over 50	Men ages 25 to 50	Men over 50
Calories	2,000	2,000*	2,700	2,500
Protein	50 g	50 g	63 g	60 g
Fat	65 g*	65 g*	88 g*	83 g*
Saturated Fat	20 g*	20 g*	27 g*	25 g*
Carbohydrates	304 g	304 g	410 g	375 g
Fiber	25 g to 35 g	25 g to 35 g	25 g to 35 g	25 g to 35 g
Cholesterol	300 mg*	300 mg*	300 mg*	300 mg*
Iron	18 mg	8 mg	8 mg	8 mg
Sodium	2,300 mg*	1,500 mg*	2,300 mg*	1,500 mg*
Calcium	1,000 mg	1,200 mg	1,000 mg	1,000 mg

*Or less, for optimum health

Nutritional values used in our calculations either come from The Food Processor, Version 10.4 (ESHA Research), or are provided by food manufacturers.

Metric Equivalents

The information in the following charts is provided to help cooks outside the United States successfully use the recipes in this book. All equivalents are approximate.

Cooking/Oven Temperatures

	Fahrenheit	Celsius	Gas Mark
Freeze Water	32° F	0° C	
Room Temp.	68° F	20° C	
Boil Water	212° F	100° C	
Bake	325° F	160° C	3
	350° F	180° C	4
	375° F	190° C	5
	400° F	200° C	6
	425° F	220° C	7
	450° F	230° C	8
Broil		Grill	

Liquid Ingredients by Volume

¼ tsp	=					1	ml
½ tsp	=					2	ml
1 tsp	=					5	ml
3 tsp	=	1 Tbsp	=	½ fl oz	=	15	ml
2 Tbsp	=	⅛ cup	=	1 fl oz	=	30	ml
4 Tbsp	=	¼ cup	=	2 fl oz	=	60	ml
5⅓ Tbsp	=	⅓ cup	=	3 fl oz	=	80	ml
8 Tbsp	=	½ cup	=	4 fl oz	=	120	ml
10⅔ Tbsp	=	⅔ cup	=	5 fl oz	=	160	ml
12 Tbsp	=	¾ cup	=	6 fl oz	=	180	ml
16 Tbsp	=	1 cup	=	8 fl oz	=	240	ml
1 pt	=	2 cups	=	16 fl oz	=	480	ml
1 qt	=	4 cups	=	32 fl oz	=	960	ml
				33 fl oz	=	1000 ml	= 1 l

Dry Ingredients by Weight

(To convert ounces to grams, multiply the number of ounces by 30.)

1 oz	=	¹⁄₁₆ lb	=	30 g
4 oz	=	¼ lb	=	120 g
8 oz	=	½ lb	=	240 g
12 oz	=	¾ lb	=	360 g
16 oz	=	1 lb	=	480 g

Length

(To convert inches to centimeters, multiply inches by 2.5.)

1 in	=				2.5 cm	
12 in	=	1 ft		=	30 cm	
36 in	=	3 ft	=	1 yd =	90 cm	
40 in	=				100 cm	= 1 m

Equivalents for Different Types of Ingredients

Standard Cup	Fine Powder (ex. flour)	Grain (ex. rice)	Granular (ex. sugar)	Liquid Solids (ex. butter)	Liquid (ex. milk)
1	140 g	150 g	190 g	200 g	240 ml
¾	105 g	113 g	143 g	150 g	180 ml
⅔	93 g	100 g	125 g	133 g	160 ml
½	70 g	75 g	95 g	100 g	120 ml
⅓	47 g	50 g	63 g	67 g	80 ml
¼	35 g	38 g	48 g	50 g	60 ml
⅛	18 g	19 g	24 g	25 g	30 ml

Recipe Index

L

M

N

ISBN-13: 978-0-8487-4477-9

ISBN-10: 0-8487-4477-2

Library of Congress Control Number: 2015942381

Printed in the United States of America

First Printing 2015

Senior Editor: Betty Wong

Editor: Rachel Quinlivan West, R.D.

Writer: Liza Schoenfein

Assistant Project Editor: Melissa Brown

Copy Editors: Jacqueline Giovanelli, Kate Johnson

Art Director: Christopher Rhoads

Senior Designer: J. Shay McNamee

Junior Designer: AnnaMaria Jacob

Executive Photography Director: Iain Bagwell

Senior Photographer: Hélène Dujardin

Photographers: Johnny Autry, Kang Kim, Becky Luigart-Stayner, Jonny Valiant

Senior Photo Stylists: Kay E. Clarke, Mindi Shapiro Levine

Photo Stylists: Katelyn Hardwick, Amanda Widis

Assistant Test Kitchen Manager: Alyson Moreland Haynes

Senior Recipe Developer and Tester: Callie Nash

Recipe Developers and Testers: Julia Levy, Karen Rankin

Food Stylists: Nathan Carrabba, Margaret Monroe Dickey

Associate Production Manager: Kimberly Marshall

Assistant Production Manager: Diane Rose Keener

Indexer: *Marrathon Production Services*

Fellows: Laura Arnold, Dree Deacon, Nicole Fisher, Loren Lorenzo, Caroline Smith